THE BUSINESS CASE FOR NETWORK SECURITY: ADVOCACY, GOVERNANCE, AND ROI

Catherine Paquet

Warren Saxe

RENEWALS 458-4574

Cisco Press

800 East 96th Street

Indianapolis, Indiana 46240 USA

The Business Case for Network Security: Advocacy, Governance, and ROI

Catherine Paquet and Warren Saxe
Copyright© 2005 Cisco Systems, Inc.
Published by:
Cisco Press
800 East 96th Street
Indianapolis, IN 46240 USA

Printed in the United States of America   1 2 3 4 5 6 7 8 9 0
First Printing December 2004
Library of Congress Cataloging-in-Publication Number: 2003115153
ISBN: 1-58720-121-6

Warning and Disclaimer

This book is designed to provide information about the business case for network security. Every effort has been made to make this book as complete and as accurate as possible, but no warranty or fitness is implied.

The information is provided on an "as is" basis. The author, Cisco Press, and Cisco Systems, Inc. shall have neither liability nor responsibility to any person or entity with respect to any loss or damages arising from the information contained in this book or from the use of the discs or programs that may accompany it.

The opinions expressed in this book belong to the author and are not necessarily those of Cisco Systems, Inc.

Trademark Acknowledgments

All terms mentioned in this book that are known to be trademarks or service marks have been appropriately capitalized. Cisco Press or Cisco Systems, Inc. cannot attest to the accuracy of this information. Use of a term in this book should not be regarded as affecting the validity of any trademark or service mark.

Feedback Information

At Cisco Press, our goal is to create in-depth technical books of the highest quality and value. Each book is crafted with care and precision, undergoing rigorous development that involves the unique expertise of members from the professional technical community.

Readers' feedback is a natural continuation of this process. If you have any comments regarding how we could improve the quality of this book, or otherwise alter it to better suit your needs, you can contact us through e-mail at feedback@ciscopress.com. Please make sure to include the book title and ISBN in your message.

We greatly appreciate your assistance.

Corporate and Government Sales

Cisco Press offers excellent discounts on this book when ordered in quantity for bulk purchases or special sales.

For more information please contact:
U.S. Corporate and Government Sales 1-800-382-3419 corpsales@pearsontechgroup.com
For sales outside the U.S. please contact:
International Sales international@pearsoned.com

Publisher   John Wait

Editor-in-Chief   John Kane

Executive Editor   Brett Bartow

Cisco Representative   Anthony Wolfenden

Cisco Press Program Manager   Nannette M. Noble

Production Manager   Patrick Kanouse

Development Editor   Andrew Cupp

Project Editor   Sheila Schroeder

Copy Editor   John Edwards

Technical Editors   Stephen Kalman, Doug McKillip, Gilles Piché

Team Coordinator   Tammi Barnett

Book and Cover Designer   Louisa Adair

Composition   Interactive Composition Corporation

Indexer   Brad Herriman

CISCO SYSTEMS

Corporate Headquarters
Cisco Systems, Inc.
170 West Tasman Drive
San Jose, CA 95134-1706
USA
www.cisco.com
Tel: 408 526-4000
        800 553-NETS (6387)
Fax: 408 526-4100

European Headquarters
Cisco Systems International BV
Haarlerbergpark
Haarlerbergweg 13-19
1101 CH Amsterdam
The Netherlands
www-europe.cisco.com
Tel: 31 0 20 357 1000
Fax: 31 0 20 357 1100

Americas Headquarters
Cisco Systems, Inc.
170 West Tasman Drive
San Jose, CA 95134-1706
USA
www.cisco.com
Tel: 408 526-7660
Fax: 408 527-0883

Asia Pacific Headquarters
Cisco Systems, Inc.
Capital Tower
168 Robinson Road
#22-01 to #29-01
Singapore 068912
www.cisco.com
Tel: +65 6317 7777
Fax: +65 6317 7799

Cisco Systems has more than 200 offices in the following countries and regions. Addresses, phone numbers, and fax numbers are listed on the
C i s c o . c o m   W e b   s i t e   a t   w w w . c i s c o . c o m / g o / o f f i c e s .

Argentina • Australia • Austria • Belgium • Brazil • Bulgaria • Canada • Chile • China PRC • Colombia • Costa Rica • Croatia • Czech Republic
Denmark • Dubai, UAE • Finland • France • Germany • Greece • Hong Kong SAR • Hungary • India • Indonesia • Ireland • Israel • Italy
Japan • Korea • Luxembourg • Malaysia • Mexico • The Netherlands • New Zealand • Norway • Peru • Philippines • Poland • Portugal
Puerto Rico • Romania • Russia • Saudi Arabia • Scotland • Singapore • Slovakia • Slovenia • South Africa • Spain • Sweden
Switzerland • Taiwan • Thailand • Turkey • Ukraine • United Kingdom • United States • Venezuela • Vietnam • Zimbabwe

About the Authors

Catherine Paquet is a freelancer in the field of internetworking and return on security investment. Catherine has in-depth knowledge of security systems, remote access, and routing technology. She is a Cisco Certified Security Professional (CCSP) and a Cisco Certified Network Professional (CCNP), and she was a Cisco Certified Systems Instructor (CCSI) with the Cisco largest training partner. Her internetworking career started as a LAN manager; she then moved to MAN manager and eventually became the nationwide WAN manager. Catherine was the course director/master instructor for the Cisco Remote Access and Security courses at the same Cisco learning partner. She was recently the director of technical resources for the same company, where she was responsible for the instructor corps and the equipment offerings in Canada, including Cisco courses. She also taught Cisco Secure PIX Firewall Advanced (CSPFA). In 2002 and 2003, Catherine volunteered with the UN mission in Kabul, Afghanistan, to train Afghan public servants in the area of networking. Catherine has an MBA with a major in management information systems (MIS).

Catherine coauthored the Cisco Press books *Building Scalable Cisco Networks; CCNP Self-Study: Building Scalable Cisco Internetworks (BSCI); and CCNP Self-Study: Building Scalable Cisco Internetworks (BSCI)*, Second Edition, and she edited *Building Cisco Remote Access Networks.*

Warren Saxe has an extensive background in profit and loss (P&L) management as general manager for a Fortune 1000 semiconductor distributor. As a top- and bottom-line-focused senior manager, he brings a unique perspective to this business decision maker-oriented book. He applies an overriding business strategy to drive IT decisions by utilizing a value-driven approach. He has extensive background in sales management, marketing management, and demand creation fundamentals. He directed a large multidisciplinary team composed of managers, engineers, sales, and marketing professionals. He was responsible for strategic and tactical planning, and he negotiated directly with CxO-level executives, both internally and with customers across many industries. He is currently focusing in the areas of security governance, risk management, and return on security investment planning. He earned his degree at McGill University.

About the Technical Reviewers

Stephen Kalman is a data security trainer. He is the author or tech editor of more than 20 books, courses, and CBT titles. His most recent book is *Web Security Field Guide*, published by Cisco Press. In addition to those responsibilities, he runs a consulting company, Esquire Micro Consultants, that specializes in network security. Mr. Kalman holds CISSP, CEH, CCNA, CCDA, A+, Network+, and Security+ certifications and is a member of the New York State Bar.

Doug McKillip, P.E., CCIE No. 1851, is president of Innovative Integrators Inc., specializing in network security consulting and training with an emphasis on routers, firewalls, VPNs, and IDS devices from Cisco Systems. Mr. McKillip has over 10 years of experience in Cisco certified training for Global Knowledge, is a leading worldwide Cisco Learning Partner, and has edited numerous books published by Cisco Press. He holds a BS/MS degree in chemical engineering from M.I.T. and an MS degree in computer and information sciences from the University of Delaware.

Gilles Piché is a security consultant in the Ottawa (Canada) area. He has provided consulting services for the Canadian federal government and major corporations in Canada for the past 15 years. Gilles has provided technical editing services to Cisco Press for a number of Cisco PIX Firewall books. In the past, he has also taught Cisco and other security courses to industry professionals in Canada.

Dedications

To my parents and sister, Maurice, Florence, and Hélène, for your encouragements: Thank you. To my children, Laurence and Simon, who are making us prouder every day: "Courage, hard work, self-mastery, and intelligent effort are all essential to successful life"—Theodore Roosevelt. And finally to my husband and constant supporter, Pierre Rivard: Thank you for giving me reasons to believe I can.

—Catherine Paquet

To my darling wife, Martha, for her kindness, understanding, and support. Her thoughtful encouragement will forever inspire me. To our sweet daughter, Amanda Pearl, who has graced us with her beautiful and tender presence. And to my family, for their wisdom, support, and boundless encouragement.

—Warren Saxe

Acknowledgments

We would like to thank many people for helping us put this book together:

The Cisco Press team: Brett Bartow, the executive editor, was the catalyst for this project, coordinating the team and ensuring that sufficient resources were available for the completion of the book. Drew Cupp, the development editor, has been invaluable in producing a high-quality manuscript. His thoughtful guidance greatly improved the quality of the book. We would also like to thank Sheila Schroeder, the project editor, and John Edwards, the copy editor, for their excellent work in steering this book through the editorial process. Many thanks to Eric Dragowski and Hoda Mohamoud for providing us with access and tools for this project.

The technical reviewers: We would like to thank the technical reviewers of this book—Gilles Piché, Doug McKillip, and Stephen Kalman—for their thorough, detailed review and very valuable input.

Our families: This book would not have been possible without the consistent and continual understanding and patience of our families. They have always been there to motivate and inspire us. We thank you all.

Each other: There were a great many hours spent researching and writing this book, and the time was made infinitely more enjoyable because of the trust and respect that exists between two friends.

Contents at a Glance

Contents

Icons Used in This Book

Network Device Icons

 CallManager

 IP Phone

 Stations

 SRST Router

 Used For:
Application Server
DHCP
DNS
MOH Server
MTP
SW Conference Bridge
Voice Mail Server

 Router

 Switch

 Layer 3 Switch

 PIX Firewall

 Gateway or 3rd-Party H.323 Server

 Modem

 Access Server

 ATM Switch

 Used For:
Analog Gateway
Gatekeeper
Gateway
H.323 Gateway
Voice-Enabled Router

 PBX/PSTN Switch

 PBX (Small)

 Cisco Directory Server

 Local Director

 PC

 Laptop

 Server

 PC w/Software

 Used For:
HW Conference Bridge
Transcoder
Voice-Enabled Switch

 POTS Phone

 Relational Database

 Fax Machine

Media/Building Icons

 Network Cloud

Ethernet Connection

Serial Connection

 Telecommuter

 Building

 Branch Office

Introduction

Developing a comprehensive business case for network security that is rooted in traditional return-on-investment (ROI) modeling can be a challenging task for even the most seasoned executive. IT managers must contend with threats inherent in operating a network, while senior business executives must determine acceptable levels of operating risk. The fast pace of technological change, coupled with ever-increasing reliance on the Internet, has created an environment that is prone to higher degrees of risk and greater vulnerability.

Threats can run the gamut from a professional hacker harboring premeditated intentions to a careless office clerk who stumbles onto a database and inadvertently deletes its contents. Appropriate equipment exists to effectively deal with known and, in many instances, unforeseen issues, but numerous challenges are inherent in implementing such equipment, not the least of which is opportunity cost. *The Business Case for Network Security* addresses the issue that funding security enhancement represents an active decision not to invest elsewhere in the corporation, and that tangible financial modeling must support security proposals. This book is an IT security-investing tool, written from a business management perspective.

An IT manager tasked with creating a business case must acknowledge that in most corporations, the IT department is not a revenue generator. IT provides a service, albeit a fundamental one, but lacking ability to directly impact sales does not excuse an IT executive from needing to present objective financial data to further his business case. And therein lies the issue to enhanced security investing. Security has an emotional bias; it is concerned with events not happening — businesses typically invest more heavily after like organizations have been successfully targeted.

A fine line exists between acting preventively and being alarmist. Determining a return on investment for security products continues to challenge both security vendors and corporate executives alike. The challenge is one of assessing ROI in a decisive business manner. This book was written to address that challenge.

There are two distinct audiences for *The Business Case for Network Security.* Attack types, technical terms, and mitigation solutions are presented in an accessible format for seasoned business executives and board members. The book is written with a minimum of technical jargon; terms are explained, equipment uses are explored, and security is represented as being akin to a core disk in a corporation's vertebrae. Narrowing the focus for this same audience, Chapter 6, "A Matter of Governance: Taking Security to the Board," is dedicated to an organization's executive management and board members. Its discussion centers on return on prevention and the greater implications facing corporations in the current environment: homeland security and the issues inherent in corporate governance.

The book's sister audience, IT management, is provided with tools to better appreciate an organization's business. The business plan is effectively positioned so that it addresses the greater needs of the company. The book guides the IT executive through his own corporation, underscoring the philosophy that even society's most fundamental pieces of political legislation must have public support before they can become law. Drawing this parallel, the book leads the IT manager through a support-garnering program and instills in him the need to educate all users on security practices.

Financial ROI modeling is a fundamental component of security investing, and the book addresses this need by utilizing situation-based surveys to ascertain a corporation's tolerance for risk. Subjective factors are quantified, and an ROI model, created to address the potential for attack, delves deeply into business case financial methodology to derive a comprehensive return on prevention.

Security policies are the keystone of enforcement, and through a process of monitoring, testing, improvement, and security self-analysis, the book strongly encourages organizations to continually assess their security posture against self-acknowledged business requirements.

This book is separated into three parts and also includes helpful appendix material.

Part I, "Vulnerabilities and Technologies," covers the following topics:

- **Chapter 1, "Hackers and Threats"** — This chapter presents a high-level overview of the cost of attacks, including pertinent statistical evidence, and explores the benefits gained from security audits. A discussion of hackers — who does it and why — leads into the issues corporations face when the hacker is an employee. The chapter concludes with a discussion of different categories of threats.

- **Chapter 2, "Crucial Need for Security: Vulnerabilities and Attacks"** — By delving further into the core of threats, this chapter, written with the corporate executive in mind, explores a wide array of vulnerabilities, including those which emanate from design, human, and implementation issues. The chapter also discusses today's most prevalent attack types and includes a discussion on attack trends and social engineering.

- **Chapter 3, "Security Technology and Related Equipment"**—This chapter presents a high-level overview of mitigation fundamentals for the corporate executive. A wide variety of equipment and technology is presented (firewalls, traffic filtering, encryption, digital signatures, strong authentication, intrusion detection and prevention systems, and self-defending networks, along with many others) in a format that is designed to be accessible for the non-technical reader.

- **Chapter 4, "Putting It All Together: Threats and Security Equipment"**—This chapter analyzes the trends of well-known threats, learned in Chapter 2, and utilizes SAFE, a best practices guide for designing and implementing secure networks, to present a variety of topology options that can help to mitigate risk, by using technologies explained in Chapter 3.

Part II, "Human and Financial Issues," covers the following topics:

- **Chapter 5, "Policy, Personnel, and Equipment as Security Enablers"**—This chapter presents an executive-level planning and policy approach to securing each facet of an organization, both its equipment and personnel. The first of two senior management surveys is also presented in this chapter; created for this book, the survey is designed to determine the corporation's aversion to network security risk.

- **Chapter 6, "A Matter of Governance: Taking Security to the Board"**—Recognizing that security is greater than the sum of its parts, and that many network security decisions are now elevated to the board, this chapter addresses an organization's most senior executives by exploring the issues inherent in security governance and return on prevention.

- **Chapter 7, "Creating Demand for the Security Proposal: IT Management's Role"**—This chapter focuses on executive and senior-level IT managers by providing them with tools to better understand the business end of their organization and presents a process to garner support and create demand for security proposals. This chapter presents the second senior management survey, which helps to further quantify the organization's net return on prevention.

- **Chapter 8, "Risk Aversion and Security Topologies"**—This chapter explores the subjective nature of risk and, utilizing information garnered from the surveys in Chapters 5 and 7, presents topology models linked to an organization's unique risk-tolerance level. The chapter also enters into a discussion on the diminishing returns of security investments.

- **Chapter 9, "Return on Prevention: Investing in Capital Assets"**—This chapter acknowledges that there are varied financial instruments that can be used to measure the value of an investment. By utilizing financial tools such as net present value and discount rate, amongst many others, this chapter provides IT management with the necessary tools to firmly substantiate the business case.

Part III, "Policies and Future," covers the following topics:

- **Chapter 10, "Essential Elements of Security Policy Development"**—This chapter delves into security policy formulation by discussing many of today's most fundamental organizational resources, including both equipment and personnel, that need to be policy protected.

- **Chapter 11, "Security Is a Living Process"**—By introducing the *security wheel,* a process that ensures continual security renewal, this chapter views prevention as an on-going investment. The chapter also delves into some of today's pertinent legal issues and ramifications and concludes with an analysis of network security strengths, weaknesses, opportunities, and threats.

The following is a summary of the appendixes:

- **Appendix A, "References"**—This appendix lists websites and other external readings that were referred to throughout this book, along with references that were utilized during the research process.

- **Appendix B, "OSI Model, Internet Protocol, and Packets"**—This appendix provides an overview of the oft-mentioned OSI model terms found in this book, namely Internet Protocol and IP packets.

- **Appendix C, "Quick Guides to Security Technologies"**—This appendix provides guides to aid the reader with quick information and reference of concepts that are covered in this book.

- **Appendix D, "Return on Prevention Calculations Reference Sheets"**—This appendix summarizes the return-on-prevention financial data presented in Chapter 9.

- **Glossary**—This glossary defines key terms used in this book.

PART I

VULNERABILITIES AND TECHNOLOGIES

CHAPTER 1

HACKERS AND THREATS

The challenge in making the business case for network security is in harnessing the abundance of data on hacking and breaches and turning it into objective matter. The business case is not built merely on revenue output, either positive or negative, nor is its foundation built on a bevy of fears. Rather, it is a melding of many divergent factors that ultimately forms the basis with which one can begin to carve out concrete numbers. This chapter begins the process by focusing on hackers and threats.

This chapter covers the following topics:

- Contending with vulnerability
- Analyzing hacking
- Threats classification
- The future of hacking and security

Contending with Vulnerability

Type **security breach** into any search engine, and a seemingly unending list of sites will be revealed, running the gamut from popular attack targets to analyses detailing the cost of mitigation and cleanup. Regrettably, it's a burgeoning field and even greater mitigation has become necessary. Not all organizational requirements are created equal, and running the gauntlet of potential vulnerabilities can quickly become alarming.

Examining the reams of readily available data requires certain objectivity; it can be challenging not to overreact to the tidal wave of potential threats. Conversely, it can be too easy to be lulled into complacency, mistakenly confident that any security an organization might have in place will effectively seal its fortress. Security is a *living* challenge, requiring continual attention. The perpetrators might not be gaining in skill or intelligence, but the tools they utilize certainly are—and worse, the tools are getting even simpler to use.

CERT, www.cert.org, a major repository for vulnerability and attack reporting since 1988, estimated security breaches in the United States totaled 153,000 in 2003, almost double the prior year and more than a sevenfold increase in three years. While the attacks have increased in number, their severity, in raw dollars required for cleanup, continues to rise. In the United States alone, $2.6 billion was spent to undo the damage created by the *code red* virus, a malicious worm that exploited a known software vulnerability in certain servers. In 2004, 74% of all businesses surveyed in the UK reported suffering at least one security incident during the prior year, up from 44% four years earlier. Sixty-eight percent of all UK businesses stated that the attacks were malicious, a marked increase from two years earlier, when only 44% reported malicious activity. Interestingly, the 2004 responses revealed that large businesses experienced far greater levels of attack: 94% reported security incidents, and 91% stated that the attacks were malicious.[1]

After a rapid rise, the increase in malicious breaches appears to be leveling off. *Information Week* queried 815 technology businesses and security professionals, and the responses revealed that 45% of the respondents had fallen victim to viruses and worms in 2003, down significantly from the 70% that were affected two years earlier.[2] Better equipment, such as firewalls and virus protection software, coupled with wider implementation helped to stem the tide. Equally significant, the increased awareness of viruses resulted in organizations implementing greater protection processes. Of concern to security watchers is that the raw figures might misrepresent certain realities: While incidents are leveling off, they still remain at a high point. Equally disconcerting is that attacks are becoming more complex. Organizations are acknowledging that while basic security tools perform well against simplistic attacks, these companies are more concerned about worms and viruses that carry lethal loads, aiming to cause widespread disruption and damage.

Unless specifically motivated, hackers aren't necessarily particular about who ends up in their gun sights. They usually take a machine-gun approach, desiring to inflict as much damage across as wide a plain in as short an amount of time as possible. In January 2003, the worm *SQL Slammer* slowed the Internet and infected 75,000 systems in only ten minutes. The net result was damage and cleanup that totaled $1 billion.[3]

A study of attacks over a two-month period in late 2002 determined that 34% of victim organizations were managerial and insurance companies, 22% were telecommunications firms, and slightly under 10% were manufacturing concerns. The attackers were not discriminating, inflicting their damage across a wide spectrum of business and industry. In addition, 82% of those attacks originated from North American soil.[4] Whether it is because access to home or workplace personal computers is more readily available in North America, or because there is simply an overabundance of overtly motivated hackers in the United States, the result is the same: A great deal of malicious activity is being perpetrated in the domestic market.

Financial figures typically represent specific costs related to cleanup and rarely include figures that are more difficult to quantify: loss of trust, and the possible long-term impact that it could have on an organization, from negative revenue growth to a punctured reputation. Collateral damage from attacks is becoming increasingly difficult to ignore, as the full extent of cleanup and potential losses mount exceedingly quickly.

One-third of companies responding to a study on *Disciplined Security* were concerned their own employees would attack them, slightly less than those fearing an attack by outsiders.[5] It wasn't that they mistrusted their employees as much as they were concerned that their users might import infected codes, or worms and viruses, and introduce them to the company network.

Cookies

Most visits to websites result in a *cookie* being generated, a tool servers use to follow their visitors back home. Information about the visit is stored on the user's hard drive and, should the same PC visit again, the website recognizes the returning caller. A cookie is similar to a good hotel concierge: It allows swift identification and remembers everything you enjoyed on your last visit. Cookies in and of themselves do not pose a danger. The risk lies in *super cookies*, which are cookies that are written into a user's portion of the registry and are available to any application or web server. Super cookies are at the core of some spyware and certain advertising tracking software.

Realizing Value in Security Audits

Public companies have long employed the services of external auditors. While specific laws and regulations require certain companies to retain independent financial auditors, many corporations engage additional third parties to monitor specific activities, such as their *quality practices.* These specialists ensure that quality procedures and regulations are adhered to in every department throughout the organization. The auditors are tasked with rooting out and reporting digressions, and they are given the authority to demand that all quality deviations be corrected promptly. The same cannot be said for the security field, where the practice of external auditing has not seen widespread acceptance. To ensure that security auditing achieves greater recognition, organizations can challenge themselves to implement third-party audits to make sure that a minimum standard for security is in effect across their companies. Only 12% of UK businesses have used external security consultants.[6] While the figure is higher in the United States, the situation isn't much healthier; only 25% of organizations arranged for external audits of their security postures.[7]

Security audits should be similar to the quality audits that are a staple of many organizations, evolving to the point where external security auditors leave no stone unturned in their search for vulnerabilities. Unlike quality audits, where incorrect practices are handily rectified, unearthing potential security vulnerabilities might be more akin to opening a Pandora's box; "While never a desirable lid to lift, an organization can confidently move forward after it has realistically determined the following items:"

- Where the company is currently
- What the company's vulnerabilities entail
- How the company can implement better security
- When the company can feel more confident that its security posture accurately reflects its risk tolerance

Although a great deal remains unknown, external auditing can aid in attempting to ascertain the most prudent projects in which a company can begin to invest. A study carried out in late 2003 determined that nearly 70% of companies used fear of liability as a justification for spending on network security.[8] It is imperative that the cornerstone of any investment be based on concrete numbers. Fear, anxiety, or uncertainty will never be the foundation of an executable long-term plan. Understanding the beast, and the organization's aversion to it, is a concrete first step.

Analyzing Hacking

Mass media has long equated hacking with criminal, destructive, and malicious acts perpetrated on computers and the networks in which equipment resides. While the descriptions are correct, they are more aptly applied to the cracker, whose intent has always been more criminal. Thought to be associated with safecracking, *cracking* is the act of unlawfully accessing a network infrastructure to perform unethical activities. Conversely, a *hacker* is defined as someone who works diligently on programmable systems until they perform optimally. But for the purposes of this book, the widely accepted term *hacker* is used to represent criminal or malicious actions directed at computer networks and hosts.

This section discusses the following topics:

- Assessing vulnerability and response
- Hackers: motivation and characteristics
- The enemy within: maliciousness and sloppiness

Assessing Vulnerability and Response

In today's fast-paced environment, the need for access, and in particular remote access, has made networks more vulnerable to infiltration than ever before. Organizations have employed independent *white-hat hackers*, professional troubleshooters, to infiltrate their networks and illustrate the damage that is capable of being inflicted. Although senior management conspires with the consultants, IT staff doesn't necessarily have knowledge of the planned intrusions. Aside from exposing an organization's weakest links, an important element of the program is to determine IT's ability to detect and deal with threats. In the Federal Bureau of Investigation/Computer Security Institute (FBI/CSI) 2003 security survey, 78% of respondents cited their Internet connection as a frequent point of attack, with their vulnerability rising markedly every year since 1999.[9]

White-Box and Black-Box Hacking

While there are many variations of company-sanctioned hackers that organizations might want to engage to independently test their systems, most fall somewhere between *white-box* and *black-box* hackers.

White-box hackers are usually given partial or complete knowledge of a network's infrastructure, while black-box hackers typically have no prior knowledge of the infrastructure they have been engaged to test or hack.

Hackers: Motivation and Characteristics

The reasons for hacking are almost as numerous as the hackers themselves, running the gamut from those simply curious and seeking peer recognition to professional types with criminal intent. Table 1-1 provides a summary of the different types of hackers.

Table 1-1   *Generic Categories of Hackers*

Types of Hackers	Description
Curious	Looks around. Typically means no harm.
Clever	Seeks challenges and potentially fame.
Professional	Acts alone or on behalf of another party. Very skilled and disciplined. Subsets of the professional hacker are as follows: • The *hacktivist*, who performs his acts as an expression of political statement. • The *cyber-terrorist*, who uses hacking as a means to carry out political and terrorist objectives.
Purist	Very skilled. On a mission to return the Internet to its original open environment.

The most innocuous in the group is the *curious* hacker, the person who wants to observe an organization simply to see what is going on. Looking at e-mail, routing activity, or delving further into proprietary information, the hacker typically means no harm.

Related, but with an additional edge, is the *clever* hacker. This type is enthralled by the cerebral challenge the hack poses. He is goal oriented, typically setting forth with a well-constructed plan to maximize destruction and minimize the probability of getting caught. When he is inside a system, the challenge has been won. A further motivation for some of these hackers is the pursuit of their *fifteen minutes of fame*; the desire to be front-page news is a lofty goal for them.

As evidenced elsewhere in society, some people will always be enthralled by vandalism, and the computer world is not immune to such individuals. Hell-bent on destruction, the attacker attempts to inflict as much damage as possible. Searching the Internet for any network that might have left open a *back door*, a method of gaining access to a password-protected system without benefit of an actual password, the attacker randomly wanders into systems and inflicts damage.

A goal-oriented type, the *professional* hacker carries out assignments. A hired hand, he bears allegiance to no particular group and, similar to the professional criminal, is disciplined and skilled. Possibly stealing documents or proprietary information, he is in and out quickly, trying to minimize damage so that he leaves as few clues as possible.

The *purist* is the individual who believes the Internet is an open communication tool, and access to it should be completely unfettered. Possibly seeing it as their personal mission, these individuals set about unlocking doors and freeing the Internet from its corporate masters.

Regardless of their motivation, most intruders gain access by finding improperly secured network borders. Whether it's a virus that is let loose on an unsuspecting network or actual tampering of a company's main website, damage can range from embarrassment and diminished reputation to concrete revenue losses. A national newspaper was the victim of tampering when its main web page was successfully breached and one of its news stories altered. Had the hackers plastered the main page with streaks of paint or foul language, it would have been simpler for the company to rectify. Not only would the newspaper have discovered the breach sooner, but the public would have been more likely to accept the obvious break-in. By choosing to falsify a lead article on the newspaper's website, the hackers were attempting to damage the company's reputation for trustworthy and objective reporting.

All hacking poses a potential financial threat. Regardless of any damage a hacker might have caused, an organization must inspect, secure, and possibly even reinstall its software and data, should it ever discover that a hacker was in its midst. It is generally understood that hackers will continue to get craftier, and the bar will continue to be raised as they try to outdo one another, for the desire of hackers is to cause disarray and widespread disruption. Protecting his network, the hapless systems administrator is wildly outnumbered by unknown attackers whose full-time preoccupation is unearthing weakest links. The plight of today's busy IT department is protecting the organization on all fronts while optimizing applications and administering the network.

The Enemy Within: Maliciousness and Sloppiness

Although commonly portrayed as a computer-centric suburban teenager, the hacker can also be internal to an organization. It can be a trusted employee with lawful access who, for reasons immaterial, commits malicious acts on the computer network. The most difficult issue for many organizations is dealing with the attacker who is already cleared and residing comfortably within its secure walls. Table 1-2 provides a summary of the enemies within.

Table 1-2   *Types of Enemies Within*

Types of Internal Enemies	Description
Disgruntled employee	Wants to inflict damage
Careless employee	Unintentionally poses a threat by his actions or omissions
Braggart	Is talkative and a show-off
Angry employee	Is quick to anger, with a strong need to fuel similar frustration in his fellow employees

The *disgruntled employee* can be found in the most unsuspecting corners. Whether a data-entry clerk in the warehouse, a marketing assistant in a new-products group, a director in finance, or a systems administrator with access to the corporate server, his ability to inflict damage cannot be underestimated. Indiscriminately deleting e-mails is tantamount to randomly shredding documents, and the potential to inflict damage can only be measured by each individual's access to the network infrastructure.

The FBI/CSI survey reveals the uncertainty organizations feel about who is doing *what* to them. While respondents feel the majority of acts perpetrated against them are from outside their organizations, they cannot be certain the acts are random—or if they're the targeted work of former employees. There remain a significant percentage of respondents who do not report intrusions to law enforcement officials.[10] The reasons are varied, from issues of perceived loss of face to not knowing which law enforcement agency is interested in hearing about them. Conversely, the joint UK PricewaterhouseCoopers-UK Department Trade and Industry survey,[11] published in 2002 and in 2004, determined that insiders were the perpetrators of that country's worst security breaches, as shown in Figure 1-1.

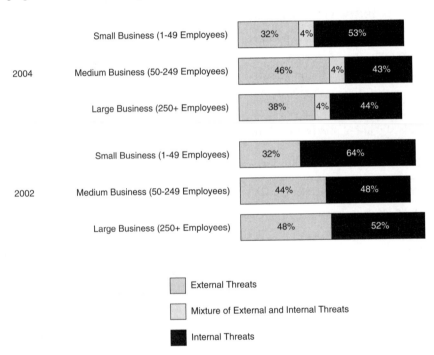

Figure 1-1 *Internal or External: Identifying the Perpetrators of Security Incidents*[12]

Former employees can pose a security concern, particularly if an organization does not have a strict policy to deal with departing staff. A company in India, solely dependent on its website for business, failed to change its network passwords after two employees departed. Angry and vengeful, they ventured to an Internet café and, over lattes and much keyboard clicking, deleted their former employer's entire customer database.

The *careless employee* is a type feared by many corporations. Never intending to cause harm, these employees unintentionally leave back doors open or innocently release information that can be helpful to potential intruders. They are underskilled or untrained IT personnel making configuration errors, front-line employees unwittingly engaging in conversations with strangers, users who unthinkingly open e-mail attachments containing viruses, and network administrators who mistakenly delete large files; they have the potential to put the company's network at risk. And they usually surface in the most unsuspecting areas. Even CEOs can add to the mayhem. At the close of an annual general meeting, a CEO left his podium and waded into the audience to converse with shareholders. Gone for only a few moments, he returned to the podium to discover his laptop missing. With the following quarter's projections loaded onto the computer, the company's proprietary information had just slipped into the wrong hands. Many times, the worst security breaches are those done inadvertently. A variety of threat-protection tools that organizations can use are explored in Chapter 3, "Security Technology and Related Equipment."

The *braggart* is someone who projects his voice while claiming victory for his latest triumph. He provides full-color commentary to everyone within earshot, even if he is in a public setting. He might have just completed a particularly difficult installation of a firewall, and in an attempt to impress his colleagues, he regales them with the specifics surrounding the configuration with which he was forced to contend. If he is known to frequent a particular pub after work, competitors—or would-be hackers—might even wander by and listen in, ensuring that they capture everything the braggart says.

Equally damaging is the *angry employee* who sits at the same bar, spewing out negative insider information for all to hear.

A subset of internal enemies can include the following:

- Recently departed staff who pose a risk should their access not be duly terminated along with their employment

- Former staff with thorough knowledge of an organization's network

Employees can be as dangerous as the average hacker, their insider knowledge enabling effortless access to the company's most vulnerable possessions. While conventional wisdom would rank the employee with high security clearance a greater risk than a lower-level employee, the reality is that the latter typically causes more damage to an organization. Finding it difficult to remember passwords, they use the same one for every program, or they write the passwords on a piece of paper and tape it to their keyboard. A hacker can do great damage with a minor password: With a crack in the door, his skills are those of a crowbar, forcing the network to open wider.

Certain security enhancements need not involve additional monetary expenditures, and they are explored in Chapter 5, "Policy, Personnel, and Equipment as Security Enablers," Chapter 7, "Creating Demand for the Security Proposal: IT Management's Role," and Chapter 10, "Essential Elements of Security Policy Development." Proactively engaging employees in becoming aware of security can create a sense of duty and individual responsibility. IT staff bear witness to the realities of hackers every day; most computer users do not. By asking for users' assistance, the organization can ensure that whatever monetary investments in security it has already made are not needlessly negated by employee carelessness.

Leakage Scenarios

With the advent of smaller and more powerful technological tools, stealing is getting easier to accomplish. Inserting a compact flash card into a laptop, similar to the memory stick found in digital cameras, or plugging a USB key into the rear of a PC, data can be downloaded in moments and slipped out of the office buried deep in a pocket. While organizations can monitor movement of large files, they typically don't implement restrictive measures unless a serious breach has occurred. Companies might be reticent to introduce highly stringent security measures, fearing that the measures could make the internal movement of information too cumbersome. Tying movement of large files to a security policy can aid in protecting both employer and employee.

The UK-PWC survey determined that more than a third of organizations harbored concerns about employees abusing their networks, yet fewer than 60% of them performed background checks as part of their hiring process. Exacerbating the issue, many used contract employees in their IT departments, resulting in few or no checks being performed. This is disturbing, because those employees are typically the ones with the most ready access to compromising data.

Threats Classification

Hackers' motivations and actions determine the type of threat they represent, whether a user in the organization inadvertently left a back door open or a disgruntled employee is hell-bent on seeking personal revenge.

The four main categories of threats are as follows:

- Unstructured

- Structured

- Internal

- External

Table 1-3 provides a summary of these categories of threats.

Table 1-3 *Threats Categorization*

Generic Threats Category	Description
Unstructured	Random hacking
Structured	Usually involves sophisticated hacking techniques
Internal	Typically performed by sloppy, oblivious, or disgruntled employees
External	Perpetrators not affiliated with the organization

An *unstructured* threat describes a hacker's search for easy prey. He doesn't necessarily target a particular site; he merely searches for one he could break into easily. Similar to the potential criminal walking down deserted streets, his eyes dart everywhere, seeking that elusive unlocked door or open window. Randomly trying door handles and running through backyards, he searches for easy prey. He doesn't necessarily have a well-crafted plan; his goal is simply to slip through the first crack he finds. In the case of the hacker, he isn't necessarily looking to take anything from you—he just wants in. But he definitely wants to hack.

For reasons known only to the hacker, your organization has struck a chord with him and, with a minor amount of work, he can set about searching for doors that might be penetrable. Going to your website and selecting the *Contact Us* option, the company's format for e-mail addresses quickly becomes evident. Searching for contact names in remote locations, the hacker might use your web page to unearth the name of a sales manager that might be lurking not too far below the surface. Failing that, he simply poses as a customer, telephones the receptionist, and requests the name of the sales manager. With that information in hand, usernames can quickly be determined, because most companies typically don't stray far from a full surname and an initial. Software is readily available to then aid the hacker in cracking user passwords.

While relatively straightforward, breaking into a system requires keen problem-solving skills and the ability to optimize such hacking tools as *war dialer*, software that places phone calls within a given range of numbers and logs which ones are answered by a modem tone.

While this might not appear to be *unstructured*, it is still a game to the hacker at this point. Gathering random bits of information and stringing them together to successfully break in can be a goal unto itself—or an evening's entertainment.

A *structured threat* is usually the work of professionals. Nothing is random about an attack; it doesn't involve wandering through deserted streets searching for an elusive unlocked door. Their plans are well crafted, their entry points into the targeted network are well defined, their tools and tactics are highly sophisticated, and their execution is generally successful.

A structured threat has a specific goal. For example, the hacker might break into a specific website on December 23 at midnight of this year and attempt to do something quite specific. He will be in and out quickly, careful to cover his tracks as much as possible.

An *internal threat* involves hacking executed by someone inside an organization. It could be an employee with malice on his mind or merely a sloppy employee who means no harm, but nonetheless, causes significant damage.

An *external threat* can be structured or unstructured and can emanate from outside an organization, typically involving all the avenues the hacker sees fit to use.

Table 1-4 provides hacking examples according to threats categorization.

Table 1-4   *Generic Hacking Classification and Examples*

Hacking Classification	Structured	Unstructured
Internal	A salesperson who, upon hearing the rumor of his imminent layoff, contaminates the CRM (Customer Relations Management) database with false information.	A user who inadvertently deletes a corporate spreadsheet because delete permission had accidentally been granted to all users.
External	A seasoned, resourceful hacker chooses a target network and proceeds to gather extensive data on it. Through his stealth detective work, he becomes familiar with the network and its vulnerabilities, eventually launching a surprise attack.	An inexperienced individual using readily available hacking tools randomly searches the Internet, on the hunt for systems with known vulnerabilities. These *script kiddies* are searching for an intellectual challenge, and they are not typically motivated by malice.

The Future of Hacking and Security

Hackers cause harm and create havoc; on that, there is general agreement. It is the future of hacking, and all that it could possibly engender, which leaves many unanswered questions.

Some people believe that the mitigation in place today provides sufficient protection. Opposing camps believe we are on the verge of anarchy. Speaking about network and Internet insecurity on a weekly national news program, David Kirkpatrick mused that while network administrators will ultimately win the war on viruses, it will be preceded by a number of powerful attacks that will severely cripple the Internet. He went on to suggest that it would serve as a wake-up call, forcing users to finally take viruses seriously.[13]

Most people already take hackers—and the viruses that they spread— seriously. But the extent to which organizations are prepared to commit funds to protect their structure remains highly individual. One person's excessive risk is another's light adventure. Understanding the threats and acknowledging the organization's aversion or comfort level with them can help to establish the firm's real cost of vulnerability. Through this process, the most prudent course of action to effectively and appropriately mitigate against unknown and unseen threats will become ever clearer.

Summary

Security breaches cut a wide swath across industry and business, and attacks are becoming increasingly more complex. Hard costs, consisting of measurable lost revenue and resultant system cleanup, continue to mount. Quantifying soft costs, including an organization's reputation and the long-term effect a breach could have on its future revenue stream, are becoming ever more important to ascertain. Organizations are beginning to acknowledge that some of their greatest liabilities lay with their staff; whether intentioned or inadvertent, it is a vulnerability that requires continual attention.

This chapter has laid the initial foundation in making the business case for network security by entering into a discussion that encompassed the following topics:

- Contending with vulnerability
- Engaging third-party security assessments
- Understanding who hacks, and why
- Addressing internal threats, whether intentioned or inadvertent
- Classifying threats

End Notes

[1]"Information Security Breaches Survey 2004, Technical Report." PricewaterhouseCoopers UK, Department of Trade and Industry UK. http://www.pwc.com/images/gx/eng/about/svcs/grms/2004Technical_Report.pdf. April 2004.

[2]Hulme, G.V. "No Time to Relax." *Information Week.* http://www. informationweek.com/story/showArticle.jhtml?articleID=12803057. July 28, 2003.

[3]Ibid.

[4]Fratto, M. "Don't Panic. Plan." *Network Computing* website. http://www. networkcomputing.com/1408/1408f1.html. May 1, 2003.

[5]Briney, A. and Prince, F. "Security Survey: Disciplined Security." *Information Security.* http://infosecuritymag.techtarget.com/ss/0,295796,sid6_ iss143_art294,00.html. October 2003.

[6]"Information Security Breaches Survey 2002, Technical Report." PricewaterhouseCoopers UK, Department of Trade and Industry UK. http:// www.dti.gov.uk/industry_files/pdf/sbsreport_2002.pdf. April 2002.

[7]Berinato, S. with research by Cosgrove, L. "The State of Information Security 2003 Survey." *CSO Magazine.* Study conducted by Pricewaterhouse-Coopers and *CIO Magazine*. http://www.csoonline.com/read/100103/survey.html. October 2003.

[8]Ibid.

[9]"Computer Crime and Security Survey 2003." Computer Security Institute and Federal Bureau of Investigation (CSI/FBI). http://www.gocsi.com/forms/fbi/ pdf.jhtml.

[10]Ibid.

[11]"Information Security Breaches Survey 2004, Technical Report." PricewaterhouseCoopers UK, Department of Trade and Industry UK. http://www. pwc.com/images/gx/eng/about/svcs/grms/2004Technical_Report.pdf. April 2004.

[12]Ibid.

[13]Kirkpatrick, D. NEXT@CNN. CNN. January 11, 2004.

CHAPTER 2

CRUCIAL NEED FOR SECURITY: VULNERABILITIES AND ATTACKS

A growing desire exists to learn more about security threats and the possible impact they can have on network and computing environments. Awareness levels in organizations both large and small are rising rapidly, as attacks are becoming more virulent and the collateral damage they cause more costly. Learning about those who threaten, and understanding what the threats can entail, is a major step toward counteracting the menace. Gauging investments in security products is not like any other; it ignites a range of discussion that will continue unabated until concrete numbers can be validated. The menace must be seen, understood, tamed, and nullified. This chapter is focused on seeing and understanding those menaces, and the following chapter concentrates on taming and nullifying them. Return on prevention (ROP) is about acknowledging the grey area that exists by understanding the threats, assessing individual tolerance to those threats, and moving forward accordingly. In keeping with the discussion, this chapter focuses on threats and attacks.

This chapter covers the following topics:

- Recognizing vulnerabilities
- Categories of attacks
- Common attacks
- Wireless intrusions
- Summary of attacks
- Social engineering
- Cisco SAFE axioms

Recognizing Vulnerabilities

It is inevitable that threats will exist. The more one is exposed to any type of interaction, be it computer networks or any aspect of everyday life, the more vulnerable one is to risk. Organizations are becoming increasingly more dependent on the Internet for their daily operations. From just-in-time manufacturing to customer service and accounts receivables, the growing reliance on the Internet results in a heightened vulnerability that needs to be continually managed. Human nature suggests there will always be an element in society that hunts for a vulnerability to exploit. Threats are external to organizations, and these threats can appear as poisoned arrows, continually airborne, searching for weak armor, or network vulnerabilities, to pierce. The best defense is stronger armor, coupled with a keen awareness of potential cracks.

Most attack vulnerabilities fall into one of the following categories:

- Design issues

- Human issues

- Implementation issues

Design Vulnerabilities Issues

Design issues encompass all network equipment, including both hardware and software. This discussion centers on the following topics:

- Operating systems

- Applications

- Protocol weakness

Operating Systems

Operating system weaknesses have been known to wreak havoc within a network. In a rush to market, operating systems (OSs) have been promoted and installed, only to reveal later that flaws within the software enabled hackers to penetrate systems with ease. A well-known flaw in an OS caused the OS to lack so much security that it allowed hackers to install malicious software and then access it remotely, with all the flexibility of a legitimate administrator.

Applications

Issues can exist in both hardware and software, but it is typically the latter that is responsible for a higher frequency of *cracks* within a system. While it does not occur as often with newer software, it was not uncommon for applications to be devoid of security mechanisms; a newly installed workstation on a network, for example, might not have required authentication for it to operate. Today, while most network-ready products arrive with built-in authentication, key steps need to be followed to ensure that proper verification procedures are enabled.

Protocol Weakness

A *protocol* is a set of rules that devices follow when communicating with one another. When network protocols were originally developed, security was not a large issue. Even today, ISPs rarely require e-mail traffic routed from a user to be authenticated. In addition, exchanges between the user's home workstation and the provider's server are usually done in clear text, enabling anyone eavesdropping on the communication to clearly see the messages.

Human Vulnerability Issues

Human issues delve into administrator and user errors, with the discussion focused on the following topics:

- Unsecured user accounts
- Unsecured devices
- Hardening devices

Unsecured User Accounts

It is not uncommon for users within an organization to be assigned network passwords when they are issued equipment. While some organizations force the user to create a new password when he first accesses the system, many companies still do not. Too often, the default password on a new system is the assignee's surname, or the company name, leaving it easy prey for a hacker. Informing a user that it is imperative to change her password might not be enough; a prompt forcing her to do so should be required. Even adept PC users can be unsure of the process to change passwords, and they might be reticent to speak up for fear of embarrassment.

Equally damaging are those users who utilize the same password for every function or, lacking a good memory, write their passwords on a piece of paper and tape it underneath their keyboard.

Unsecured Devices

Hackers are well aware that many new devices, from firewalls to routers and everything in between, often leave the factory with both the username and password preset to *admin* or another similar word. Because a tremendous amount of work is involved in just installing the new devices, the network administrator might not prioritize the resetting of the factory default passwords. But prior to the unit going live, changing the passwords can help to mitigate a vulnerability scanned for by most hackers.

Hardening Devices

Devices, operating systems, and applications often arrive set to behave in an open and trusting manner. It is the responsibility of the systems administrator to *harden* a device; this is the process of ensuring that all possible leaks get plugged. For example, some routers, by default, broadcast pertinent configuration information such as their network addresses, and host name. While publicizing that information internally might be expedient for the network administrator, broadcasting that same data on the Internet connection would only aid the hacker in his reconnaissance. By immediately deactivating the discovery protocol, unnecessary broadcasts are curtailed. At minimum, the interface, which faces the Internet, must stop such broadcasts.

Implementation Vulnerability Issues

Implementation issues deal with policy creation, configuration, and enforcement. This discussion focuses on the following topics:

- Password policy
- Access integrity
- Extrapolating policy intent
- Policy enforcement challenges
- Peer group communication

The proceeding discussion on security policy is presented as it relates to attacks. A greater analysis of policy and procedures can be found in Chapter 10, "Essential Elements of Security Policy Development."

Password Policy

Password integrity and password expiration are vital to security, and it is critical that users understand what is expected of them. If the system accepts alphanumeric passwords or requires a concocted password derived from a combination of numbers and characters, it is incumbent upon the corporation to consistently relay that information to its users. While it might be noted in a security policy, continually reminding users can only aid in overall adherence to the program.

Access Integrity

To effectively maintain a secure border, communication with employees is essential. Certain seemingly innocuous actions could represent a breach of security and, unless otherwise advised, might continue to occur. A user should be cognizant, for example, that under no circumstance is it permissible to disconnect a fax machine and borrow its analog telephone line to connect his laptop to the Internet. Although a user might want to do this when the network is down, utilizing an analog line could open a back door into the network once it is live again.

Extrapolating Policy Intent

Technology often precedes formal policy, requiring employees to understand the intent of company guidelines and ensure that they conduct themselves within the spirit of the guidelines. Even if a situation is not explicitly mentioned, or there is a lack of formal written policy, an employee should be able to discern between acceptable and unacceptable behavior.

For example, wireless hubs are relatively inexpensive, and an employee might decide to purchase his own for office use so that he can still be connected while freely moving about the department. He might justify his actions by concluding that the personal expenditure has increased his productivity, so the company shouldn't have an issue. But inexpensive wireless hubs typically ship from the manufacturer with the encryption option not yet activated, and the employee's actions could place the corporation in a highly vulnerable position.

Organizations do not customarily allow unauthorized devices to be installed on their internal networks. Even if it was not specifically detailed in a policy, an employee should have been able to draw that inference.

Policy Enforcement Challenges

An organization faces many challenges, not the least of which is the consistent implementation of its policies. When the corporation is experiencing high employee turnover or has numerous varied-sized remote offices, periodical challenges to policy enforcement might exist. Even where formal policy is not lacking, various departments, or remote offices, could have differing interpretations of the same rules.

Equally important as a written policy is the policy's consistent implementation throughout an organization.

Security policies are explored in detail in Chapter 10.

Peer Group Communication

Organizations continually stress the need for open lines of communication between departments but, in some instances, open dialogue *within* departments can be even more critical. A large enterprise acts as an example when it separates its IT department by responsibility. A typical IT group could be divided in the following manner, spreading responsibility, for example, over four distinct parties:

- **Workstations group**—Includes all in-house and remote users
- **Network infrastructure group**—Includes, but not limited to, routers and Ethernet switches
- **Network security group**—Typically includes firewalls and security policy
- **Network communications group**—Includes WAN (wide-area network), head office–to–branch office communication

While each group bears an enormous responsibility, they all are, at their core, intricately interrelated. A policy that encourages communication and strives for consistent implementation will be better prepared to deal with the unknown.

Categories of Attacks

Preparing for known attacks is relatively straightforward: Equipment can be put in place, logs can be monitored, and IT personnel can be trained and placed at the ready. Dealing with new attacks can be more problematic, but history shows that these attacks seem to take their cue from the past. Acknowledging historical trends can go a long way in preparing for the unknown.

This section first covers the human component and then covers the following categories of attacks:

- Reconnaissance attacks
- Access attacks
- Denial of service attacks

The Human Component in Attacks

Try as hackers might, it is generally difficult for them to completely cover their tracks. They can be successful in somewhat obscuring their trail, but analysis performed after an attack has enabled targeted organizations to see how, where, and possibly why they were attacked, allowing these companies to take necessary measures to plug leaks and ward off similar future attacks. In an effort to expose unlawful activity, many organizations have proactively taken the lead in advising security interest groups. Organizations such as CERT Coordination Center routinely publish wrongdoing, enabling systems administrators to perform preemptive measures that could better secure their networks.

But *human nature* will continue to play a major role in most organizations: Systems to protect the perimeter are purchased and associated equipment which protects the interior are installed, and until an attack occurs, an organization can begin to feel a comfort level that it is doing everything possible to fortify itself against intrusions. Typically, it is right at that point where human nature begins to assume a greater role.

The most comprehensive equipment can't help secure an organization if someone goes home at night leaving a back door open. Complacency typically creates exposure, and an organization's weakest link might be the execution of standard security practices in each of its departments. Human nature dictates that until a breach occurs, until perceived exposure exists, complacency can be masked by thoughts that one is doing the right thing.

By reconstructing an event, network forensic specialists illustrate how reconnaissance attacks, access attacks, and denial of service attacks were carried out on a targeted organization. Through this process, these specialists can act as an enabler, helping the organization to move forward.

Figure 2-1 depicts a generic corporate network, as well as the possible network devices and systems that it uses against attacks. Devices that typically perform targeted tasks are also referred to as *appliances*. These include, but are not limited to, routers, switches, VPN concentrators, remote access servers, and intrusion-detection sensors. These devices are discussed further in Chapter 3, "Security Technology and Related Equipment."

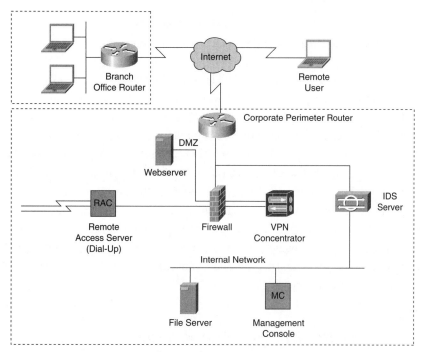

Figure 2-1 *Topology of a Generic Network and Its Components*

Reconnaissance Attacks

Reconnaissance is the observing, gathering, and analyzing of information about a specific area or device. It is often associated with wartime, when participants in a conflict would collect intelligence on their enemy in an attempt to capitalize on the enemy's vulnerabilities. In IT, reconnaissance invariably precedes a structured attack; the hacker rarely skips this intelligence-gathering step when planning to break into a network.

Through reconnaissance, the hacker collects as much data as possible about the network and hosts that he wants to break in to. As an example, the hacker can do the following things:

- Search for network addresses of possible targets

- Determine the operating system

- Drill down to the version of the operating system

- Determine the applications that are running on the possible targets

The wily hacker has access to a wide array of readily available tools that can aid in determining both the live network hosts and their respective network addresses, also known as *IP addresses*. IP is the underlying communication protocol used on the Internet and by most organizations (see the following Tech Tip regarding IP addresses). A great deal of effort, and many steps, are required to unearth such data, but when the data is in hand, the hacker is in a position to identify diverse information, from the vendor of the operating system to the version that is installed on a workstation. Proceeding to the manufacturer's or CERT website, the hacker will search for information concerning significant flaws pertaining to the equipment. It is generally accepted that equipment will experience issues from time to time, and manufacturers post solutions, or *patches*, to the issues on their websites.

Tech Tip: IP Addresses = Network Addresses

An IP address is an address assigned to individual hosts on an IP network. Each address consists of a network number, an optional subnetwork number, and a host number. The network and subnetwork numbers together are used for routing, and the host number is used to address an individual host within the network or subnetwork. An IP address is also called an Internet address.

Figure 2-2 shows a hierarchical addressing scheme using IP addresses.

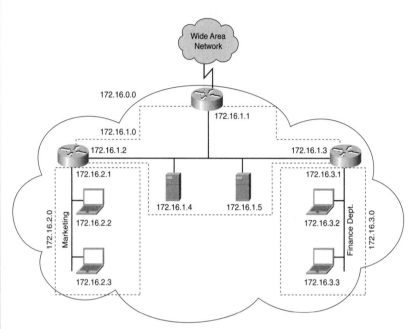

Figure 2-2   *Hierarchical Addressing with IP*

An example of a host IP address is 172.16.3.8, where the components are as follows:

172.16 represents the network.

.3 represents the subnetwork.

.8 represents the host.

Even the most ardent network administrators have their hands full running their networks, and they don't necessarily apply *patches* that would immediately address system known issues. Relying on human nature, the hacker assumes that at least one patch is yet to be installed, so he attempts to determine on which *ports* the host is listening. A port, which makes a service accessible, is similar to a door, and certain ports are always open so that traffic can flow easily. For example, an outgoing mail server usually receives e-mail messages on its port 25, a file transfer server usually listens on its port 21, and a web server usually welcomes browser requests on its port 80.

The server should only be listening to ports that are relevant to it, and ports that are not needed should be turned off. This is part of hardening a device, as described earlier in this chapter and as shown in Figure 2-3. Active ports that are not required can be an invitation to hackers. Ultimately, the more ports the server leaves open, the more its exposure is increased. This is important to note, because many servers arrive with multiple ports open, by factory default. If a network only requires a handful of ports for its e-mails, file sharing, and web surfing, but doesn't close the remainder, the organization is more vulnerable than it needs to be. It would be equivalent to the shopkeeper who opens his front door for customers but also leaves every door and window open in the back.

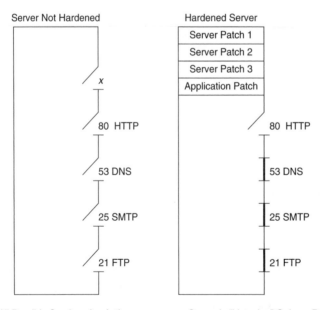

Figure 2-3 *Process to Harden a Web Server*

Mapping the Topology

The hacker's goal during a reconnaissance attack is to do one or more of the following things:

- Discover all hosts on the network

- Discover services (ports) on those hosts

- Determine the OS and the versions of software running on the identified hosts

If the hacker can drill that far into the network, he might eventually be able to plan his assault from multiple fronts.

Network reconnaissance is a fundamental part of information gathering. Similar to the potential criminal who wanders into the same bank branch every other day for two weeks studying the movement of guards and staff in the hopes of exposing vulnerability, he is signaling his intent. Discovering a pattern of *harmless* intrusions on your network might be a telltale sign of intent to cause damage. Chapter 3 discusses tools that can alert a systems administrator to possible intent.

Access Attacks

An access attack is a breach, widely considered to be a major assault on a network. Using data collected from a reconnaissance, an *access attack* puts knowledge into motion and executes on specific vulnerabilities.

Capitalizing on Protocol Vulnerabilities

A hacker might decide, for example, to capitalize on a protocol vulnerability by sending the following items:

- A specially crafted packet bearing the same source IP address as the destination IP address

- The same source port number as the destination port number

The workstation to which the packet was addressed, becomes stuck in a loop when trying to reply to the source address—because the source address is also itself—and the result is full CPU consumption.

Packets are further expanded upon in Appendix C, "Quick Guides to Security Technologies."

Access Stratagems

Conversely, a hacker might use a Trojan horse (a program that purports to do one thing, but is actually doing something malevolent in the background). Inadvertently activating the malicious code concealed in an e-mail, for example, a pop-up window presents an enticing tag line: *Click here to see cute puppies.* When the code is activated, puppies instantly appear on top of what was already on the screen. In the short time the user is enjoying the dancing puppies, a program is diligently running in the background, accessing the user's e-mail address book and sending it back to the originator, typically a *spammer*, an individual or organization that sends unsolicited commercial messages. With multiple new address entries in its customer contact database, the program goes on to send the same Trojan horse to an ever-expanding list of victims. The concept of a Trojan horse is expanded on later in this chapter.

Access attacks are unmitigated acts of trespassing, the hacker's equivalent of unlawful entry into secured sites.

Denial of Service Attacks

Unlike a typical attack, where a hacker wants to gain control of a system to use it for specific purposes, a hacker attempting to conduct a denial of service (DoS) attack does not necessarily need to gain access to the targeted system to wreak havoc. He merely needs to overload a system or network so that it cannot provide service any longer. DoS attacks can have different targets, ranging from the simple, *bandwidth consumption*, to the more complex, *resource starvation.* Some of the classifications for DoS attacks are application DoS, network-based DoS, and distributed denial of service (DDoS).

Denial of service encompasses a range of exploits, any of which are capable of stymieing normal network activities. Its goal is to effectively quash network resources including, but not limited to, processors, memory, storage drives, and bandwidth. It can also include instances where Internet URL directories are purposely corrupted, resulting in Internet traffic being diverted to a third-party website, as evidenced in Figure 2-4, when a user requests the web page www.stropsekin.com, but is unwillingly directed to www.environment.org. Domain name hijacking is discussed later in this chapter. In essence, denial of service (DoS) represents those acts that prevent the use of a network or cause a system to be inaccessible. Similar to other kinds of attacks, they are not necessarily carried out by an external party, nor are they necessarily done intentionally.

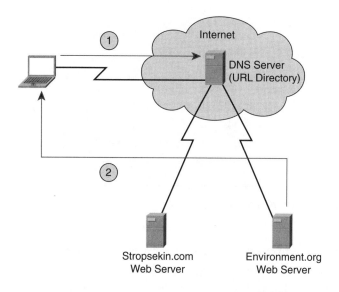

Figure 2-4   *Domain Name Hijacking*

Buffer Overflow and Bandwidth Consumption

In an attempt to create a chaotic situation, a hacker might fire off very large data strings in his effort to overwhelm a targeted server, performing an action known as *buffer overflow*. The hacker is aware that the server has a finite amount of memory and processing power and, as an example, sending an illegally large payload in a *ping* request could result in a buffer overflow. That particular buffer overflow attack is called *Ping of Death*, ping being a tool that determines whether a network device is online, as shown in Figure 2-5. Similar to naval sonar, a signal is sent and the return of the signal bouncing off an object is used to gain information.

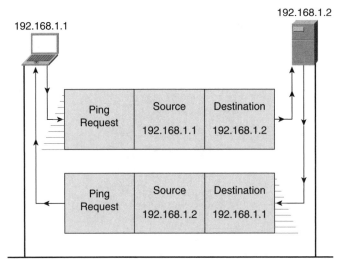

Figure 2-5 *Ping: Request and Reply*

Specifically, to effectively transmit a very large ping, the ping typically needs to be broken into smaller chunks; upon reaching the destination, the server reassembles the chunks. But the size of the reassembled ping, or chunks, is so far beyond the processing capacity of the Internet Protocol that the buffer, in this example, overflows and effectively shuts down the targeted system. Even those servers with seemingly endless processing power and equally ample memory resources can be stymied if the buffer becomes overloaded.

Mail Bomb

A *mail bomb*, another DoS attack, is an attempt to direct enormous numbers of e-mails to a single user or system with the goal of overwhelming and derailing the targeted system.

Though typically intentional, a mail *storm* can be an inadvertent DoS initiated by an internal party. Preparing to be absent from the office for jury duty, an employee might, for example, want to advise those contacting him that he will be unreachable for a number of days. Activating the *out of office* and *reply to all* options in his e-mail program, he also activates *auto-confirmation*, because he wants to ensure that the original sender opened his reply e-mail and understood the response would be delayed.

While these tools are useful when users check their e-mails regularly, they can tax a system if not monitored closely. It is not uncommon for large organizations to e-mail company-wide memos, and when both *reply to all* and *auto-confirmation* are activated on a recipient's e-mail, the result can be overwhelming. If a corporation has 4000 users, the auto-reply feature will, in this case, send out the recipient's jury duty note to all 4000 users on the network. Worse yet, an auto-confirmation will be sent back to the original recipient, after each of the 4000 users opens his or her e-mail. When the auto-confirmation is received, it sends an auto-reply in response. If any of the 4000 users are similarly out of the office and have their e-mail set up in a comparable fashion, the domino effect can be devastating to a network, grinding it to a halt from the fantastic flurry of e-mail activity. While checks and balances are typically in place to expose unusual activity, significant damage can still be inflicted in the interim.

Domain Name Hijacking

Domain name hijacking has become prevalent, and while fixes have been published, the allure of hijacking a domain name can be too great a magnet for many a hacker; the resourceful ones will likely root out new avenues to keep redirecting traffic. A famous case involved traffic destined for a sportswear manufacturer that was redirected to an environmental website. An odd twist on DoS—because the prospective visitor had seemingly reached the intended site—it would take repeated attempts before realizing that the diversion had been deliberate and done without the visitor's consent.

Distributed Denial of Service

While a DoS attack is straightforward for even a novice to initiate, a *distributed denial of service (DDoS)* requires barely more expertise. Where a DoS attacks from a single point, a DDoS recruits other computers across numerous networks, resulting in an attack from multiple fronts.

A hacker initiates his plan by searching for a network he can compromise. Performing reconnaissance and pinpointed access attacks, he locates a vulnerable system and loads specific hacking software onto it. The attacker activates the newly loaded program to work in stealth mode, so a systems administrator performing a routine examination of the network wouldn't necessarily notice the malicious application. As shown in Figure 2-6, the newly recruited *handler*, also known as master, searches its network for peer workstations that can be compromised and plants malicious software to turn the workstations into agents. The hacker continues his search for additional vulnerable networks until he has successfully breached, for example, eight networks. If each of the 8 workstations he compromised is able to find 99 others, he will have amassed an army of 800 workstations spread over 8 different networks from which to launch his attack.

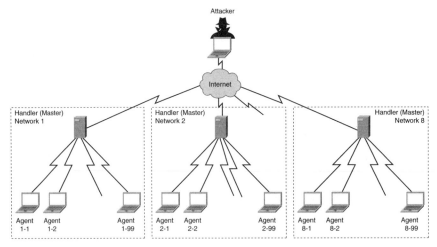

Figure 2-6   *Mounting a Distributed Denial of Service Attack: Recruiting Accomplices*

Typically choosing a famous website as his target, the hacker adds a twist to his plan. He sends a request to the website, knowing that its reply will always be sent to the originator's network address. The hacker's twist is that he involves an unaware third party, typically another well-known website, and modifies that source, or originator network address, in his requests.

With 800 workstations, from various networks, preprogrammed to send 1000 *header-modified* requests simultaneously (an information-carrying ping that appears more legitimate to the about-to-be-breached server) to the target, www.skoobnozama.com is not only overwhelmed, but the server's automatic response to the requests is also returned to the falsified address— www.mitciv.com—as shown in Figure 2-7. The hacker will have successfully used 8 unwilling networks, and 800 of its workstations, to send 800,000 requests to the www.skoobnozama.com website and worse, force the breached website to unwittingly attack another website, www.mitciv.com, with the mandatory 800,000 replies.

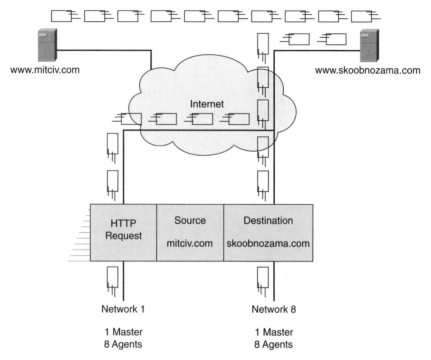

Figure 2-7 *Distributed Denial of Service Attack*

In summary, forensic analysis allows organizations to understand how and why they were attacked, typically resulting in higher walls being erected after a breach. Certain organizations can be reticent to react in such a manner because, some might surmise, the movement of hackers is so quick that the game is perpetually being ratcheted up a notch, and hackers will be looking forward to their next complicated attack rather than looking to the past. But history tends to repeat itself, as hackers seem to look to the past to figure out how they are going to attack in the future. Whether *social engineering* is the old conman's game or *reconnaissance* is similar to the petty criminal scouting a sleeping neighborhood searching for unlocked doors, human nature suggests that people tend to pull from their store of knowledge when they chart a path for the future. Organizations would be wise to do the same.

Additional Common Attacks

The list of possible attacks is endless, with new ones surfacing each week and older ones being resurrected, richly peppered with unique twists to make them more explosive in their reincarnated state. Hackers typically drive new attacks, pushing the envelope at every turn, because their main preoccupation is to wreak havoc. While an exhaustive analysis of attacks could fill its own book, the goal of this section is to provide a basic overview of some common attacks, understanding that many newer ones are often subsets or combinations, of what already exists. The discussion includes the following topics:

- Footprinting
- Scanning and system detailing
- Eavesdropping
- Password attacks
- Impersonating
- Trust exploitation
- Software and protocol exploitation
- Worms
- Viruses
- Trojan horses
- Attack trends

Footprinting

Performed during the reconnaissance stage, *footprinting* is the process of identifying a network and determining its security posture. The hacker attempts to create a layout of the IT operation, by mapping out the following items:

- Geographical location of corporate IT assets
- Related companies—extranet—to find weakest links
- Phone numbers assigned to corporate analog
- Names of employees, usernames, and e-mail addresses

Individually, each parcel of information could be deemed somewhat innocuous. By combining these pieces, the hacker is able to draw a map that can roughly determine the architecture of the overall system and its security infrastructure.

Scanning and System Detailing

Scanning and system detailing, part of the reconnaissance stage, is the process of probing for live servers, determining which ports are active, and drilling down further to discover details regarding applications and versions running on the system.

The hacker, for example, might be running a reconnaissance overnight, as shown in Figure 2-8. By using port-scanning software, a report can tell her which stations are live and what ports the stations are listening on. If the report states that the system is listening on ports 21, 25, and 80, all well-known ports, she can surmise that the equipment is most likely a server. By drilling down further and determining the operating system, she can confirm her suspicion. Utilizing that information, she can then search for known vulnerabilities inherent in the operating system, as well as the particular version of the OS.

Eavesdropping

Eavesdropping is a traffic-analysis program that sniffs (monitors), records, and analyzes network traffic. As shown in Figure 2-9, the hacker uses software that does the following things:

- Listens to all communication on a network

- Captures each bit of every transmission

- Uses a protocol analyzer to reassemble packets of information, allowing it to read e-mails, for example

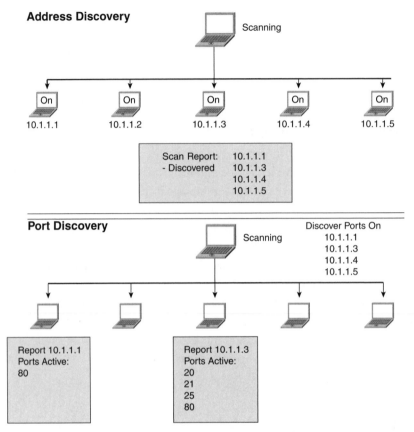

Figure 2-8   *Reconnaissance Attack: Scanning a Network*

Communication between the CEO and CFO

"...the current blackout period prevents us from making a press release
regarding the $12M contract we just signed with our Asian client."

Figure 2-9   *Hacker Eavesdropping on a Communication*

Eavesdropping can quickly reveal usernames and passwords, enabling the hacker to eventually impersonate a user to gain entry into the network.

Password Attacks

A *password attack* is a process the hacker employs to learn user passwords.

Discovering a legitimate username within a network is only valuable if the hacker can also determine the user's password. Depending on how well the hacker knows the user, he might first go through the obvious list: given name, company name, birth date, maiden name, and family names. Many systems use a *three-strike* access rule, whereby the system locks out the user after his third failed authenticating attempt. If the hacker were unable to establish the passwords, he might favor an attack known as a *brute-force attack*, which uses a process that tries seemingly endless combinations of letters, numbers, and symbols in an attempt to determine a user password. This technique works particularly well when the three-strike rule has not been implemented.

Conversely, if the hacker is an insider, he might opt to walk by a workstation and see whether the user wrote her password on a slip of paper and taped it to her keyboard. Alternatively, an insider could also be aware of certain tools that provide access to encrypted password lists on a network, such as password decryption tools, which can take advantage of weak encryption algorithms.

Impersonating

Impersonating describes the person or persons who unlawfully assume a legitimate user's credentials for the purposes of deceiving a computer network.

The hacker might *sniff* on a network (monitor its traffic) in an attempt to uncover a username and its accompanying password.

Conversely, the hacker might opt to steal a purse, wallet, or personal digital assistant (PDA) that belongs to a network administrator, knowing that many people keep pertinent access information close at hand.

With this sensitive data, the hacker would be able to access the targeted network with the full authority to run it. After the attack has been carried out, the hacker has minimal fear of being caught, because analysis after the fact will attribute the breach to the impersonated user. However, exhaustive forensics could ultimately reveal the true hacker.

Trust Exploitation

A *trust relationship* exists when two systems, possibly operating within the same organization or, as an example, two separate organizations that connect for *just-in-time* processes, grant certain two-way access privileges to each other. A user authorized on server X would be provided with privileges on server Y, with both systems openly allowing the other in. The premise is that if a user is precleared on one system, that gives her automatic right, or trust, to access the other system. *Trust exploitation*, as shown in Figure 2-10, can occur when a hacker, who might have been unsuccessful in his attempts to break into server X, discovers he is able to penetrate server Y and, exploiting the trust that is inherent between the two systems, successfully works his way back to server X and inflicts damage.

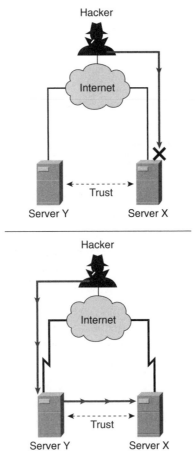

Figure 2-10   *Trust Exploitation*

Software and Protocol Exploitation

It is not uncommon for flaws to exist in software and operating systems. While vendors are thorough in their research and development, the possibility exists that product containing flaws could be shipped to an end user. Similar to most other industries, software manufacturers are quick to respond, issuing patches for the flawed software. The wily hacker, aware that his targeted organization uses the affected software, relies on human nature when he surmises that most network administrators are very busy and might not install the needed patch the moment it is published. Taking advantage of that window, the hacker attempts to break into the system, exploiting the flaw in the software.

When major software revisions are initially made available, organizations can decide to delay implementation until the inevitable quirks, or issues, have been determined and a less problematic version of the software revision is available.

Another type of exploiting occurs when a tool is used for something other than its original purpose. *Pinging*, for example, was created to aid network administrators in determining whether equipment was live on their networks. While they could have walked around the facility and seen for themselves, it was not only faster to send a signal and see whether the appliance responded, but networks were also quickly becoming geographically larger, and walking around to check on equipment was becoming a poor option. Hackers seized the checking tool and used it for their own nefarious purposes.

Worms

A *worm* is a program that potentially contains malicious code that continually replicates itself as it works its way through networks. Although worms self-propagate, unlike viruses, worms are not designed to impose harm on their host systems.

The primary goal of a worm program is to replicate itself on as many networks as possible, sometimes gathering data, possibly e-mail address books, from each of the breached systems.

Worms can quickly create a DoS attack by bottlenecking networks. The Melissa worm in 1999 wreaked havoc and stymied systems as it literally wormed its way through networks, duplicating itself whenever it came into contact with a target. It would worm its way into the targeted user's e-mail address book and then forward itself to the first 50 addresses it found. The worm would arrive at each new victim's computer disguised as e-mail from someone the victim seemingly knew. Not surprisingly, the unsuspecting user would open the e-mail and the worm would perform the same act: Each worm found 50 new addresses, reattached itself, and 2500 new victims were attacked. Those 2500 victims each found 50 more to infect and, quite rapidly, the aberrant e-mail propagated throughout the Internet on the backs of address books, leaving bottlenecked systems in its wake.

Viruses

A *virus* is a software program that strives to generate great harm by corrupting files or functionality on a system. Early-generation viruses required the help of an unwitting accomplice, typically a system user, to propagate itself. But viruses have matured and now often include worm-like characteristics that enable self-generating replication. Code Red was a prime example of this type of hybrid. It acted like a virus by dynamically generating new web pages on infected web servers that made the claim *Hacked by Chinese*. In its sister role as a worm, it also self-propagated and spread itself to other networks, continually seeking new web server victims in its path of infection.

Trojan Horses

A *Trojan horse* is a malicious program that masquerades as a legitimate one, purporting to do one thing in the foreground while it is doing something malevolent in the background. A Trojan horse is a popular means of disguising a virus or worm, as described in the puppy example in the section "Access Stratagems," earlier in this chapter.

Attack Trends

Combination malicious attacks, known as *combo-malware*, are becoming more prevalent. By combining the most destructive elements from past attacks with the most effective tools available today, hackers are able to combine worms and viruses that replicate faster, cause greater damage in shorter periods of time, and leave fewer clues for forensic analysts.

While the industry should anticipate attacks to become more sophisticated, most hackers themselves likely will not. Regrettably, the tools available, along with easily obtainable elementary instruction guides, make attacks a pastime in which too many could effortlessly engage. The tools that carry out malicious activities are more powerful with each new iteration, as illustrated in Figure 2-11. Hackers' technical abilities need not be as advanced as in the past, because their tools are now so automated and powerful that they can carry out the attacks.

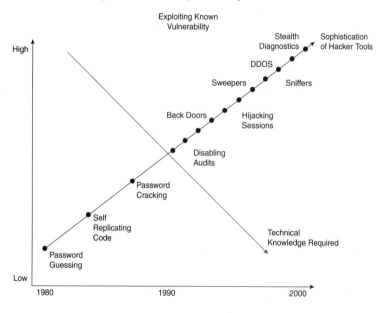

Figure 2-11 *Inverse Relationship Between Hacker Knowledge and Hacking Tools (Source: "Cisco Networking Simplified," 1-58720-074-0, Cisco Press)*

But a small minority remains that relishes the cerebral challenge that a breach poses. The reality for organizations is that they must contend with this element and use mitigation tools to deal with those who perpetually strive to unearth innovative ways to breach even the most sophisticated intrusion-prevention systems. A basic key for most organizations is to first acknowledge their weakest links and then implement procedures to fortify them, ensuring that any future programs are built on terra firma.

Wireless Intrusions

Wireless networks have simplified daily rituals for many people, from the remote user whose laptop is configured to borrow any wireless signal it can detect regardless where he might be to the office-bound professional who can shift to multiple locations within a building and always maintain his wireless connection. While much has changed in the new office realm, attacks perpetrated against wireless systems have not. Notably, some of the so-called traditional attacks can still be used against wireless systems and, of more concern, these attacks are also less complicated to stage. In many of the following examples, wireless access points (WAPs) are deployed throughout an office. A WAP is a wireless hub, layer 1 device that provides physical connectivity—in this case, through radio frequencies instead of unshielded twisted-pair cable. Some common types of wireless intrusions are as follows:

- Wireless eavesdropping
- Man-in-the-middle wireless attacks
- Walk-by hacking
- Drive-by spamming
- Wireless denial of service
- Frequency jamming
- The hapless road warrior

Wireless Eavesdropping

A hacker attempting to eavesdrop in a wired environment must be physically connected to her target's network infrastructure, as opposed to being in a wireless situation, where she need only be in the vicinity. Yet she would still face issues, such as contending with possible broadcast interference and the uncertainties inherent in sending signals around concrete walls.

An activity known as *war driving* could easily be referred to as drive-by eavesdropping, because it typically involves an individual driving an automobile, attempting to log on to wireless networks, as shown in Figure 2-12. It's not an illegal act, because radio frequencies used by LANs (local-area networks) are unlicensed public frequencies. Unless an organization could prove that a war driver was acting with intent, compiling information for an attack, it could prove difficult to bring such a hacker down.

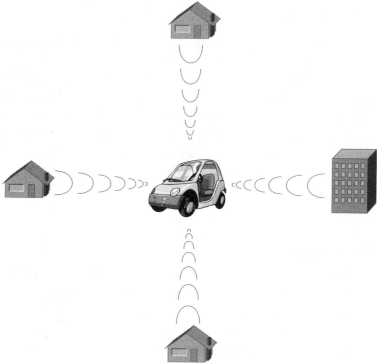

Figure 2-12 *War Driving*

Man-in-the-Middle Wireless Attacks

A typical wireless office has wireless access points scattered about its building, and with so many signals available, equipment is generally configured to attract the strongest signal each time it boots up. Hackers have been known to position their own wireless access point just outside an office window, resulting in a workstation being more attracted to the hacker's hub than an office antenna, which could be farther away. Called a *man-in-the-middle* attack, the rogue access point can reveal invaluable information—for example, usernames, associated passwords, the network's authentication request mechanism, and so on—while the unsuspecting user attempts to connect to his supposed network.

Walk-By Hacking

In his article "Walk-by Hacking" in *The New York Times Magazine* (July 13, 2003), Eric Sherman relayed the story of his short stroll along The Avenue of Americas in Manhattan. Armed with his laptop and a $40 network interface card, he connected to 13 different networks along a 45-foot stretch of sidewalk. Of those 13 networks, only one-third were using encryption. While connecting shouldn't necessarily be equated with breaking in, the hacker can still engage in disruptive activity, namely, bandwidth hogging. Borrowing a network's bandwidth for the hacker's own, possibly innocuous, activities can slow the network's pace in its own office.

Drive-By Spamming

A person who engages in sending spam e-mail could be a prime candidate for stealing bandwidth. Possibly reticent to initiate mass mailings through his own outgoing mail server, or simply lacking enough bandwidth himself, the hacker parks his vehicle in close proximity to the targeted network, connects to his wireless signal, and sends e-mails. He not only minimizes his own costs, but he also reduces the likelihood of getting caught, because the sender will technically be the breached network. Similarly, spammers can also spoof the receiver address so that it is the same as the sender address. As a result, the victim receives messages that appear to have been sent by himself.

Wireless Denial of Service

To carry out a DoS in a wired environment, a remote hacker must crack through an organization's firewall. In a wireless environment, the hacker need only position himself in close proximity to the building to initiate network contact and begin his acts of intrusion. His job is even easier to execute if the corporation has not yet activated encryption on its wireless network devices.

Frequency Jamming

An attack that is more prone to a wireless environment is *frequency jamming*. The hacker attempts to overload every frequency over which the network is broadcasting, bringing all internal activity to a standstill.

The Hapless Road Warrior

Many laptop users spend a certain amount of time away from their office but still have the need to connect with their organizations while on the road. To ensure ease of use, wireless network cards installed on laptops are configured to search and capture every available signal they can locate. Similarly configured is e-mail software, which immediately begins to synchronize the moment its network card makes a connection.

While convenient, problem situations can arise. For example, a CEO of a medium-sized public company was working on his laptop during a drive through a high-end residential neighborhood when he noticed his e-mail begin to synchronize. When the car drove through an intersection, it suddenly stopped synchronizing. A block later, his e-mail started to synchronize again and, as the car drove along, it stopped again. On its third attempt to connect, the reason became clear: The e-mail program was designed to synchronize as soon as its network card found a wireless signal to borrow. Driving through the neighborhood, the CEO's laptop kept locating signals emanating from the wireless LANs installed in neighborhood homes. Because the vehicle was moving, it lost signals as quickly as it picked them up. Had the car been stationed in front of a wireless home, he could have sent e-mails all afternoon, provided that the network was not protected with an encryption option.

Social Engineering

An individual who purports to be someone he is not, or who assumes a persona and proceeds to engage insiders in verbal and written conversation for the express purpose of infiltrating their organization, is understood to be engaging in *social engineering*. These individuals possess persuasive communication powers, ably convincing their targets to reveal confidential network information. The social engineer rarely employs technology in the pursuit of information. The tool of choice is similar to that of the old-time conman: fast-talking conversation.

Social engineering is not a new phenomenon. Kevin Mitnick, a self-proclaimed social engineer, has publicly stated that he rarely used his technical expertise to garner information. He simply employed an endless range of communication tactics.

Examples of Social Engineering Tactics

The conman initiates telephone contact with an organization's IT department, claiming to be an official with the company's service provider. He speaks with authority, stating that he was delayed by an off-site project and couldn't return to his office in time to perform a required diagnostic analysis of the network. And therefore, he doesn't have the network passwords with him. Requesting the help desk agent's assistance, he asks for a favor: Could she provide the current network password so that the analysis could be done remotely? The help desk agent succumbs to the tired and weary technician, and she supplies the requested information.

Conversely, the conman can pose as the network administrator and contact a user in a remote office. He informs the branch employee that due to system maintenance performed overnight, his account needs to be reset right away. Peppering the conversation with technical jargon, he gives the employee every reason to trust him. When he inevitably asks for the password, the user doesn't hesitate to supply the requested information.

The conman has also been known to employ aggressive telephone tactics. Posing as a senior manager, she will intimidate a help desk agent, forcing the agent to divulge proprietary access information. Try as the agent might, when a senior manager is threatening him, the inclination is to provide the demanded passwords.

With millions of customers using personal identification numbers (PINs) daily to carry out financial transactions, the banking community was confronted with vulnerability in its ATM network. While the community fortresses had high walls, conmen focused on the bankers' weakest link: their customers. Assuming that the consumer wouldn't suspect an official request for information, the social engineer wily conned individuals into providing the keys to their personal safes. Posing as bank officials, the conmen made telephone contact with consumers and convinced them to expose their PINs. Swiftly responding to the attacks, the banking community informed their customers that under no circumstance would a bank representative ever telephone them and request that they reveal their PIN. But the damage had been done.

Social engineers have been quick to capitalize on the growing trend to outsource nonkey functions. A typical small- to medium-sized business (SMB) in cost-reduction mode might decide to maintain an in-house IT department for its key infrastructure needs, but to outsource such perceived minor functions as its help desk. Handling calls from a branch office whose network is down, or a remote user who can't access her e-mail, the help desk is seen as a quick-fix department, which is best handled by a third-party provider specializing in the field.

Depending on the service provider the SMB engages, the technicians fielding calls might be the weakest link in the chain. Possibly overwhelmed on a particular day, needing to get users off the telephone and get back online, they skip in-depth identification probes and unwittingly release proprietary network access information to an intimidating, angry, senior-sounding voice on the telephone. It is important to note that this scenario could exist even if the department remained in-house. Third-party services can impose authentication processes that are more stringent than those an organization might initiate, or enforce, in-house.

Using third-party relationships can be quite safe, assuming that the company has a verifiable track record and that rigid rules tie back to an enforceable security policy that doesn't tolerate shortcuts.

The conman has many faces, changing his identity and calling card as the situation warrants. The best protection is a specific and enforced security policy that dictates what, if any, information can be handed out. Most importantly, the document should detail how someone must present himself or herself to be in a position to even seek information. With all parties aware of the policy, the help desk representative can have the necessary strength to stand tall against the belligerent senior manager.

Summary of Attacks

Table 2-1 provides a summary of common attacks and their characteristics.

Table 2-1 *Attacks and Characteristics*

Attack Type	Category of Attack	Description	Occurrence	Impact	Complexity
Footprinting	Reconnaissance	Determines network topology and its security posture.	Medium	Low	Medium
Scanning and system detailing	Reconnaissance	Probes for live ports, determines where they are listening, and finds the equipment that is doing the listening.	High	Low	Medium
Eavesdropping	Reconnaissance	Sniffs, records, and analyzes network traffic.	Low	High	High
Password attack	Access	Process that discovers passwords.	Medium	High	Medium
Social engineering	Access	Individual who creates a persona to convince insiders to reveal confidential information.	High	High	Low
Impersonating	Access	Unlawfully assuming a legitimate user's credentials to deceive a network.	Low	High	Medium

Table 2-1   *Attacks and Characteristics (Continued)*

Attack Type	Category of Attack	Description	Occurrence	Impact	Complexity
Trust exploita-tion	Access	Hacker engages penetrable system to exploit the trust it has with his true target, which is impenetrable on its own.	Low	High	High
Software and protocol exploita-tion	Access DoS	Exploiting known OS flaws or using tools in a manner for which they were not designed.	Medium	High	Medium to high
Worm	Access DoS	Self-duplicating program that collects data from systems it breaches.	High	Medium to high	High
Virus	Access DoS	Strives to generate harm by corrupting files or functionality in a system.	High	Medium to high	High
Trojan horse	Access DoS	Malicious program that masquerades as a legitimate one.	Medium	Medium to high	High
Datadriven attack	Access DoS	Uses a virus or Trojan horse.	Medium	Medium to high	High
Session hijacking	Access	Taking over a session between two workstations.	Low	Low to high	Very high

continues

Table 2-1 *Attacks and Characteristics (Continued)*

Attack Type	Category of Attack	Description	Occurrence	Impact	Complexity
Man-in-the-middle attack	Access	On a wired network, hacker gains access to the medium, sniffs packets, modifies them, and reinserts those packets on the network.	Low	High	High
Session replay	Access	Records data of an exchange between two parties and later replays the session to deceive the victim.	Low	Low to high	Medium to high
Wireless eaves-dropping	Reconna-issance	Sniffs, records, and analyzes wireless network traffic.	Low	High	Medium
Wireless man-in-the-middle attack	Access	Used in a wireless environment, as an example, a hacker can set up a rogue network in an attempt to intercept traffic.	Low	High	Medium to high
Walk-by hacking	Access	User who connects to an unprotected WAP to either use its bandwidth or to hack the organization.	Medium (Could be high, but few tend to take advantage of it)	High	Low

Table 2-1   *Attacks and Characteristics (Continued)*

Attack Type	Category of Attack	Description	Occurrence	Impact	Complexity
Drive-by spamming	Access	Walk-by hacker who uses the victim network to send out spam e-mail.	Low	Medium	High
Wireless DoS	DoS	Walk-by hacker who launches a DoS, for example, a SYN Flood attack, against a local server.	Low	Medium to high	Medium
Frequency jamming	N/A	Not necessarily done with malicious intent. Could be simply noise or interference on the same channel used by the WAP. But it could also be a direct attack on the radio frequency.	Low	High	High

Most attacks share some common components, not the least of which is patience on the part of the hacker, because many attacks require intricate planning. A DDoS attack, for example, is generally preceded by a reconnaissance attack and an access attack, as shown in Figure 2-13.

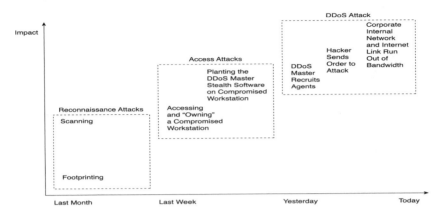

Figure 2-13 *DDoS Attack Example: Plan Through to Execution*

Cisco SAFE Axioms

Cisco's SAFE blueprint, a best practices guide for designing and implementing secure networks, enables organizations to determine the type and level of security that should be implemented throughout their networks. The SAFE blueprint addresses the enterprise as a whole and identifies and examines each major facet of a security-conscious network. The SAFE blueprint aids organizations in realizing a security environment that can accurately reflect their desired security posture.

It would be foolhardy to look at the infrastructure of a network and categorically declare that certain facets were either out of a hacker's reach or simply held no interest for him. The dismal reality is that every aspect of a network is a target. Whether it's an appliance, a server, a link, or the network itself, every element and component is potentially in a hacker's gun sights. Regrettably, nothing is immune from attack.

Using Cisco's SAFE blueprint, this section considers the following targets:

- Routers

- Switches

- Hosts

- Networks

- Applications

Routers Are Targets

A router, at its core, is an interface between networks. Routers are intelligent devices, widely used from small network environments to large Internet service providers. By using routing protocols to share information with neighboring routers, they keep data circulating on corporate networks and the Internet. They forward data or packets within networks on a *hop-by-hop* basis, with each router along a route determining the next hop to send the data.

Routers not only maintain a table of available network routes, but they are also able to distinguish between an organization's large network and all of its subnetworks. Using their knowledge, routers determine the most efficient route to use when sending data between senders and receivers.

Routers' support of multiple protocols and their ability to interconnect networks, coupled with their continual *broadcasting* or *multicasting* to that effect (they are commonly stationed at the edge of complex data networks), make them highly susceptible to attack.

Protecting routers is a critical element in security deployment, requiring those responsible for routers to be acutely aware of their inherent vulnerabilities. By keeping abreast of the latest threats and most pertinent router protection information, security professionals work diligently to safeguard their systems.

Switches Are Targets

Switches help to control congestion in a system by breaking traffic into smaller, logical, and more manageable units. Most users within large organizations typically direct the vast majority of their network traffic to destinations within their own workgroups. For example, switches can contain traffic within a finance department by linking its workstations to printers and other equipment that service only its department. When workgroups are segmented, system speed and efficiency are optimized, because the number of users sharing the same equipment has been limited.

While departmental switches are interconnected to allow the flow of information between workgroups, the switches never do so unless requested. The goal of a switch is to ease overall congestion and to optimize system performance by compartmentalizing as much data as possible.

Switches create the physical backbone for a LAN and would be a target for hackers desiring to disrupt a network. It is highly recommended that network administrators take measures to protect switches from potential hackers. The following list covers switch security basics, but it is not meant to be an exhaustive representation:

- It is best to avoid configuring switches using a network connection, particularly if the communication is in clear text. Use encryption for in-band configuration or configure the switch as *out-of-band*, as described in the sidebar "Out-of-Band and In-Band Management."

- Ensure that access to configuring switches is restricted to system administrators.

- Unless required, deactivate discovery broadcast.

Out-of-Band and In-Band Management

Out-of-band refers to an administrator who is directly connected to the configuration port of a switch and who doesn't use network media to send configuration commands.

In-band refers to the method of sending management and configuration commands to a network device using the same medium and communication protocol as those used by user data.

See Figure 2-14 for in-band and out-of-band management illustration.

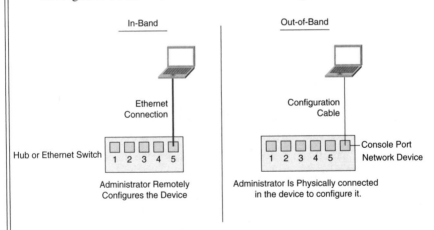

Figure 2-14   *Out-of-Band and In-Band Management*

Hosts Are Targets

Hosts are intelligent devices that comprise, but are not limited to, servers, mainframes, and computers that make services available to other computers on a network. They often provide services such as www, e-mail, and file download capabilities. Unfortunately for hosts, they are easy targets.

Generally accepted practice for hardware and software vendors is their issuance of patches and fixes for their installed base of product, whenever it has been determined that issues have arisen. Failure to subscribe to an automated notification service means that a network administrator never knows when alerts will be published, and he therefore must always be on the lookout for patches that are relevant to his equipment. Just as importantly, he must be prepared to install the patches as soon as he is made aware of an issue.

Network administrators are faced with the following fundamental issues:

- Security notices are issued haphazardly, and it's critical that most be addressed urgently.

- A wide array of equipment is typically under their control, and most appliances need to be handled separately.

- Equipment is usually purchased from a multitude of sources, resulting in diverse hardware with different operating systems and applications. Patch alerts arrive from a vast array of suppliers, with little or no uniformity to them.

Hosts provide services, such as www, to other computers on a network and, as a result, become highly visible to hackers. While other components continue to be targets, they are not generally as vulnerable. The job of a router, for example, is to move data from one host to another host. The end result is that the destination, and not the path taken, becomes the more vulnerable device and, ultimately, the more obvious target.

Networks Are Targets

Networks bring diverse components together and allow them to communicate and share information in an efficient manner. Networks connect computers with printers and connect servers with innumerable communication devices, while at the same time allowing users and resources to exchange information and perform tasks.

A planned DDoS can have certain appliances in its gun sights as it executes an attack on a network, but it doesn't necessarily view the network itself as a target. But as evidenced in Figure 2-15, a well-executed DDoS can have as great an impact on an overall network as it could have on individual appliances. A hacker launches a DDoS attack through the master, along with 100 recruited agents.

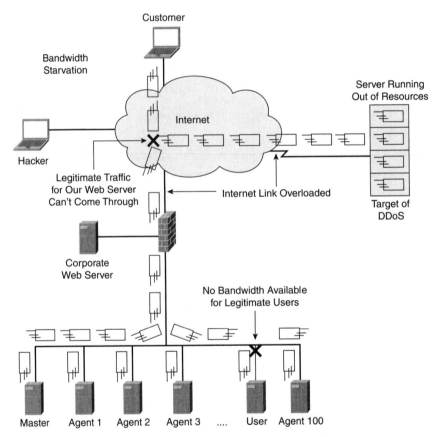

Figure 2-15   *Networks Are Targets: Bandwidth Starvation*

A DDoS disrupts regular network traffic and, by the time the administrator is notified that traffic is crawling, the damage will have been done, as follows:

1   The outbound traffic, on a mission to cause more harm, not only disrupts internal network traffic but also probably uses most of the network's Internet bandwidth, stymieing all potential incoming traffic that might be headed for the company website.

2   When the attack reaches its destination, the DDoS and its onslaught of data consume any available bandwidth. The server runs the risk of crashing because of resource starvation.

Some of the most frustrating attacks are those that cannot be predicted or stopped. The effects of a DDoS could be muted somewhat by effective coordination within an organization's ISP.

Applications Are Targets

An application, or software, is a program that both servers and computers use to perform tasks.

Programs are highly complex, and software manufacturers have, at times, found it challenging to produce them without flaws. Commonly referred to as *bugs*, these flaws have run the gamut from innocuous errors to potential disasters. A well-known bug allowed hackers to remotely access servers; hackers were recognized as administrators and granted full network privileges, including configuration.

CERT and similar agencies regularly post security advisories. Because potential hackers routinely check the same sites, or even get automated notification detailing the latest flaws, it is advisable to follow the guidelines in the reports, which typically suggest applying patches immediately.

Summary

Threats will inevitably exist. Regardless of a hacker's motivation, recognizing that systems are inherently vulnerable is a fundamental first step in deciding what an organization is prepared to tolerate. This chapter focused on the following topics:

• Recognizing vulnerabilities

• Understanding attack types

- Understanding attack processes
- Acknowledging power-of-persuasion attacks
- Recognizing that every part of a network is a potential target

Making the business case for security investment involves many components, not the least of which is determining an organization's real cost of vulnerability. In today's climate, it is not yet possible to rule out threats, but the desired level of mitigating them can potentially limit any impact they could possibly inflict. The following chapter advances the discussion by addressing threats directly and detailing how an organization can protect itself.

CHAPTER 3

SECURITY TECHNOLOGY AND RELATED EQUIPMENT

Advances in security technology are being made at a rapid pace as the challenges posed by those desiring to cause harm continue unabated. Gains made on the technology front have seemingly pushed hackers back from the front lines, forcing them to find better cover and become ever craftier in their relentless pursuit of disruption.

Entering into a discussion regarding appropriate security equipment is an important component of the planning process. But it is fundamental to note at the outset that no single piece of hardware or software contains an overall solution. The key is a combination of technology, policy, and compliance building blocks that can aid an organization in its quest to solidify a comprehensive security foundation.

This chapter covers the following topics:

- Virus protection
- Traffic Filtering and Firewalls
- Encryption
- Authentication, authorization, and accounting: AAA
- Public key infrastructure
- From detection to prevention: intrusion-detection systems and intrusion-prevention systems
- Content filtering
- Assessment and audit

Virus Protection

Antivirus software, also known as AV software, helps to protect networks and PCs against known viruses. Norton, along with other well-known AV software vendors, assigns a threat level to viruses based on particular criteria. It looks at the contagion possibility for every pertinent virus and attempts to ascertain the damage each could cause.

Viruses are then slotted into a risk level, ranging from very low to very severe.[1] The software scans incoming and outgoing e-mails, network communications, operating systems, user files, and so on. It attempts to uncover patterns, or *signatures*, a specific sequence of characters, knowing that every virus has its own trademark. It alerts the user if one is found. While AV scanning is an essential part of a first-line defense program, it is important to note that viruses are continually becoming more complex. In an attempt to avoid exposure, they embed themselves so deeply in programs that detection becomes increasingly more difficult.

AV analyses are generally done on hosts—servers and workstations—but they can also be network-based, using a dedicated device to analyze the bit-sequence of traffic as it passes live across a wire. Although it is possible to have a device dedicated exclusively for network-based AV, that functionality is often found in a technology that is explored in the section "From Detection to Prevention: Intrusion-Detection Systems and Intrusion-Prevention Systems," later in this chapter.

Organizations traditionally performed AV software updates either weekly or monthly; today many choose to update daily. An *AV engine*, the mechanics behind scanning, refers to software that is installed on hosts. It performs the actual work of rooting out viruses. Part of that role involves maintaining update schedules that a network administrator might have requested, be it checking for virus updates every Friday at noon, as an example, or every day at 6:00 a.m. Its sister, the signature file, is the database that is downloaded from the AV vendor at the times requested.

Until recently, antivirus software was only effective when signatures were known and antidotes had been created. Very similar to infectious diseases, a virus had to be discovered, or diagnosed, before a relevant antidote could be developed. Virus definitions periodically downloaded from AV vendors are those antidotes. Second-generation AV scanners had intelligent features built into the scans (also known as heuristic scanners) in an attempt to have them notice irregularities, even those they weren't yet programmed to discern. Some scanners are also capable of performing network analyses, vetting all live traffic as it travels to its destination. The scanner can alert the system administrator if it suspects a virus.

Attaining virus protection includes five steps, as shown in Table 3-1.

Table 3-1   *Virus Protection*

Step	Antivirus Vendor Action	Organization's Reaction
1	Virus is discovered or diagnosed, or AV software is enabled to *forward-think*, acting intelligently in its search for the unknown.	Virus was brought in (by e-mail attachment or corrupted network connection) or allowed entry through (inadvertent) open back door.
2	Virus is detected or begins to propagate.	IT alerted to as-yet unknown issues in network.
3	Infection begins to take hold.	Organization is under attack.
4	Antidote is developed.	Signature is recognized by AV software.
5	Antidote is disseminated.	Antivirus software is ready to vet all incoming and outgoing traffic.

While the inclination might be to load as much scanning capability as possible, some issues are inherent in having unnecessary scans. Certain software might declare a virus was discovered, but you might find that it was a false positive. Time, resources, and system availability lost determining whether a virus existed can quickly spiral. Excessive scanning can also slow the system, encouraging users to find shortcuts to speed up the network, ultimately opening back doors.

Utilizing More Than One Brand of AV Software

Rather than increasing the amount of scanning, certain organizations have found it useful to install one brand of AV software on the e-mail server and firewall and another brand of AV software on the workstations. If both brands claim to be 99% effective, using two different ones should ensure a greater-than-99% chance of recognizing a virus.

Traffic Filtering and Firewalls

The logical progression for network protection begins with the hardware immediately at hand, typically the PC, and progresses to the more complex, the network, as follows:

- Basic filtering:
  - Routers
  - Switches
- Advanced filtering:
  - Proxy server
  - Stateful firewalling

Basic Filtering

Basic filtering is efficient, but it offers only simple protection. It performs two actions as it checks the source and destination IP addresses of traffic and declares, for example, that any information from source A to destination B is free to pass through. It works quickly, deciding almost instantly whether traffic can move to its destination. Its analysis does not probe any deeper than necessary.

Routers

At their core, routers act as interfaces between networks. They are intelligent devices that connect like and unlike LANs and have the ability to support multiple protocols. Routers are used extensively throughout networks large and small; their primary role is the efficient movement of traffic. Security optimization was never considered a prime feature, but Figure 3-1 illustrates how a router can avoid security missteps. By ignoring ping requests emanating from the Internet and, as an example, not advertising its routing table, the router can ensure that it doesn't inadvertently advise would-be attackers of its vulnerable position. Recent iterations of certain routers have firewall capabilities built in, but typically they are only activated in branch or remote offices, where a stand-alone firewall might not be economically feasible or necessary. Conversely, a central office would continue to have greater speed and safety requirements, which would necessitate using dedicated routers and firewalls.

The design of an optimally secure network typically includes a firewall that resides behind a perimeter router, as evidenced in Figure 3-2. While the firewall is a stand-alone device, a stateful firewall, covered in the section "Advanced Filtering," later in this chapter, can be built into the router.

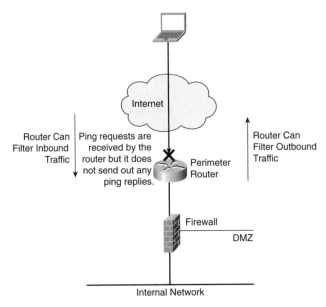

Figure 3-1 *Avoiding Security Missteps with a Perimeter Router*

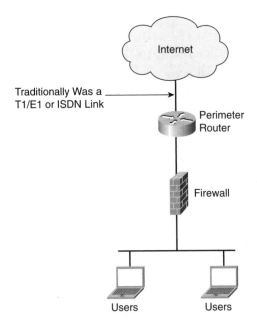

Figure 3-2 *Security Design: Perimeter Router as First Line of Defense and Firewall Providing Internal Network Protection*

Routers can be placed at multiple points along a network, but perimeter routers are typically found positioned at the edge, performing basic address filtering and acting as the first line of defense.

Switches

Switches provide logical segmentation of physical networks; they compartmentalize data by breaking traffic into smaller, logical, and more manageable units.

Switches are an integral part of improving network traffic; they have evolved significantly in the last decade and today play a highly versatile and consequential role in networks.

Private Virtual LAN

Switches enable private virtual LAN (PVLAN) capabilities by ensuring that traffic is not allowed to flow between servers. Configured in this manner, switches dictate the flow of traffic. As shown in Figure 3-3, traffic received by Port 2 must be passed to Port 1. Absence of a PVLAN could result in an attack against one server quickly escalating into a breach of the other. The switches help prevent a hacker who, having breached server A, attempts to mount an attack against server B.

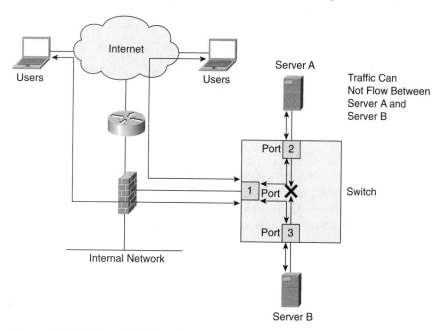

Figure 3-3   *Using a Switch to Create a PVLAN*

Port Security

Port security provides protection at the physical level by configuring ports on a switch to accept incoming traffic only if it originates from a predefined Media Access Control (MAC) address, as shown in Figure 3-4. For more on MAC addresses, refer to the sidebar "Tech Tip: MAC Addresses."

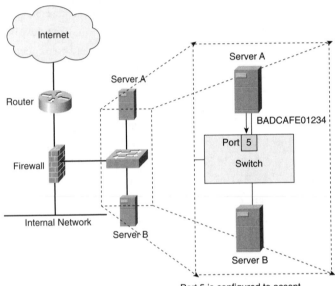

Port 5 is configured to accept traffic originating only from MAC Address BADCAFE01234

Figure 3-4 *Port Security Filtering MAC Addresses*

Tech Tip: MAC Addresses

Network interface cards, commonly known as NICs or network cards, physically connect workstations to networks. Each card has a 48-bit number burned in its memory that is known as the physical, or MAC, address of the NIC. MAC addresses are usually presented in hexadecimal notation, illustrated by a 12-character code, such as BADCAFE01234 or 42-3F-C2-3A-23-AA.

Advanced Filtering

Advanced filtering systems can provide significant increases in network security. The following discussion centers on proxy servers and firewalls, and their ability to provide enhanced security.

Proxy Server

Proxy servers are similar to firewalls—they keep unwanted traffic from entering an internal network. Operating at the software level, a proxy server would, as an example, intercept internal traffic headed to the Internet, create a new session for that message, and then resend the new message to its intended destination, as shown in Figure 3-5. When delivering a reply to the message, the Internet server would send it to the proxy server because, from the Internet server's point of view, the proxy server was the original sender. Upon receipt, the proxy server would go back to its earlier session and forward the reply to the true originator. While the process provides sound protection, it is less efficient, because the server has to manage two concurrent sessions.

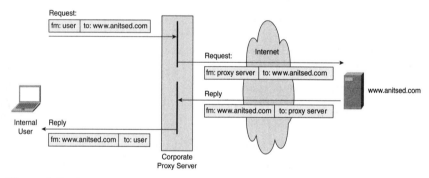

Figure 3-5   *Proxy Server at Work*

Stateful Firewalling

A firewall prevents intruders from gaining access to internal systems. It allows for a single point of delivery from an organization to the Internet, and it allows controlled access from the Internet to network-attached hosts. Rules for access are established, and any transaction that falls outside the prescribed rules is blocked.

Networks were once said to be *crunchy on the outside and soft on the inside*, implying that barriers that protected the network from the outside environment could create a difficult, or crunchy, experience for a prospective intruder. Internally, networks were thought to be soft, because hubs, switches, and routers were the only separators between departments. Internal security needs were not considered to be nearly as demanding as external requirements.

Today, interdepartmental firewalls are becoming increasingly more prevalent as organizations grapple with the need to proactively protect strategic data-sensitive divisions, such as Finance, R&D, and Human Resources, as illustrated in Figure 3-6.

Stateful firewalling looks at the state of a session when two devices are communicating and determines whether a transaction is beginning, ongoing, or ending. If, for example, a transaction had just completed but reams of data continued to flow in, the firewall would block incoming traffic.

A firewall monitors all traffic exiting an internal network, and records the following data:

- Source IP address
- Destination IP address
- Source port
- Destination port
- Sequence number of packets
- Additional pertinent data

When traffic returns, the firewall matches the traffic to what the firewall had originally recorded in its state table, as evidenced in Figure 3-7. If a corresponding match is found, the firewall allows the traffic in. Otherwise, the traffic gets blocked. This process is similar to an apartment security guard who relies on recognition of tenants to determine who can enter the grounds.

A new firewall, not yet configured, has a default behavior that allows requests to leave a network and returning traffic to come back, but it does not allow requests originating from outside to gain entry. Conversely, public websites that rely on communication generated externally are configured to accept messages initiated outside its network. Messages are sent to a demilitarized-zone (DMZ) web server, placed just outside its internal network, as shown in Figure 3-8.

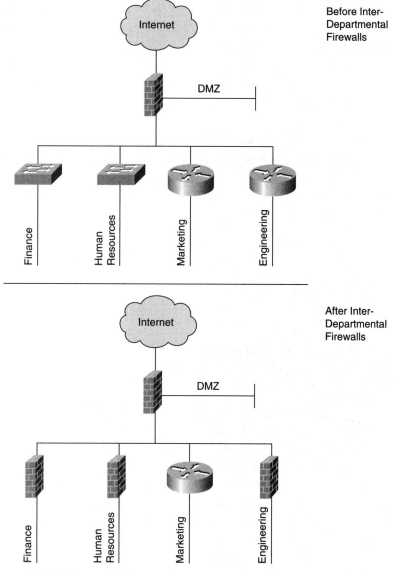

Figure 3-6 *Before and After Interdepartmental Firewalls*

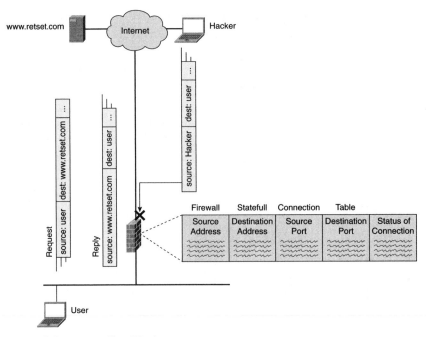

Figure 3-7   *Firewall at Work*

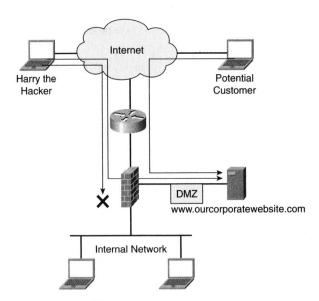

Figure 3-8   *Firewall and DMZ*

Filtering Summary

Table 3-2 provides a summary of the different characteristics of filtering equipment.

Table 3-2 *Filtering Equipment and Characteristics*

Name	Protection	Processing Speed After Security Option Activated	Configuration Complexity
Routers	Low to medium	Slow to medium	Low
Switches	Low to medium	Fast	Low to medium
Firewall	High	Fast	Low to high
Proxy server	High	Slow	Medium to high

Encryption

Encryption turns messages and data into a format that is unintelligible to unauthorized parties. A key is required to decipher encrypted files, ensuring that only an authorized recipient, as evidenced in Figure 3-9, can decipher their contents. The key is instrumental to the process, and while it is kept well guarded, it can be vulnerable if it remains in service too long or if an excessive amount of data was encrypted by it. The longer a key is exposed, the simpler it could be to spot a pattern.

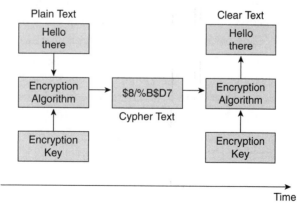

Figure 3-9 *Encryption Process*

The lifetime of a key is decided by time usage or amount of data encrypted, as shown in Table 3-3. After it expires, parties negotiate another key.

Table 3-3   *Encryption Key: Examples of Lifetimes*

Device	Default Key Life (Time)	Default Key Life (Size or Size/Seconds)
Cisco PIX firewall	28,800 seconds (or 8 hours)	10 MB per second in 1 hour
Cisco router	3600 seconds (or 1 hour)	4,608,000 KB

Three common encryption applications found in industry are as follows:

- Encrypted virtual private network (VPN)
- SSL (Secure Sockets Layer) encryption
- File encryption

Encrypted VPN

A VPN is a tunnel created between office networks (site-to-site) or between a remote user and her office network, as shown in Figure 3-10. A connection is created at the edge of a network allowing access as if the user were physically connected on-site.

VPN provides secure communication over the Internet. It is particularly useful for organizations with many remote users, allowing them to avoid higher costs typically incurred with T1 communication lines or frame relays.

A growing need exists to ensure that data is not vulnerable during transmission. Because IP packets, also referred to as datagrams, can be manipulated during transmission, tools to protect them are required. IP Security (IPSec) addresses that issue. Table 3-4 represents methods IPSec uses to provide security.

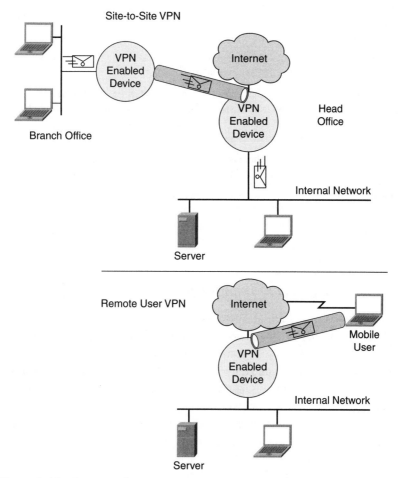

Figure 3-10 *Encrypted VPN: Site-to-Site and Remote User*

Table 3-4 *Mechanisms for Authenticity, Confidentiality, and Integrity*

Method to Ensure	Result of Method	Tools Used
Authenticity	Verifies that the sender of the packets is the legitimate sender	Authentication mechanisms
Confidentiality	Ensures that packets are not readable during transmission, and even more specifically, not readable to anyone but the intended receiver	Encryption algorithms and keys
Integrity	Ensures that packets are not manipulated during transmission	Message digests, or *hashing**

*Hashing preserves the integrity of a message by converting its contents into a format that can only be understood by the receiver. Refer to the sidebar "Example of a Secure Data Exchange."

Example of a Secure Data Exchange

A firm needs to electronically transmit a purchase order to its supplier, but it is concerned that a hacker could tamper with the data while the message is in transit. To counter this issue, the firm creates a hash—a process that uses an algorithm to convert data into a fixed-length result (regardless of whether the data is a short e-mail or thousands of pages of text, a hash is always the same fixed length). Both the sender and receiver share a predetermined special key, or shared secret, ensuring that no one other than the intended receiver can read the message in its proper form. The process of hashing is similar to a butcher grinding a solid piece of meat. When he has turned it into ground beef, any attempt to reverse-engineer the grinding proves fruitless—it is a one-way function. As illustrated in Figure 3-11, hashing typically includes the following steps:

1   Sender creates the message and, using the shared key, implements the hashing algorithm.

2   The file is transmitted, along with the hash results.

3   The receiver opens the message and, using the shared key, determines his own hash results.

4 The receiver next compares the hashing result he created with the one the sender included with his message and, if they match, the receiver knows the message was not altered during transmission.

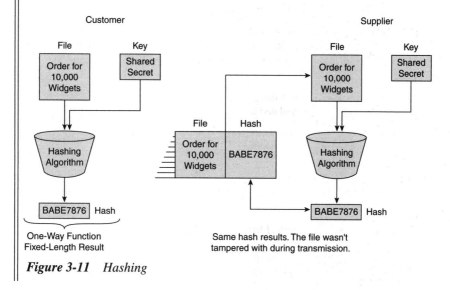

Figure 3-11   Hashing

VPN Concentrator

A VPN concentrator is optimized to manage multiple user- and session-encryption profiles, and it is the appliance most suited to terminate remote-access IPSec VPN tunnels. But if an organization only requires a minor number of tunnels to be terminated simultaneously, a firewall or router could be called upon to perform the task.

SSL Encryption

A typical visit to a merchant site on the Internet does not require encryption until checkout. Shopping carts can be filled, but when the merchant prompts the user to enter payment information, the session requires encryption; the user's browser would have to support SSL (Secure Sockets Layer). Similarly, when performing online banking, most merchants require sessions to be encrypted at the login page. SSL works at the software, or application, layer ensuring that every required session is protected, regardless of the quantity of sessions in play.

Online banking, for example, invariably makes users more security-conscious than simply browsing innocuous web sites from their PC. Acutely afraid that a mere click of their mouse could send their funds in any number of directions, users want assurance that transmissions are secure. SSL encryption is used, providing a *key* that is valid for only one session. Each time a connection is made to an online banking or similar site, a new key is dynamically negotiated between the workstation and the server at the destination. Specifically, the URL at most websites begins with "http://", as shown in Figure 3-12, but at the login page of banking sites, the URL begins with "https://"—the difference being the added *s*, as shown in Figure 3-13. A small lock icon on some browsers appears in the display of icons that run across the bottom of the user's monitor, stating "SSL Secured (128 bit)," giving the user assurance that the transmission is secured, as shown in Figure 3-13.

Figure 3-12   *Browsing the Internet: SSL Encryption Not Required*

Figure 3-13   *Browsing the Internet: SSL Encryption Required for Online Banking*

File Encryption

Users who send and receive files utilize encryption algorithms to protect their information. *Pretty Good Privacy (PGP)* and GNU-PGP are commonly used third-party encryption software. In the most basic form of file encryption software, the sender and receiver of a specific file would both share the same secret and, should the file be intercepted, the illegitimate reader would only see gibberish— only the intended receiver would hold the key that would allow the file to be deciphered and read in clear text.

While encrypting files is recommended to ensure confidentiality, it is not required to encrypt a session or a communication link. In Figure 3-14, an IP packet header is transmitted in clear text, and only the data in its payload is encrypted.

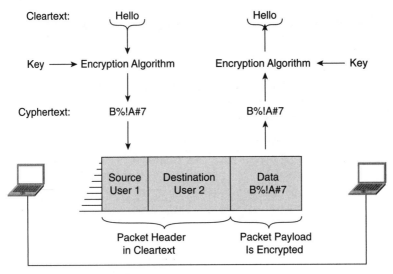

Figure 3-14   *File Encryption Process*

Authentication, Authorization, and Accounting: AAA

Establishing a user's identity and determining where he is allowed to venture and what he might be entitled to do when he has reached his destination is a multipronged process. Authentication, authorization, and accounting addresses these fundamental issues:

- Authentication asks *Who are you?*

- Authorization asks *What are you allowed to do, and when?*

- Accounting asks *When, where, and how long were you there?*

Authentication

Authentication is the process of verifying that someone, or something, is really who or what he says he is. The following are pertinent topics that discuss authentication:

- Passwords and access cards

- Strong authentication and biometrics

Note that public key infrastructure is covered in the section "Public Key Infrastructure," later in this chapter.

Methods for Authenticating: Passwords

Two main types of passwords exist: static and one-time. Static passwords are used, for example, when logging on to an Internet service provider (ISP). The required password is typically embedded in the automated login procedure, and after a short while, the user likely doesn't remember that a password is even used in his connection process. Even a password with a limited lifetime, 30 or 90 days as an example, would still be considered a static password.

Conversely, one-time passwords (OTPs) used to require a great deal of user intervention, making them cumbersome to manage. Participating parties were provided computer-generated password lists, and each new communication required the next password on file to authenticate the transaction. Distribution of the lists was problematic, and finding a safe and efficient avenue to deliver them to participants was getting increasingly more difficult.

When OTPs evolved to a digital format, distribution improved exponentially. The initial design was a credit card–sized variety that later evolved into a fob token. It was similar to a remote-access key-chain attachment for an automobile, as shown on Figure 3-15. Soft tokens are in wide use today, with passwords loaded on a user's personal digital assistant (PDA). Whichever mode manages passwords, the method of authenticating is the same: Serial numbers are assigned to individual cards or tokens, registered to one user, and finally synchronized with the authenticating server. Passwords are preset to change every 60 seconds, for example, and the lists are saved in the memory of both token and server. When a token is activated, password rotation begins on both ends and continues regardless of whether the user is transmitting. Tokens have large memory banks and can store hundreds of thousands of passwords at a time, ensuring multiple months of continuous usage.

Token Card

Token Fob

Soft Token

Figure 3-15   *Examples of One-Time-Password Tokens*

It is worthwhile to note that tampering with physical tokens is pointless. They have a built-in feature that renders the token useless should an attempt be made to open it. If one were stolen, there would still be no cause for concern, because a token requires *strong authentication* before it can perform a task. Strong authentication is discussed in the section "Strong Authentication," later in this chapter.

Methods for Authenticating: Access Cards

Special-purpose cards have long been used to restrict physical access to suites or buildings, ensuring that only authorized persons can gain entry. But early-generation card readers didn't delve deeply into identification, and if a card was swiped that matched the legitimate list for entry, the holder was allowed in. The conundrum facing organizations was that the swiper wasn't necessarily the rightful holder, and worse, the organization had no means of making a further determination.

Contactless, or proximity, cards were similar to early-generation special-purpose cards, except they included a small antenna coil that negated the need for physical contact between the card and reader. Stuffing the card in a rear pants pocket, a user would typically swing her hips in the direction of the hip-height card reader, allowing for hands-free entry into a restricted area.

Smart cards also open doors, but they have more intelligence on-board. They are outfitted with their own memory and processing power and can store a vast array of information, from a user's fingerprint and iris scans to her medical files.

Strong Authentication

Strong authentication requires more than a simple match on a verification device to allow a user into a restricted area; it demands a two-factor authentication method. Any two items from the following list can suffice for strong authentication, but the emphasis is on the initial three:

- What a user knows
- What a user has
- What a user is
- What a user does

A password or PIN is something a user would know, while a token (bank card, key, or fob) is something a user would have. To initiate a transaction with an automated teller machine, it is necessary to have a hard piece of identification (a bank card) along with a soft piece of identification (a PIN), as shown in Figure 3-16. In an earlier example of a security fob, should a two-step authentication be required, a subsequent theft would not be cause for concern because any attempt to use a fob would be futile — without the addition of a PIN, access would not be granted.

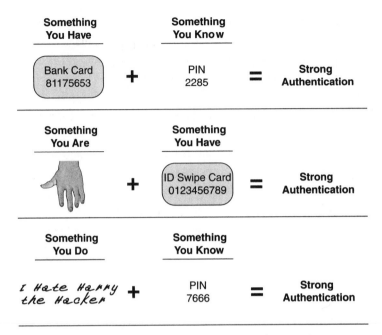

Figure 3-16 *Examples of Strong Authentication Implementation*

Static biometrics, including iris, face, fingerprint, and hand geometry, are based on characteristics that typically change only glacially. They are part of what a user *is*. As part of strong authentication, entry to a building can require a user to input his PIN and, after the PIN is accepted, prompt him to place a specific finger on a scanner to verify his identity.

Something you do is relatively new to the list, although it remains possible that some of these functions, including voice, signature, and keystroke dynamics, could be learned. While a forger could learn to imitate a signature, it would be more difficult to re-create certain nuances, such as the amount of weight delivered per square centimeter of down stroke.

Evolving from standard access control to a system that uses strong authentication is relatively straightforward: Incorporate an additional step. For example, prompt a user to enter his PIN into a card reader keypad immediately after he has swiped it.

USB Token

A USB token is similar to a smart card, but rather than inserting a wallet-sized card into a PC, a token is instead plugged into its USB port. Physically possessing a token would not be enough to gain entry; a PIN would be required to authenticate it.

Bio-Token

A bio-token, also known as a pseudo-token, uses biometrics to confirm a user's identity and, delving deeper, it uses its built-in scanner to authenticate the user's identity. For example, a lawful user's thumb image is permanently stored in a bio-token, and each time he attempts to gain entry to a secured site, he must present his thumb to the token's built-in scanner. The token performs a comparison between the live thumb and what it has stored in its memory, granting access if it establishes a match.

Authorization

An authorization server contains *rules* for an organization that specify who is allowed access, and where and when they are allowed to go. When a user signs on, he provides his identity to network devices, which in turn check his access level with the authorization server. Any new attempt to perform an action results in the rules being consulted prior to granting said access. The process is efficient, because authentication and authorization often reside on the same server.

Computers that act as access control servers (ACSs) running mission-specific software are usually responsible for the authentication process, the accounting process, and some aspects of the authorization process.

Accounting

Accounting is the process of gathering data to determine the following items:

- What resource access did a user occupy or which networks did he visit, and when did it happen?

- What was the consumption—the length of time the user was there and the amount of data that was downloaded?

The data is used to determine tracking (of users), auditing, trends analysis, capacity planning, billing, and cost allocation.

If it was determined that 75% of remote-access users were members of the sales department, the corporation might decide to allocate the bulk of expenses to that group. The accounting process would ensure that communication costs and IT staff required to support the remote-access infrastructure were legitimately allocated.

Alternately, if the organization was an ISP firm, the accounting might be geared toward trends analyses. If strain on bandwidth was found to be greatest from 8:00 to 11:00 p.m., the ISP might decide to offer better rates to clients prior to 8:00 p.m. and after 11:00 p.m. to avoid investing in bandwidth expansion. Or, if the firm did want to consider capacity planning, it might decide to monitor the trends more closely for 90 days before deciding what should be done.

While every organization is encouraged to maintain accounting logs for prescribed periods of time, the sheer volume of data can make it challenging to review on a timely basis. For many organizations, logs provide useful information on bandwidth usage, as well as who has been where, when, and for how long. Equally important, accounting logs can be invaluable in aiding network forensics should an attack occur.

The accounting process is usually performed on the same server that is responsible for both the authentication and authorization processes. That same server acts as the repository for all activity logs.

Public Key Infrastructure

Public key infrastructure (PKI) is a set of policies, procedures, and techniques that verify, enroll, and certify users in a security system. PKI applies public key cryptography and key certification to verify and authenticate each party involved in an electronic transaction to ensure that secure communication is provided.

Readers might be familiar with the term *digital certificates*—they are at the core of PKI.

An issue of great concern in cryptography is how best to distribute the keys. At the risk of greatly oversimplifying a topic that can fill volumes on its own, PKI addresses this issue by establishing that a user can have a private and a public key, and the latter would reside on a central server known as a *certificate authority (CA)*. Any file that is encrypted with the private key can only be deciphered with the corresponding public key (which could reside centrally). Conversely, any file that is encrypted with a specific public key can only be deciphered by its corresponding private key. An example, as shown in Figure 3-17, is as follows:

1   User A wants to send a file to user B.

2   User A prepares the file, and requests user B's public key to encrypt that file.

3   User A sends the message, confident that only user B has the capability to decipher the file with his private key. (As a note, a central server would typically demand proof of user A's identity before releasing user B's public key.)

4   User B uses his private key to decipher the note.

5   If the note were intercepted, it would be undecipherable to anyone but user B.

6   Should user B reply to user A, the reverse set of transactions would occur.

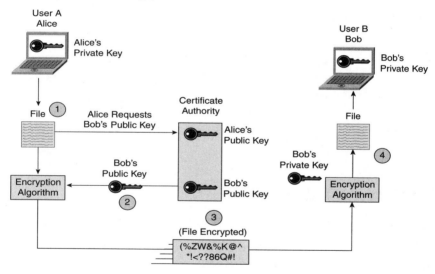

Figure 3-17   *Public and Private Keys at Work*

If a senior executive wanted to send a file to her staff and, given the nature of its contents, wanted to ensure that each recipient was assured of the validity of the information, she would sign it with her digital signature, which would allow recipients to verify the sender's authenticity and confirm that the message itself was never altered. For further details on digital signatures, refer to the sidebar "Tech Tip: Digital Signatures." Upon receiving the note, the recipients would request the sender's public key from the CA. Successfully deciphering the file would confirm that the signature was created by the executive's private key.

Tech Tip: Digital Signatures

Digital signatures use two processes that were presented earlier in this chapter: hashing and encryption. A digital signature is the hash of a message, which is encrypted using the private key of a sender, as shown in Figure 3-18. A digital signature provides assurance that a signed file not only came from the person who sent it but also that it was not altered since it was signed.

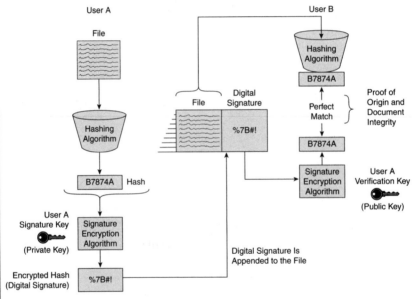

Figure 3-18   *Digital Signature Process*

Every system has its vulnerabilities, and PKI is not immune. While it is a highly reliable encryption method, if a key has yet to be registered and an untrustworthy party is privy to not only that knowledge but also the CA's enrollment process, the remote possibility exists that the infiltrator could pose as the rightful owner of the public key. Multiple safeguards can help prevent impersonation, including, but not limited to, human intervention, telephone confirmation, and e-mail verification. Biometrics is one of the strongest forms of authentication, and partnering it with PKI is a solid step toward eliminating that security threat.

From Detection to Prevention: Intrusion-Detection Systems and Intrusion-Prevention Systems

Basic intrusion-detection systems (IDSs) are passive devices that view incoming activity traveling along a wire. The only action required of them is to advise a management console about suspicious activity, although invariably by the time the alert is delivered, the attack could already be under way. The next-level device takes the best of IDS and includes an avenue for action: Intrusion-prevention systems (IPSs) perform real-time detections and have the capability of acting, rather than being relegated to merely advising.

Each appliance warrants a greater understanding, and the following sections provide a top-level overview of both. The topics covered are as follows:

- IDS overview
- Network- and host-based IDS
- IPS overview
- Target-based IDS

IDS Overview

IDS monitors traffic on a host, or network, in an attempt to identify intrusions or undesirable traffic that could represent hostile activity. It searches for the following items:

- Aberrant attack signatures and virus patterns that could indicate hostile activity is already under way.
- Traffic-anomaly detection—The same source has possibly sent multiple requests to the targeted server in a matter of seconds.
- Protocol-anomaly detection—A packet is malformed or its declared contents are in direct conflict with where the packet is attempting to be delivered.[2]

Detecting Attacks

The IDS does not act as a filter with information flowing through it. Rather, using its sensing interface, it takes a snapshot of data as it goes across a wire and performs its examination on that *copy*, ensuring that its analysis doesn't delay network traffic. The process is similar to the one described in Chapter 2, "Crucial Need for Security: Vulnerabilities and Attacks"—Sniffing software ordered a workstation's network interface card to copy all traffic that was traveling along the particular physical network. This is illustrated in Figure 3-19. The sensing interface typically operates in stealth mode, making it more difficult for an outsider to detect it. Appliances need IP addresses to facilitate communication with each other, but stealth-mode IDS interfaces operate without an IP address, resulting in a hacker not being able to confirm its presence or make it an attack target. The hacker cannot attack what he cannot address.

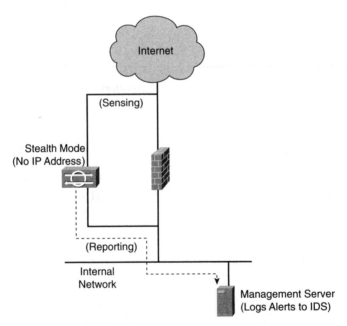

Figure 3-19   *IDS Implementation*

IDS should be able to detect the following items:

- **Reconnaissance attacks**—Specifically, pinging, probing, or mapping with port sweeps.

- **Exploit attacks**—For example, high numbers of login attempts, all from the same source address, within a short time period, or malformed packets—those with overlapping fragments or impossible addressing.

- **DoS attacks**—For example, a hacker can send multiple requests to a server, knowing that it needs to open a new session to deal with each request. The attacker won't complete any of his requests, but he'll keep initiating new ones. Ultimately, the server's resources are pushed to the limit, overloaded by requests and corresponding open sessions, and it crashes. For additional analysis, refer to Chapter 2.

- **Abuse**—The sensor could continually search for specific text strings. For example, a company concerned that employees might e-mail proprietary files could stop any transmission that contained specific trigger words.

Classifying and Reporting Attacks

When a possible attack has been detected, the IDS sensor proceeds to determine the severity of the threat, ranging from benign to severe. The incident is reported to a management server console, the central repository for IDS sensor activity, as shown in Figure 3-20, which either logs the activity or activates an alarm.

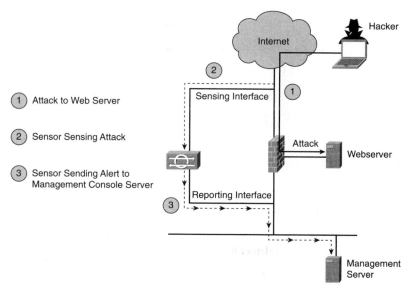

Figure 3-20   *Role of IDS Management Console*

A management server console collects information from a multitude of sensors situated on its network. Sensor A might report a minor issue and, while it might be considered insignificant, if sensors B and C were to also report issues, the management console has the ability to put the incidents together to achieve a wider perspective, as illustrated in Figure 3-21. The management server console is expanded upon in the section "Audit Tools," later in this chapter.

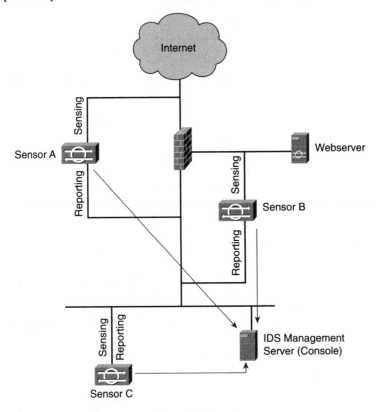

Figure 3-21 *IDS Management Console Direct Reports*

Network- and Host-Based IDS

Network-based IDS (NIDS) monitors traffic as it moves along a network wire, as shown in Figure 3-19. In addition to NIDS, it is advised that host-based IDS (HIDS) be used. A HIDS is typically installed on a mission-critical server, such as DMZ web servers, to monitor traffic that is coming to the station, as illustrated in Figure 3-22.

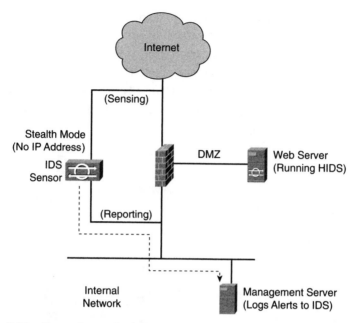

Figure 3-22   *Protection on Both Fronts: Network-Based IDS and Host-Based IDS*

NIDS and HIDS are optimized when used together on a network. HIDS is concerned strictly with its own workstation or server and, as a result, is better equipped to deal with a direct assault. Should it sense suspicious activity, NIDS has the ability to send an alarm to the management console, which can then take aggressive action. An ideal preventative situation places a HIDS on critical hosts and uses a NIDS to oversee the complete network.

IPS Overview

While the term *IDS* is still prevalent in network- and host-based IDS, the characteristics necessary to take remedial action are more reflective of intrusion-prevention systems (IPSs). This signals the evolutionary process currently under way, from IDS to a more feature-rich IPS.

An IPS behaves similarly to an IDS but with a key added benefit—the IPS has an ability to act and can potentially block an attack. Rather than copying data moving along a wire before being able to analyze it, IPSs situated on servers can analyze data as it comes through, deciding instantly whether to allow it to pass. If, for example, the IPS software detects a DoS attack because it was bombarded by the thousandth request from the same source (and had been preconfigured to react at the 1000-request level), it can drop the packet (as it had also been preconfigured to do in this example) and, as shown in Figure 3-23, it might also be preconfigured to close all open sessions to eliminate the possibility of a crash.

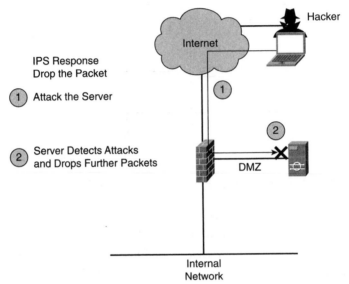

Figure 3-23   *IPS Drops Packets to Curtail Attack*

IPS sensors still retain the option of simply alerting the management console server, as evidenced in Figure 3-20, or they could send an *RST* (Reset) packet, an action that would forcibly finish or terminate the stalker's session, as illustrated in Figure 3-24.

Should an IPS sensor determine an attack is under way, it can shun the incoming data by sending a command to its firewall, telling the firewall to block specific incoming source addresses. *Shunning* is the act of dynamically modifying the firewall, as illustrated in Figure 3-25.

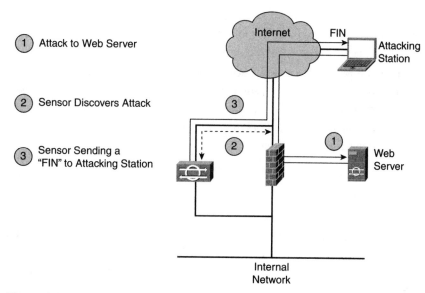

Figure 3-24 *IPS Terminates Suspicious Session*

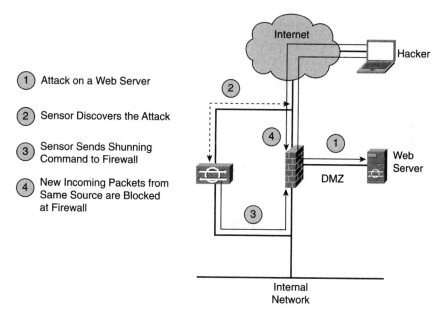

Figure 3-25 *IPS Shunning Attack*

False positives can be a common occurrence before sensors are *trained*, a process that teaches sensors what they can safely skip. As an example of a false positive, a legitimate query directed to a corporate database could have a bit pattern that is similar to a well-known attack. The systems administrator can train the sensor to override its concerns and accept traffic from specific sources. Ultimately, both IPS and IDS sensors should, with high accuracy, differentiate between acceptable and potentially harmful traffic, eventually eliminating false positive alarms and only escalating actual attacks.

Target-Based IDS

When a sensor reports suspicious activity, a target-based IDS can provide automated just-in-time analyses of each targeted host to determine whether a compromise has occurred. The target-based IDS system, shown in Figure 3-26, examines hosts that are presumed to be under attack and attempts to ascertain their potential vulnerability.

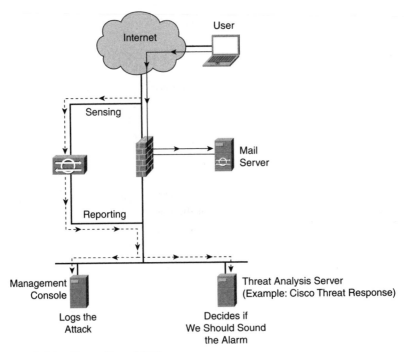

Figure 3-26   Target-Based IDS

A target-based IDS takes the following items into account:

- The type of device being targeted
- The type of operating system installed
- The patch history of the OS and the current status of the patches

This analysis results in fewer false positives while also ensuring speedier remedial action if an intrusion occurs, thereby limiting the potential resultant disruption of either situation.

Content Filtering

Content filtering sets limits on where users can venture on the Internet and can help to increase productivity while decreasing the organization's potential for negative exposure. Content filtering also serves to reinforce the message that office Internet access is granted for business use and that any general-purpose use is at the discretion of the organization.

This section discusses the following content-filtering topics:

- URL filtering, including filtering tools and administering outgoing traffic
- E-mail content filtering

URL Filtering

Uniform Resource Locators (URLs) enable users to reach any site on the Internet. In an office setting, the lure of the Internet can be so intense that it can get in the way of normal-course activities. Users are attracted for a variety of reasons, including the following:

- Online personal banking needs
- Personal financial trading of stocks, bonds, and other related instruments
- Desire to visit potentially nefarious or inappropriate sites
- Employment opportunities

- Determining what to prepare for dinner
- General retail shopping
- Boredom

According to IDC Research, in excess of 30% of office Internet use is not business related.[3] Another somewhat alarming study revealed that 70% of Internet pornographic traffic occurs during regular business hours.[4] The latter statistic is potentially more problematic because, depending on the sites the user visited, the organization itself could face certain issues. If the user was found to be downloading illegal images, the reputation of the organization, notwithstanding any possible legal implications, could be threatened.

Filtering Tools

Multiple sources offer filtering software tools, and some of the leading brands have reviewed in excess of 5 million websites. These filtering tools query the sites for content, with business environment suitability in mind, and slot them into categories. The vast database of said websites is made available to clients, who are then able to customize Internet access to fit their organizational needs.

Using these tools allows organizations to specifically deny the types of sites they want to have precluded from their users' access—after users are made aware of the Internet Acceptable Use policy, which is discussed in Chapter 10, "Essential Elements of Security Policy Development." The major tools have at least 80 categories, with multiple subsections within each one. For example, a major category might be gambling, which is then broken down further into casino gambling, lottery sites, betting houses, off-track betting, and so on. While an organization might want to eliminate gambling on the Internet, it might not have an issue with employees checking their lottery tickets. The filtering software would allow the systems administrator to stop traffic going to identified gambling websites, while still allowing users to check their lottery numbers.

Most major vendors issue frequent updates, some even daily, as their mission to categorize new sites continues unabated, as evidenced in Figure 3-27. Searches can also include sites that might only have changed their Internet address in an attempt to elude filters.

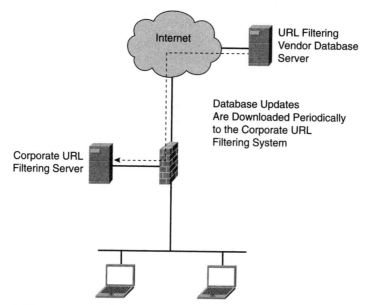

Figure 3-27   *URL Filtering Updates*

Administering Outgoing Traffic

In Cisco's case, as shown in Figure 3-28, after URL filters are installed, outgoing traffic headed to the Internet (step 1) is delayed momentarily at the firewall, as destination permission is sought from the URL filtering server (step 2). The server checks the organization's policies (step 3) and sends a message to the firewall (step 4), either granting or blocking access. Regardless of the outcome, the firewall *caches* the response (step 5), a process that stores the answer in its short-term memory so that if another user makes the same request, the firewall can deal with it more quickly. If the filtering server were to deny the request, a terse message would be sent to the user advising her that access had been denied (bottom step 6). Other implementations have browser traffic transiting through a proxy server, which also acts as a URL filter.

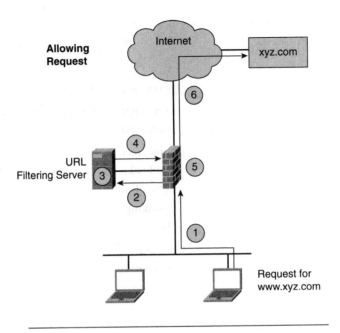

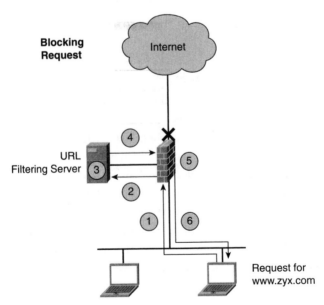

Figure 3-28   *URL Filtering Process*

As shown in Figure 3-29, the systems administrator can customize the software in a variety of ways to meet her organization's unique requirements. Customization can include the following items:

- Blocking or limiting access by one or both of the following criteria:

  - Time of day. For example, users might be granted unlimited access, certain site types not withstanding, prior to 8:00 a.m. and after 6:00 p.m.

  - Time-based quota. For example, recognizing that staff can use the telephone to perform personal banking if they cannot access the Internet, an organization might allow its employees limited daily Internet access for personal banking. Less time will likely be spent on personal activities, and the access might be greatly appreciated.

- Determining individual requirements by user, workstation, group, or network. For example, an organization might decide that its finance department requires full Internet access to keep tabs on its clients' financial positions or that its engineers need full access to effectively gather research. However it decides, filtering software can allow specific users or entire workgroups varying types of access.

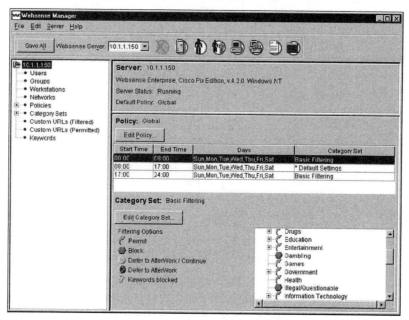

Figure 3-29 *Customizing URL Filters*

E-Mail Content Filtering

An e-mail content-filtering server, which can be situated either before or behind the firewall, acts as an intermediary between a network and the outside world. In Figure 3-30, e-mail messages are first sanitized, and *clean* messages are then passed to the mail server located on the DMZ. E-mail content filtering acts as a defense against unwanted e-mails, including spam, junk, hoaxes, viruses, chain mail, and other similar types.

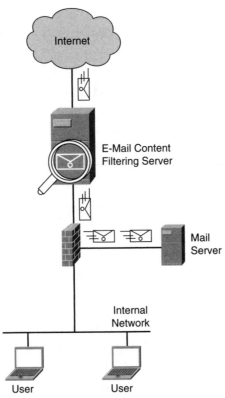

Figure 3-30 *E-Mail Content Filtering*

An e-mail content-filtering server can be programmed to examine e-mail file attachments, effectively filtering nonbusiness transmissions. Changing filenames so that a music extension appears to be a text document does not fool the filter; a routine check can reveal the actual contents.

Should a security threat be discovered, the e-mail message would be deleted, quarantined, or *cleaned*, a process that removes the attachment and forwards the body of the e-mail to the internal messaging system for delivery. An appropriate message might advise the recipient that an attachment had been removed for security purposes.

Additional filters are on the market that specialize in blocking possible malicious coding. An example might be a Java or ActiveX filter, which would typically examine a web page requested by a user and ensure that it is free of malicious coding.

Assessment and Audit

Secure environments use assessment tools in a preventive manner to ensure that vulnerabilities are highlighted internally, and potential issues can be avoided. Audit tools are typically used post-incident; they collect data and report on the data, providing a wealth of information that organizations can use in the future. This section explores the following topics:

- Assessment tools
- Audit tools

Assessment Tools

To effectively identify potential vulnerabilities in desktops, servers, and infrastructure devices, assessment tools are used to perform distributed or event-driven probes of network hosts, such as routers, switches, servers, and firewalls, as shown in Figure 3-31. Assessment tools conduct detailed analyses of network components and identify their weaknesses.

If a systems administrator is pressed for time, she can choose to focus on specific targets rather than engage in full-scale system-wide testing. Appliances such as web servers, for example, might garner more frequent testing because their proximity to the Internet can result in greater vulnerability. Equally susceptible are new devices that typically arrive from the factory with all ports open. They must be *hardened* immediately after installation, a process that determines which ports are open contrasted to which ports the appliance is listening on; closing those it doesn't require reduces unneeded exposure, as discussed in Chapter 2. Similar to a retail store that has every access and fire door open, the system would notify the server about open doors (ports), knowing that legitimate traffic can come through the front door and that other doors left open might only attract undesirables.

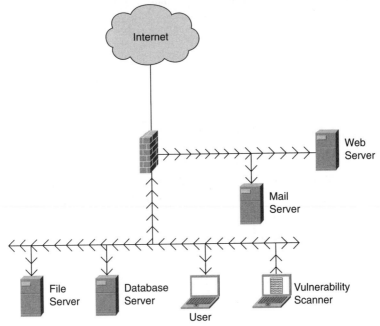

Figure 3-31   *Assessment Tool Conducts Vulnerability Scan*

The assessment tool performs a scan and produces a report that prompts a manager to determine the importance of each system and assign a corresponding value that can eventually lead to a risk score. The purpose of the assessment tool is to help the system administrator determine where best to allocate her resources and time.

Penetration Analysis

Organizations can employ third parties, known as *white-hat hackers*, to perform rigorous testing of their structures. These are firm-sanctioned hackers who use every tool available to break into a target's system and test the robustness of their shield. The white-hat hacker's mission is to determine where vulnerabilities exist and suggest appropriate solutions that address them. Figure 3-32 illustrates an analysis that could be used.

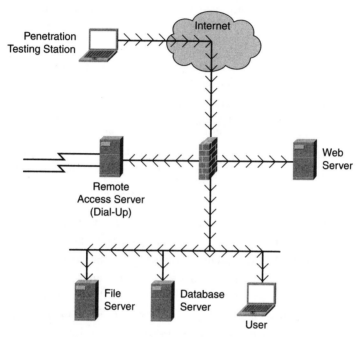

Figure 3-32   *Network Penetration Testing*

Table 3-5 lists possible assessments when the analysis is used.

Table 3-5   *Example of Work Done by White-Hat Hackers*

Activity Performed by White-Hat Hacker	Plan Employed to Carry Out Process
Host vulnerability assessment	A wide scan of the network is carried out. Reconnaissance is done to obtain a picture of the network and its vulnerabilities. It is followed up by a breach of the system: an access attack.

continues

Table 3-5 *Example of Work Done by White-Hat Hackers (Continued)*

Activity Performed by White-Hat Hacker	Plan Employed to Carry Out Process
Wireless security assessment	A hacker might sit in your parking lot and attempt to hack into your network. Alternately, he might try a *man-in-the-middle attack* by setting up a wireless laptop directly outside your office in an attempt to redirect wireless traffic to his covert network—revealing confidential passwords and pertinent network information.
Security response assessment	This assessment determines how well-equipped a company is to respond to security threats by the speed to which they respond to said threats.
Security awareness evaluation	This evaluation uses well-honed social engineering skills to extract confidential information from unsuspecting company staff.

Dealing with security vulnerabilities can be akin to working in a hospital emergency room—a new crisis can erupt, easily trumping an issue that a systems administrator might be attempting to solve. Giving the greater emergency the priority it requires could result in the lesser issue being forgotten. Thorough review processes include *ticket assignments*, a method that prioritizes issues by urgency and assigns formal tracking numbers that are continually monitored, ensuring that every issue is eventually addressed.

Audit Tools

Audit tools collect, analyze, and correlate security events. This section covers the following audit tool topics:

- Normalizing
- Correlation tools
- Log analysis
- Forensic analysis
- Luring the enemy

Normalizing

The installed base of security software can be so extensive on certain systems that it is not uncommon for different appliances on the same network to report vastly different explanations of security incidents. It can be challenging for a system administrator to distinguish between a true emergency on one piece of equipment and an unknown, but possibly innocuous, event on another. Software is available to manage the diverse security postures of network appliances by creating a common format for similar types of alarms. This has been dubbed *normalizing*, and it is effective in permitting a system administrator to properly assess security situations, allowing her to respond more efficiently. Normalizing can also serve to reduce the possibility of duplicate events by generating just one notification of a ping sweep, as an example, rather than having every piece of equipment on a network sounding off alarms about the same event.

Correlation Tools

IDS and IPS sensors are in contact with the management console server, instantly relaying any pertinent information. An IDS sensor might detect a small event and, in its normal course, report it to the server. Another IDS sensor on the network might detect a similar, almost innocuous, event, and it too relays the information to the management console server. Analyzed individually by the management console server, these two events might be seen as being inconsequential. But when a correlation tool analyzes the two events, it would become obvious that a possible attack was on its way, as shown in Figure 3-33. The correlation tool can analyze the two events concurrently and, by using real-time event data along with vulnerability assessment data and asset value, it can identify threats and attacks and manage them in real time. The individuals responsible for defending the network would also be alerted to the possible wrongdoing.

Network Intelligence (http://www.network-intelligence.com), NetForensics, and ArcSight (http://www.arcsight.com) are examples of vendors that provide products that transform raw log data into meaningful event information.

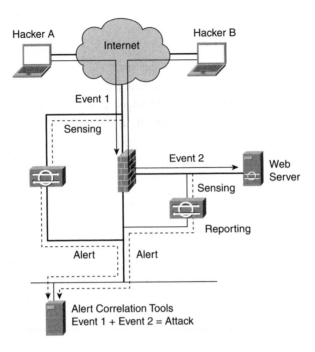

Figure 3-33 *Correlation Tools*

Log Analysis

A system log, commonly referred to as a *syslog*, is the central repository for all operational and configuration-oriented network events, as shown in Figure 3-34. Syslog messages can run the gamut from notification that a cable has been disconnected to an urgent message that a suspected breach is under way. Software sorts the events by type and severity and can contact the system administrator should a situation warrant it.

Vendors of comprehensive log analysis include FirewallAnalyzer (http://www. eiqnetworks.com) and NetIQ (http://www.netiq.com). Log analysis functionality is also provided by ArcSight, NetForensics, and Network Intelligence.

Forensic Analysis

When an attack has occurred, system administrators are encouraged to treat the infected area as a crime scene. Violated equipment has to be quarantined—an *image*, or copy, is taken of a hard drive, for example, and all necessary investigations are carried out on the copy—and network events need to be analyzed. Correlation tools are used to determine whether it was an isolated event or whether multiple attacks took place concurrently. As shown in Figure 3-33, if a web server were attacked, its log and history files would be analyzed and the investigation would proceed to the firewall. If further analysis confirmed that the malicious transaction did come from the firewall, its logs would be examined, and the logical progression would continue next to the ISP. The trail would keep following the thread backward until it eventually reached the intruders.

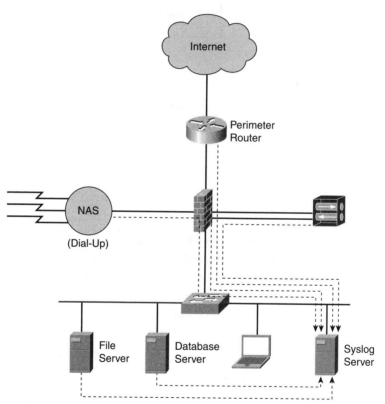

Figure 3-34   *Syslog Server: Network Management Repository*

Niksun (http://www.niksun.com) is one vendor that provides forensic analysis tools that can perform a variety of functions, including evidence gathering, selective archiving, and selective traffic replay.

Luring the Enemy

Organizations have employed *honeypots*, decoys that are deliberately installed on networks to lure and trap hackers. A server or network segment is intentionally riddled with vulnerabilities consisting of interesting files and information and then loaded with tracking software, enabling a hacker's movements to be effectively logged. They serve the additional purpose of diverting intruders' attention from mission-critical devices.

Additional Mitigation Methods

Organizations can mitigate threats in a variety of ways, and this section considers a number of them, as follows:

- Self-defending networks
- Stopping a worm
- Automated patch management
- Notebook privacy filter

Self-Defending Networks

The need to deal with unknown threats has emerged as one of the larger issues facing networks and those who administer them. Much of the equipment discussed so far has explored the issue of dealing with known threats; unknown threats are another matter. The goal of self-defending networks is to bridge that gap and begin a process that protects networks from threats that are still unknown.

This section discusses the following two main components of Cisco's self-defending networks:

- Cisco Security Agent
- Cisco network admission control

Cisco Security Agent

Cisco is offering software called Security Agent (SA), which works to identify unknown threats by searching for abnormal or atypical behavior. The software is installed on a PC or server, and should the tool detect irregular activity, it takes corrective action to deal with the issue. It is an IPS.

Unlike virus-checking software that is signature based—which requires continual updates for it to be effective—SA is an automated defense system. It does not rely on continual updates for it to be an effective protection program.

Cisco Network Admission Control

Network admission control (NAC) is the second layer of defense whereby the network itself acts as the defense. The protection comes from the router, or eventually the switch, wireless access point, or VPN concentrator. Network appliances used in a NAC role are referred to as Network Admission Devices (NADs).

The network, or in this case the router, asks a connecting laptop for the version of its antivirus (AV) software and the security policy it is running. The router, in its NAD capacity, checks with the head office policy server to ensure that the versions are current. The policy server is an ACS responsible for obtaining and evaluating the security posture credentials from the connecting client. The policy server provides the appropriate network access policy to the NAD, based on the client's system posture.

The router has the ability to carry out policy enforcement to ensure that noncompliant laptops—those not running up-to-date versions of AV or security policies—are put into quarantine. For example, consider that the router finds that the laptop is not compliant and places it in quarantine. In quarantine, a remediation server applies the latest patches and AV software to the laptop. After compliance is assured, the laptop is granted access to the corporate network.

A trust agent must be installed on the laptop so that it can communicate its security status to the enforcing appliances or, in this example, the router.

Stopping a Worm with Network-Based Application Recognition

Worms are capable of causing great problems for both networks and the people who administer them. The ability to recognize a worm, and then be able to do something about it before it completes its planned mission, is a benefit that most organizations would appreciate being able to implement.

Network-Based Application Recognition (NBAR) is a feature on Cisco routers. NBAR can police traffic based on applications, and should it ever be determined that certain packets might be malicious, it has the ability to drop the identified packets. Rules can be developed that, as an example, would filter out readme.eml files and stop them from being downloaded. (Those files were associated with the NIDMA worm.)

NBAR is an effective tactical tool that can be used to block malicious packets while patching or establishing defenses against worms. Other similar products are available that can aid in minimizing the impact of attacks and help to clean up from the after-effects.

Automated Patch Management

Applying patches in a timely manner can be somewhat problematic because of the sheer amount of hosts that need to be patched and the irregularity of patch issuance—patches are available only when an issue has been discovered. In normal-course situations, network administrators need to first be aware of the existence of a patch and then set aside time to perform the necessary work. The need for just-in-time patching becomes crucial whenever a worm, virus, or "hole" in a system is detected.

Using a process of automated patch management (APM) can ensure that patches are applied as soon as they are available, notwithstanding specific rules that network administrators can implement regarding noncritical daytime patching of highly used servers, as an example. APM can ensure that a patch is tested before it is applied and that rollout and rollback options are available should the patch need to be removed precipitously because of incompatibilities. Using annual subscription services, patch-management servers are kept abreast of the most currently available patches. Subscription services can ensure that patches are reliably deployed on an organization's servers, desktops, and roaming laptops.

APM can markedly reduce the number of hours a typical IT department would likely have to invest tracking patches manually for the vast array of equipment on a network. For example, it would greatly reduce the amount of time required for a network to effectively deal with a virus infection.

The following four key steps are followed whenever a virus or worm is suspected:

Step 1. Containment

Step 2. Inoculation

Step 3. Quarantine

Step 4. Treatment

Containment is a crucial first step in the long path of identifying the precise nature of an issue. A process of antibody, or antivirus, development follows it, and the issue is effectively isolated and a patch is ultimately applied. In this case, APM would be a crucial element in preventing the propagation of the virus by distributing the requisite patch in a timely fashion.

Tech Tip: Worm Propagation

Worms use the systems they inhabit as platforms to continue infecting other systems. The speed at which worms propagate can be so fast, as in the case of the Slammer worm, that network congestion issues are typically the result—Slammer was launched on January 25, 2003, and in 31 minutes, it infected approximately 75,000 victims. Figure 3-35 depicts the world immediately before the initial Slammer attack, and Figure 3-36 shows the amount of infected hosts after 31 minutes. Of concern to industry watchers was that while a patch had been developed and distributed, it had not been widely applied. This type of network congestion is analogous to automobiles on a freeway, should a city's inhabitants all decide to vacate a city at the same time, using the same road. Serious congestion would result.

Figure 3-35   *Slammer Immediately Before Initial Attack*

continues

> ### *Tech Tip: Worm Propagation (Continued)* 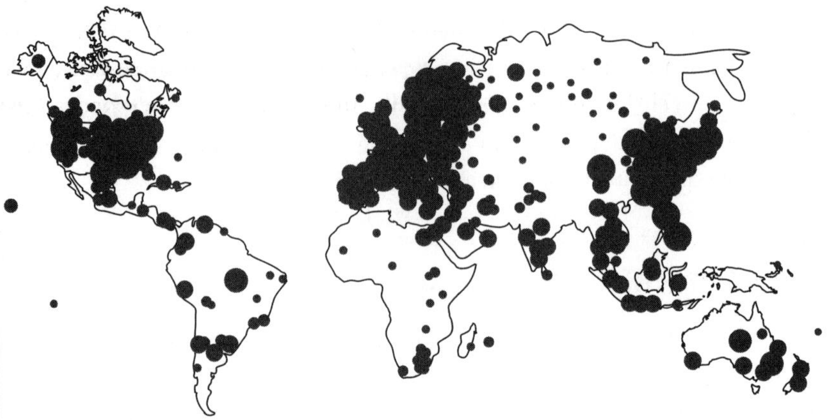
>
>
> **Figure 3-36**   *Slammer after 31 Minutes*
>
> Worms continue to propagate ever faster, as witnessed by the Mydoom worm that was launched in January 2004. It propagated itself at a far quicker rate than Slammer had done only a year earlier.

Notebook Privacy Filter

Nonoffice use of laptops used to be relegated to those business travelers who relentlessly crisscrossed oceans and continents on the way to their next appointment. But the prevalence of wireless networks encourages everyday users to work from any location that their laptops can locate a wireless signal, including such diverse settings as offices, home networks, and even coffee shops. This situation has necessitated the need for notebook privacy filters, thin opaque plastic sheets—referred to by 3M as Notebook Privacy Filters—that can be placed over a user's screen, ensuring that only those persons who are situated directly in front of a screen can view its contents.

A concern facing many users, particularly business users, is intellectual property (IP) protection. A senior executive reviewing confidential documents on his laptop while sitting comfortably in an airplane seat can be the victim of snooping by curious people seated around him. Harris Interactive recently conducted a survey on this issue, and it discovered that 42% of business travelers are fearful of their seatmates' wandering eyes; concerned flyers are perpetually trying to shield their work from others. In an interesting twist, nearly as many respondents, 40%, admitted to looking over to see what their seatmates were working on. That figure is up markedly from the 11% of respondents who admitted to the practice in 2001.

Products such as notebook privacy filters can lend a greater degree of confidence to those users who need to work on private or sensitive documents in public settings.

Summary

Business plans produced by an organization's various departments can differ in their approach, scope, and depth, but at their core, they share a fundamental element: Projections are essentially based on objective financials. The challenge in making a business case for network security is deriving a model from an ambiguous and ever-changing minefield of potential threats.

The discussions in Chapter 2 and in this chapter have centered on recognizing threats, acknowledging vulnerabilities, and understanding the multitude of equipment and tools available to mitigate risks. Building awareness is the fundamental thread that runs through each discussion. That knowledge is used in coming chapters to create and substantiate objective figures from the morass of readily available subjective matter.

This chapter focused on tools, applications, technology, and processes. It delved into areas organizations might decide to protect, limit access to, validate, sense, or filter. The discussions included the following topics:

- Using antivirus software
- Understanding traffic filtering
- Using encryption
- Implementing authentication, authorization, and accounting
- Using PKI and digital signatures

- Proliferating sensors throughout the network
- Recognizing the benefits of URL filtering
- Using assessments and audits

The following chapter uses data from both this chapter and the previous one to present pertinent mitigation tools that can effectively aid in fortifying an organization.

End Notes

[1]Norton website, http://www.norton.com, February 2004.
[2]Snyder, J. "Taking Aim." *Information Security.* January 2004.
[3]Websense website, http://www.websense.com, February 2004.
[4]Ibid.

CHAPTER 4

PUTTING IT ALL TOGETHER: THREATS AND SECURITY EQUIPMENT

The discussion to this point has centered on potential threats and the technology and equipment that can be used to guard against attacks. This chapter takes that information and offers a range of security topologies that organizations can implement to reflect their tolerance for risk. Risk tolerance determination is explored in Chapter 5, "Policy, Personnel, and Equipment as Security Enablers," and Chapter 7, "Engaging the Corporation: Management and Employees."

This chapter covers the following topics:

- Threats, targets, and trends

- Lowering risk exposure

- Security topologies

Threats, Targets, and Trends

Many types of attacks have been discussed in the previous chapters, and while new ones might be appearing on a regular basis, older ones are not necessarily dying off—they are being reused and reinvented in ever-destructive ways. Table 4-1 lists some of the attacks that have been addressed in earlier chapters and states whether their frequency is on the rise, declining, or holding steady.

Table 4-1 *Threats, Targets, and Trends According to CSI/FBI**

Well-Known Threat	Primary Target	Trend
DoS	Servers	Declining
Unauthorized access	Servers	Declining
System penetration (usually preceded by a network reconnaissance attack, which can include password attacks)	Network	Steady
Sabotage	All	Declining
Virus	Servers and workstations	Declining

*"CSI/FBI Computer Crime and Security Survey 2004." Computer Security Institute and Federal Bureau of Investigation (CSI/FBI). http://i.cmpnet.com/gocsi/db_area/pdfs/fbi/FBI2004.pdf.

It is relevant to note that certain statistical data regarding attack activity can be somewhat contradictory—different sources reveal differing attack trends. For example, the 2004 E-Crime Watch Survey, conducted by *CSO Magazine* in cooperation with the United States Secret Service and the CERT Coordination Center, reports that attacks are up 46%, whereas other organizations report downward trending.

At first glance, the data appears to be conflicting. But delving further, the data reveals a landscape that is being better protected by tools and equipment such as antivirus (AV) software, IDS, IPS, and so on. If organizations were to scour their logs for all attacks that were attempted against their networks, most would likely discover that while the numbers of attacks were on the rise, the damage that had been inflicted had been substantively decreased because of the equipment that had been put in place.

Organizations that have invested in IT security prevention equipment over the last number of years will have experienced the positive trending that has recently been reported. Sustaining an environment that is focused on preventive measures continues to pose a challenge, as attacks, and attackers, will forever attempt to find vulnerable points that can be penetrated.

There might not always be agreement on attack trends, but following them ensures that an organization is always aware of existing threats. An appropriate infrastructure, aligned with an organization's tolerance for risk, can be effectively developed to address the bevy of ever-present threats.

Lowering Risk Exposure

Equipment is available to address most risks, and while new and reinvented threats will inevitably continue to abound, implementing fundamental security appliances and practices throughout the system can aid organizations in their attempts to mitigate such threats.

Additional measures can also be taken to reduce the risk of attack and to ensure that hackers cannot clandestinely use an organization's network. Refer to the sidebar "Tech Tip: Being a Good Netizen."

Tech Tip: Being a Good Netizen

Organizations that connect to the Internet can be unwittingly serving as participants in denial of service (DoS) attacks. Simple measures, such as filtering addresses, can help to reduce risk. These were discussed in Request for Comments (RFC) 1918 and RFC 2827. RFCs are a series of documents that describe Internet protocols and related equipment. They can be found at http://www.ietf.org/rfc.

In brief, filtering ensures that perimeter equipment does not allow private addresses to cross the Internet boundary. Private addresses, such as 10.0.0.0 and others, are only meant to be used on internal networks and should never find their way to the Internet. Correspondingly, they should never originate from the Internet either.

RFC 2827 is best summarized as follows: A perimeter router or firewall must ensure that packets arriving from the Internet, and having originated from outside the network, do not bear a source address from their own internal network. Filtering consistent to this policy should be implemented.

Table 4-2 borrows threats from Table 4-1 and provides an appropriate type of technology that can effectively mitigate a particular type of attack. It lists the equipment in which the mitigating technology is primarily found, along with a fair substitute—other equipment that can be effectively used to also provide similar mitigation, albeit invariably to a lesser degree.

Table 4-2 *Mitigation Technologies*

Threat	Mitigation Technology	Recommended Equipment	Fair Substitute
War-dialers	Strong authentication	Access Control Servers	—
DoS	IDS	NIDS sensor	Router and firewall running IDS, routers with NBAR
	IPS	HIDS	
	Filtering	Router	
	Rate limitation	Provided on ISP equipment	

Table 4-2   *Mitigation Technologies (Continued)*

Threat	Mitigation Technology	Recommended Equipment	Fair Substitute
Unauthorized access	Stateful firewalling	Firewalls	Routers with firewall feature set
	Filtering	Routers	
	Intrusion detection	HIDS	
Man-in-the-middle attack	Encryption	VPN concentrator	Routers and firewall with VPN (IPSec) capabilities
	PVLAN	Switches	
Network reconnaissance	IDS	NIDS sensor	Routers with IDS
	IPS	HIDS	
	Filtering	Routers with access control list	
	Encryption	IPSec—Only IPSec traffic would be allowed inbound to corporate network.	
	Hardening	Automated patch-management systems	
Password attack	Strong authentication OTP	Access control servers	Local authentication with strong passwords
IP spoofing	Stateful firewalling	Firewall	Routers running firewall feature set
	RFC 2827 filtering RFC 1918 filtering	Routers	
Packet sniffers	Switched infrastructure	Switches	—
	Intrusion detection	NIDS sensor HIDS	
	Encryption	VPN concentrator	

continues

Table 4-2 *Mitigation Technologies (Continued)*

Threat	Mitigation Technology	Recommended Equipment	Fair Substitute
Trust exploitation	Private VLAN	Switches	—
	Firewalling	Firewalls	
Worm	Content filtering	—	—
	Virus scanning	—	
	Intrusion detection	—	
Virus	Content filtering	—	—
	Virus scanning	—	
	Intrusion detection	—	
Trojan horses	Content filtering	—	—
	Virus scanning	—	
	Intrusion detection	—	
Application layer attack	Up-to-date patching	Automated patch-management system	—
	Intrusion detection	HIDS	
Port redirection	Intrusion Detection	HIDS Firewall	Router
	Filtering	—	

Security Topologies

Cisco has developed a best-practices guide, called SAFE, for designing and implementing secure networks. The guide addresses different-sized organizations, from small- and medium-sized businesses (SMBs) to large enterprises. Cisco also addresses specific situations, or issues, of functionality, in an attempt to aid organizations in determining the type and level of security that should be implemented throughout a network.

The SAFE series of best-practices can assist the reader in joining the vulnerabilities that were discussed in Chapter 2, "Crucial Need for Security: Vulnerabilities and Attacks," and the network security mechanisms that were discussed in Chapter 3, "Security Technology and Related Equipment." Using the network models presented in the SAFE series, readers can learn how to combat security threats originating from both inside and outside the organization. Through the use of a modular design, they can create a scalable, corporate-wide security solution.

This section considers the following topics:

- SAFE blueprints
- SAFE architecture
- Using SAFE

SAFE Blueprints

The Cisco website (http://www.cisco.com/go/safe) provides a multitude of readily available SAFE blueprints, including the following:

- **SAFE: A Security Blueprint for Enterprise Networks (SAFE: Enterprise)** — Provides information on designing and implementing secure networks for large organizations.

- **SAFE: Extending the Security Blueprint to Small, Midsize, and Remote-User Networks (SAFE: SMR)** — Provides information on designing and implementing secure networks for small organizations or networks, which can include branches of larger organizations, or stand-alone operations. It also provides information on remote-user networks, such as those for mobile workers and teleworkers.

- **SAFE: VPN IPSec Virtual Private Networks in Depth (SAFE: VPN)** — Provides information for designing and implementing enterprise IP security (IPSec) Virtual Private Networks (VPNs).

- **SAFE: Wireless LAN Security in Depth (SAFE: Wireless)** — Provides information for designing and implementing wireless LAN (WLAN) security in networks.

- **SAFE: IDS Deployment, Tuning, and Logging in Depth (SAFE: IDS)**—Builds on the information in high-level design guidance for NIDS sensor placement, host-based IPS implementation, and secure syslog messaging by discussing in detail other IDS and logging design considerations and best practices.

- **SAFE: Worm Mitigation (SAFE: Worm)**—Describes best practices for containment and mitigation techniques and technologies that can be used against worms.

- **SAFE: IP Telephony Security in Depth (SAFE: IP Telephony)**—Provides information for designing and implementing secure IP telephony networks.

SAFE Architecture

Many SAFE blueprints are available, and while all hold great value, this book focuses on SAFE: Enterprise and SAFE: SMR.

This section explores the following topics:

- SAFE: A security blueprint for enterprise networks
- SAFE: Extending the security blueprint to small, mid-size, and remote-user networks

SAFE: A Security Blueprint for Enterprise Networks

The blueprint for enterprise networks emulates, as closely as possible, the functional structure and requirements of enterprise-sized networks and allows scalability and redundancy.

Scalability ensures that components can be added without needing to dismantle the current SAFE architecture that is in place on a network. Redundancy recognizes that certain appliances on a network could be considered mission-critical and that the security topology must have room to meet the demands of those types of requirements by doubling-up equipment.

SAFE uses a modular architecture that allows designers to address individual blocks of a network module-by-module, rather than requiring designers to contend with the entire enterprise every time security is addressed.

In Figure 4-1, the first layer of modularity is illustrated, with each block representing a functional area of the enterprise. As a side note, because the Internet service provider (ISP) module is not implemented by an organization, it is not discussed here.

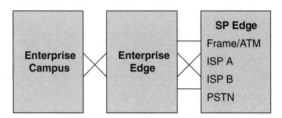

Figure 4-1   *Enterprise Composite Module*

Networks found in large organizations today typically consist of two fundamental functional areas: campus and edge, as shown in Figure 4-2. Because both areas are significant in size and complexity, the Cisco SAFE blueprint addresses each of their issues by subdividing them into specific modules that address each functional area. For example, the campus functional area typically includes a server module, a management module, a building distribution module, and similar modules. This modular approach helps to ensure that undivided attention is delivered to one vital aspect of the network at a time.

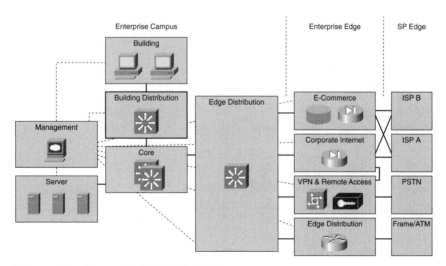

Figure 4-2   *Enterprise SAFE Block Diagram*

The primary role of SAFE blueprints is to ensure that mitigating functions are specific to the particular threat that a network module addresses.

SAFE: Extending the Security Blueprint to Small, Mid-Size, and Remote-User Networks

The SAFE blueprint for small- and medium-sized businesses and remote-user networks (SMRs) is similar to that available for enterprise networks, except that it is sized for smaller networks. SMRs can include branches of large enterprises or stand-alone small- to medium-sized security installations.

The SAFE document also provides pertinent information on remote-user networks.

The SAFE enterprise model represents the most comprehensive security blueprint. Figures 4-3 and 4-4 illustrate how the smaller models take their lead from the enterprise offering.

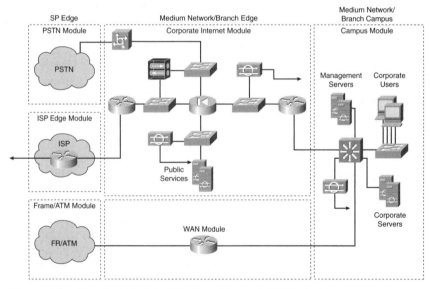

Figure 4-3 *Detailed Model of Medium Network SAFE Architecture*

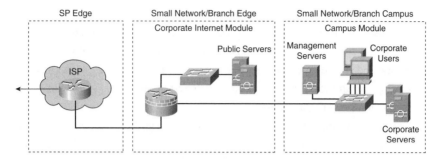

Figure 4-4   *Detailed Model of Small Network SAFE Architecture*

Using SAFE

Every organization has an operating and network structure that is somewhat unique, and it might not always be possible to slot requirements into one particular model, as described earlier in this chapter. The SAFE enterprise modular approach provides an effective solution to that issue by allowing security functions to be implemented modularly across a network. Network security topology models that address three general levels of risk aversion (basic, modest, and comprehensive), are presented in this section with risk tolerance itself being further explored in Chapters 5 and 7.

This section considers the following three network security topology models that organizations can use in their search for the most appropriate fit:

- Basic network security topology
- Modest network security topology
- Comprehensive network security topology

Basic Network Security Topology

Two organizations will likely have different definitions of what might constitute a basic network security topology model, particularly if they operate in different industries. Each of the three models presented in this section can be used as guides when developing security models in-house, but they are not meant to represent definitive solutions. For example, one organization might consider a straightforward firewall as constituting basic protection, whereas another might assume that a firewall would need to incorporate NIDS, among other offerings, to be called basic.

At a minimum, it is expected that workstations—be they stand-alone, networked, corporately owned, or situated in users' homes—are equipped with virus-protection software. The same is true for servers, regardless of whether they are connected to the Internet. Any server that is used for finance, engineering, general administration, or any operational function should be equipped with a host-intrusion prevention system.

All organizations that connect to the Internet, regardless of their size, should install a firewall. Stateful firewalls, as discussed in Chapter 3, cost as little as a few hundred dollars for a basic unit.

Modest Network Security Topology

Modest network security topologies are different for large enterprises and SMBs, resulting in the shopping lists for each being presented in separate tables.

Table 4-3 presents a modest security model for an enterprise network. It corresponds with Figure 4-2.

Table 4-3 *Shopping List for a Modest Security Model in an Enterprise-Size Network*

Module	Function	Security solutions
Campus	Network management	HIDS
		Virus scanning
		OTP server
		AAA services
		SNMP server (read-only)
		Network log server
		Switch
	Building distribution	Switch
	Building access	Switch
		Host virus scanning
	Corporate users	Core switch
		Virus scanning
	Corporate servers	Switch
		HIDS

Table 4-3 *Shopping List for a Modest Security Model in an Enterprise-Size Network (Continued)*

Module	Function	Security solutions
Edge	Edge distribution	Switch
	E-commerce	Router (FW)
		NIDS
		HIDS on servers
		Firewall
		Switch
	Corporate internet (DMZ)	Edge router
		Firewall
		DNS server
		http/FTP server
		Layer 2 switches
		NIDS appliance
		SMTP server
		HIDS
	WAN	Router
	Remote access and VPN module	NIDS
		VPN concentrator
		NIDS
		Firewall
		Router

Table 4-4 presents a modest security topology for an SMB. Table 4-4 corresponds with Figures 4-3 and 4-4.

Table 4-4 *Shopping List for Modest Security for a Medium-Sized Business*

Module	Function	Security Solutions
Campus	Network management	HIDS
	Corporate users	Core switch
		Virus scanning
	Corporate servers	Switch
		HIDS

continues

(133)

Table 4-4 *Shopping List for Modest Security for a Medium-Sized Business (Continued)*

Module	Function	Security Solutions
Edge	Corporate internet (DMZ)	Edge router
		Firewall*
		DNS server
		http/FTP server
		Layer 2 switches
		NIDS appliance
		SMTP server
		HIDS
	VPN and remote access	Dial-in server
		VPN concentrator
	WAN	WAN router

*To be considered basic, a perimeter firewall should come equipped with additional features such as basic IDS and basic VPN capabilities, which are available from vendors such as Cisco on its PIX Firewalls.

Comprehensive Network Security Topology

One of the main attributes of a comprehensive topology structure is redundancy. A resiliency that is a fundamental part of the operation is built in so that if anything should occur that would cause a system to fail—for example, poor configuration or physical failure—backup equipment would immediately take over operations. For example, Figure 4-5 illustrates a network redundancy situation, where a primary firewall is backed up by a standby firewall. Known as *stateful failover*, the job of the standby firewall is to continually check on the status of the primary firewall. The moment the standby firewall notices an issue with the operation of the primary firewall, the standby immediately takes over all functioning from the primary unit.

While the topology of a comprehensive security network could resemble that of a modest topology—with the main difference being equipment redundancy built into the plan—every organization has its own unique set of requirements. The possible list of equipment that could be found on a comprehensive security topology is potentially endless. The list is wholly dependent on the amount of redundancy and resiliency an organization might require.

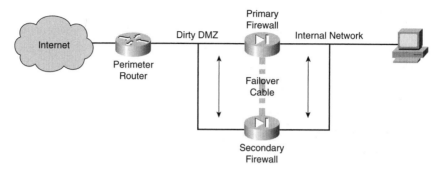

Figure 4-5 *Firewall Redundancy Through Stateful Failover*

In essence, a comprehensive security topology is the ultimate of alternates. Every relevant appliance and component is backed up, and additional componentry can also be included, as shown in Figure 4-6.

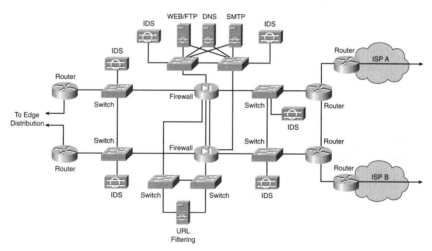

Figure 4-6 *Example of a Comprehensive Network Topology*

Summary

It is inevitable that threats will continue to exist. Understanding the magnitude of threats, the equipment that is typically targeted, and whether a particular threat is on the decline or the increase can aid organizations in determining the appropriate equipment to install on their networks.

Cisco publishes SAFE blueprints that organizations can use to proactively develop security systems to suit individual requirements. The SAFE blueprints are modular in their approach, allowing organizations to implement corporate-wide security solutions that are highly scalable.

This chapter explored the following topics:

- The issues inherent in threats, targets, and trends

- The equipment that can lower risk exposure

- The various security topologies that organizations can use as effective guides

Every organization is built differently, both in physical characteristics and ability to tolerate risk. The discussion in Chapters 2 and 3 centered on potential attacks and equipment that can help mitigate them. While this chapter provides security topologies and specific modeling that organizations can implement across their networks, it is vital to note that security policy development and enforcement are equal partners in the fight against potential attacks. The security policy development and enforcement topics are discussed throughout the rest of the book, primarily in Chapter 5, "Policy, Personnel, and Equipment as Security Enablers," Chapter 6, "A Matter of Governance: Taking Security to the Board," and Chapter 10, "Essential Elements of Security Policy Development."

Creating an effective business case for network security uses all this information, along with return-on-investment (ROI) modeling that is found in Chapter 9, "Return on Prevention: Investing in Capital Assets," to develop a proposal that is comprehensive in nature and financially sound in structure.

PART II

HUMAN AND FINANCIAL ISSUES

CHAPTER 5

POLICY, PERSONNEL, AND EQUIPMENT AS SECURITY ENABLERS

Enhanced security, as a field of business, is still relatively young. Security audit firms are burgeoning, swiftly heeding the call of urgency in many organizations. The auditing process can reveal many evils, not the least of which is an insufficient security policy framework. Given the threats that exist today, organizations would be well served with security policies that take the corporation's unique structure into account and create procedures that work to increase its business flexibility.

Making the business case for network security requires acute awareness of process flow. The course of business must not only be protected, but business processes should also be improved upon with every policy formulated.

Corporations are beginning to place greater emphasis in this area, recognizing that security policies are the backbone in substantiating a well-formed business case. The widest possible array of security equipment might still struggle to protect a system if its employees are not versed in preventive safety techniques. A policy should reflect the needs of an organization and encourage those elements that could help to grow its business. In essence, security, and its policies, should act as business enablers.

This chapter is the precursor to formal policy formulation (which is covered in detail in Chapter 10, "Essential Elements of Security Policy Development"). It explores key areas that policies should address, from equipment utilization and employee awareness programs to querying senior management on internal best practices. Most importantly, it can serve as a benchmark for ascertaining an organization's current security posture.

This chapter covers the following topics:

- Securing the organization: equipment and access
- Managing the availability and integrity of operations
- Implementing new software and privacy concerns
- Regulating interactivity through information and equipment control
- Mobilizing the human element: creating a secure culture
- Creating guidelines through the establishment of procedural requirements
- Determining rules and defining compliance
- Securing the future: business continuity planning
- Ensuring a successful security policy approach
- Surveying management

Securing the Organization: Equipment and Access

After equipment is installed and personnel are trained, spotting vulnerabilities demands the incessant task of analyzing minutiae. Whether it is log analysis, password control, physical building access, or strict rules governing departing employees, to name only a few, concentrating on details can help to ensure that security cracks are revealed and handily rectified.

The discussion in this section centers on the following topics:

- Job categories
- Departing employees
- Password sanctity
- Access

Job Categories

Many organizations use job categories to determine the scope of system access to grant individual users. A field salesperson with remote access might need to regularly check e-mail and search for marketing tools, but she should not necessarily be able to generate finance reports from the accounting department. Defining access by job category can help to preserve data integrity and ensure that unauthorized users, whether internal or external, cannot make unlawful contact with applications, operating systems, and networks.

Departing Employees

Recently departed employees can pose a risk if their access is not summarily terminated. In the flurry of activity that can surround a departure, laptops, keys, credit cards, and other physical property are collected, and the local manager might arrange to change the front door lock and forward the company credit card to the finance department. But a long-distance calling card might struggle to find its way back to the communications division. Similarly, advising the IT department to sever access privileges is not always high on a manager's alert list. Given the potential for damage that a recently departed employee could inflict, IT notification of user de-access should be prioritized appropriately. Outlining a procedure for departing employees, even those transferring departments, ensures that unlawful, yet still authorized, access does not occur.

Password Sanctity

The process of disseminating user passwords needs to be securely controlled. Users should be instructed, if not required, to change passwords on a regular basis and to choose words or characters that are not easily identifiable. Equally important, users should extend the same respect to passwords as they do their personal bank card PINs. The sanctity of passwords is of paramount importance; mishandled, they can represent the weakest link in a once-formidable chain.

Access

Physical access continues to play a significant role in network security. Installing floor-to-ceiling barriers might be deemed appropriate to protect a server room and, depending on the organization, securing air ducts leading to the room might also need to be considered. Certain organizations might find it appropriate to institute a *clean-desk* policy, ensuring that employees remove all paper and books from their desktops before they leave work for the day. Similarly, a *closed-blind* policy can ensure that wandering eyes outside a building cannot view its interior.

Sensitive areas must be defined and access appropriately restricted, and visitors or noncompany persons must never be left to wander a building alone. A branch office of a large enterprise, the former workplace of one of the authors, was visited late on a Friday afternoon by a photocopier service technician. He approached the receptionist and informed her that he needed to perform regular maintenance on the office copier. Not wanting to disturb her any more than necessary, he asked her to point him in the direction of the copier. She gratefully complied and returned to planning her weekend, and the technician wandered down the hall to service the equipment. Moments later, the receptionist attempted to place an outgoing call, but she could not get a dial tone. She walked over to a nearby phone, but still no dial tone was available. She consulted a manager, and together they walked to the telephone equipment room. The photocopier was located in the same room, but the technician was nowhere to be seen. They immediately noticed that the rack holding the PBX telephone switching equipment was empty. The technician had made quick work of snatching the PBX and had apparently exited through a rear door. Maintaining a strict visitor policy through the use of badges, visitor accompaniment, and employee vigilance can help to better ensure a secure environment.

Security issues can vary markedly by organization, ranging from the handling of hazardous materials to ensuring that IT equipment is protected against widespread power disruptions. Planning sessions that fully consider an organization's unique requirements can aid in forming the foundation of a well-constructed security policy.

Managing the Availability and Integrity of Operations

Maintaining availability and ensuring integrity of both physical and logical equipment are the bedrocks of operation management. Its goal is to protect the organization from interruption to its regular business activities and to minimize risk of system failure.

Safeguarding information requires that measures be in place before users begin to interact with one another or the Internet. For example, an organization could only ensure the integrity of its database if its appointed agents, typically in-house IT staff, were the sole persons responsible for loading software and performing maintenance on the system. Individual users would not be allowed to download or install software on their workstations, laptops, or local networks. IT would assume that responsibility, along with the task of deploying appropriate antivirus software throughout the network and its appliances.

IT staff would also ensure that discarded hard drives, prior to being recycled or trashed, get *sanitized*, a process that overwrites each block of a disk drive and fills it with 0s.

Safely managing the vast amount of information organizations typically generate requires that a consistent set of practices be instituted to ensure the following items:

- Systems are backed up regularly, preferably daily.
- Backed-up data is stored off-site, possibly using service providers who specialize in collecting and storing tapes and CDs. Whether in-house or third-party, storage facilities should be located in geographically secure areas.
- Thorough logs are maintained, enabling audit trails to be followed should an attack ever occur and forensic analysis required.

Managing security operations should include a systematic process of checks and balances, which can reduce the probability of unauthorized modification or misuse of equipment. Policies should ensure that no individual could perform all the following functions:

- Request a service
- Approve the required funds for the service
- Interview all vendors, contractors, or product providers
- Place the purchase order for the service or product
- Approve and make payment to the vendor
- Reorder the service

A chain of responsibility ensures that multiple individuals must give their consent before plans are put in motion. While it has the potential to become overly bureaucratic, the end justifies the means—checks and balances are the keystone of efficient operations, security or otherwise.

Implementing New Software and Privacy Concerns

This section addresses issues to be considered when implementing both custom and vendor-supplied software, and the integrity of data during transmission. The discussion centers on the following topics:

- Custom and vendor-supplied software
- Sending data: privacy and encryption considerations

Custom and Vendor-Supplied Software

The task of determining appropriate software for a company network can be challenging. Many organizations have invested untold sums assigning internal teams to test a litany of vendor offerings, only to decide that no single product could meet their unique requirements; the organizations were then relegated to writing their software. It's an expensive process that can be fraught with its own set of potential security issues.

Regardless of the route an organization might follow—in-house, custom-written software or off-the-shelf vendor-supplied software—certain fundamentals must be met. For example, extended password protection might not be of interest today, but in the future, unforeseen circumstances could force an organization to change its security posture. It is prudent to ensure that basic privacy options are included in current software and can be implemented without necessitating wholesale structural changes.

Custom programs should include the following items:

- During the development stage, creating a program that identifies potential security holes and implements an effective process to plug them

- Prior to production, running acceptance testing to root out unforeseen programming errors

- Postproduction, initiating a process that continually searches for newly created holes, and plugs them

If an organization plans to use off-the-shelf software, it is best to select a program that requires the least amount of modification. Well-known brands should have most holes plugged before the product is released to market, but by virtue of their brand-name status, these products can also attract more attention than lesser-known brands; this can result in hackers searching for holes even more diligently. In instances where issues surface after the product has a widely installed customer base, manufacturers are typically quick to issue patches to correct problems.

Postinstallation software modifications could potentially create back doors, because changes never occur in a vacuum. In typical situations, one change usually begets another, and the computing world is not immune to the domino effect of changes. The less software is modified, the fewer unexpected and unforeseen changes will result.

Change Control

A process that documents all changes, regardless of how minor a particular change might seem, can help to counter a negative impact a change might pose to a system. Commonly known as *change control*, it is a process that allows organizations to retrace their steps, from approval and security assessment of the proposed change to system backup, implementation, and monitoring of the change. Should an issue ever result from the change, determining the source of the issue should be less challenging to ascertain.

Sending Data: Privacy and Encryption Considerations

An organization might not need to encrypt every communication it sends out. Adding steps to any process naturally slows a system, and while it can seem inconsequential, encrypting and decrypting a communication still requires time and effort for both the sender and receiver.

Organizations can dictate a practice to streamline file encryption by developing a policy that states which communications are to be protected. The approach might consider the sender or the type of file being communicated. For example, a rule might state that e-mails from the CEO or files from the finance department are automatically encrypted. Conversely, an organization might consider encrypting all data it sends out, regardless of importance, to avoid inadvertently singling out its most sensitive transmissions to hackers. When a process becomes policy, less chance exists for confidential data to inadvertently be communicated in clear text.

Similar to a corporation's automatic encryption of particular users' e-mails, a program should be established that ensures the safe handling of users' public keys and certificates. The program should also include a process that revokes the keys and certificates when they are no longer required.

Regulating Interactivity Through Information and Equipment Control

Consistency is the key to effective communication of most messages. Whether it is a senior executive consistently repeating a specific objective or the simple labeling of documents to create an expectation, the need for employees to adhere to guidelines is of paramount importance.

This section considers the following topics:

- Determining levels of confidentiality
- Inventory control: logging and tagging

Determining Levels of Confidentiality

Most organizations regularly e-mail and courier envelopes and documents they deem to be sensitive in nature. Labels such as private, personal, protected, confidential, and secret are used to ensure that documents are afforded appropriate respect. The decision to label and choose terminology is generally made by the sender.

Regulating interactivity attempts to define a process users can call upon to determine the following items:

- When a situation or file warrants labeling
- What label to use—private, confidential, secret, and other similar markers

This process sets expectations. It allows e-mail users to effectively prioritize incoming traffic. It also allows the mailroom to appropriately segregate and distribute internal mail, and reception staff to effectively handle couriers and pass confidential packages to the intended receiver or the appointed agent.

At a minimum, three security communication classifications should be used, and the security level should be noted on each segment of the communication, including the envelope, e-mail, file, and actual document. The latter is particularly important in the case of e-mailed documents, where the receiver is more likely to generate a printed copy of the confidential file. An accompanying comments section should note that sensitive documents should only be printed on a dedicated printer, when the user is available to immediately collect the documents.

Inventory Control: Logging and Tagging

It might seem odd to individuals uninvolved in the process, but maintaining up-to-date and comprehensive inventory listings of all hardware, software, and data assets can be challenging. It is particularly difficult for large enterprises with remote offices, but it is advisable to develop centralized practices or to construct a controlled decentralized process whereby every department has one IT-sanctioned individual who can perform the necessary work. The process would strive to curtail aberrant network additions and to protect the organization against unknown equipment vulnerabilities, because an IT department cannot protect equipment it does not know exists.

In an attempt to sidestep perceived bureaucracies, the following mistakes might be made:

- Departments might be tempted to purchase and install their own network equipment, unwittingly creating a possible conflict with centralized security measures.

- Departments that independently install certain equipment and software could unwittingly cause negative implications, similar to two doctors prescribing prescription drugs for a patient, although neither is aware of the other's involvement. The computing pairing would likely not result in a fatal error, but it could serve to undermine security by creating back doors.

- Users could install personal wireless hubs, enabling them to wander from their workstations but still be connected. As discussed in Chapter 2, "Crucial Need for Security: Vulnerabilities and Attacks," this could inadvertently result in a breach.

Enforcing a consistent program that logs every piece of equipment, both hardware and software, can serve to remind all employees that equipment purchases must be approved and sourced centrally. The logging and tagging of equipment can help to thwart those who attempt to undermine a company's security measures by purchasing and installing appliances and software locally. Most importantly, manufacturers issue patches for their equipment immediately upon learning of a flaw. If the IT department were not fully aware of all equipment on the company network, fundamental patches might not get applied.

Mobilizing the Human Element: Creating a Secure Culture

The development of a secure computing environment requires high-level sensing, detecting, filtering, authenticating, encrypting, and authorizing equipment to be purchased and disbursed across an organization's appliances and systems. The process of establishing an enhanced security environment reaches well beyond physical equipment in an attempt to bring together an organization's most diverse component: its people.

This section considers the following topics:

- Employee involvement
- Management involvement: steering committee

Employee Involvement

It is becoming increasingly incumbent upon organizations to foster a culture that embraces security as an employee-initiative program, rather than a set of top-down rules imposed on users. Most employees have a genuine desire to maintain a positive working environment, and if they are informed about issues and understand what is at stake, they are more likely to become vigilant participants in the security process. Employee education can spell the difference between creating a security culture and merely installing equipment to build a security system.

Education can take many forms, but setting a tone can begin the moment an individual joins an organization. By incorporating security expectations in every job description, or statement of duties, individuals not only understand what is expected but also recognize the organization's commitment to having its employees accountable for security. The more prominence the statement is given on a job description, the greater its impact for each employee.

Orientation programs can be ideal forums to begin the process of disseminating security information, allowing new users to acknowledge the following policies of an organization:

- Internet policy
- E-mail policy
- Hardware and software policy
- Physical security policy

In recent years, organizations have become more diligent in checking business and personal character references during the hiring process. They delve deeper into resumes, substantiating employment periods, academic degrees, and other pertinent claims a prospective employee might make. Certain organizations are extending this practice to include contract, part-time, and temporary workers, ensuring that agencies that provide such people perform exhaustive identity checks before they are approved for work.

Management Involvement: Steering Committee

Organizations can have departments that are so diverse that it can be challenging to get its different factions moving in the same direction. From R&D and finance to warehousing and investor relations, finding common ground can be a challenge unto itself. While security is not the great leveler, it is an element that runs through every fabric of an operation. Every user is capable of wreaking havoc, and every individual is responsible for the sanctity of security practices.

Creating a security culture can be enhanced by the formation of an inter-departmental senior-level security steering committee. The direct involvement of leaders from distant groups can create positive ripple effects in the organization. Senior managers can do the following:

- Bring pertinent issues to the fore

- Be required to understand the needs of other departments, and the organization, in their quest to achieve a process that benefits all

- Provide a reliable litmus test to determine whether potential solutions are overly restrictive and could result in negative implications, such as users circumventing the rules

- Have a stake in the process, which makes them better equipped, and more inclined, to ensure implementation in their own departments

The steering committee concept can be a positive forum for senior managers to develop corporate policy in an area that is normally outside their sphere of influence. No single entity of an organization is an island, and bringing senior managers together under one umbrella can have a twofold effect: It can help to ensure the organization's security, and it can create an avenue for the pertinent corporate discussions that naturally ensue.

Creating Guidelines Through the Establishment of Procedural Requirements

The structure of security policies should not appreciably differ from other procedural documents an organization might construct. Policies should be formulated by a group consisting of security and company experts; the latter should comprise a cross section of senior managers who lead major departments within the organization. While Chapter 10 focuses on policy content, this abbreviated overview is concerned with fundamental structure. Specifically, every policy should attempt to answer the following questions:

- What is the policy about, and how does it get accomplished?

- Who owns the policy?

Policy Fundamentals

Every policy component should explicitly state what it is attempting to achieve. If a particular process uses technology to realize its goal, a short summary detailing the role of the equipment should be provided to enable the reader to garner its purpose. Equipment usually requires human intervention, and policies should detail all that is required of users to ensure proper use and compliance; the users need to know unequivocally what is expected of them, including the potential consequences for noncompliance.

Policies should contain defined review dates, ensuring that their core components are continually reevaluated and updated.

Determining Ownership

Every process needs an *owner*, an individual who is ultimately responsible for a function or job. Whether the process is equipment, networks, software, appliances, or databases, clearly defining roles and responsibilities can avoid the inevitability of postattack finger pointing.

The sales department, as an example, might believe that it owns the customer relationship management (CRM) software, and the engineering department might justifiably assume that it has responsibility for its highly specific plotter equipment. But the IT department likely has a different view of both situations. Should an attack be the result of improper loading or installation, which department would be at fault? Different levels of responsibility must be considered: Operators of the sales tool or engineering printer might not consider security their issue, but unless otherwise specified, owning either should entail complete accountability. To resolve this dilemma, an organization might declare two owners for specific situations: The user would be responsible for populating fields with data, and the IT department would be accountable for operability, ensuring that data is backed up every evening and that patches are applied as soon as they are published. This process would ensure that the equipment user is responsible for determining security classifications and secure handling of documents produced on the equipment, while IT is responsible for the security of the physical equipment itself.

Ownership is not about placing blame. Rather, it is concerned with assigning complete responsibility, ensuring that no individual or department can ever say, "I thought someone else was supposed to do it." Ownership defines accountability, and in so doing promotes a culture that is steeped in prevention and responsibility.

Determining Rules and Defining Compliance

Users within a corporation must abide by its rules, making it incumbent upon the organization to ensure that its policies are logical, fair, ethical, and germane to computing and security jurisprudence. Corporations must ensure that they act not only within the law but also within the spirit of the law. This section considers the following topics:

- Corporate compliance
- User compliance

Corporate Compliance

Issues have recently surfaced that bring new emphasis to the phrase "acting within the spirit of the law." Many have argued that laws governing corporate behavior shouldn't necessarily dictate strict rules of conduct, because rules can be misinterpreted, misunderstood, or simply gotten around. It is argued that because one cannot misconstrue the spirit of a law, the business community might be better served by a system that encourages adoption of that spirit.

The Internet has made various materials more accessible than ever, and certain copyrights can prove difficult to protect. While legislation is working hard to keep up with technological advancements, enforcement can be another issue. Corporations have long respected copyright laws on software, ensuring that counterfeit copies of software are forbidden on company property. But inappropriate e-mail and file deletions are still a relatively new issue, and only recently have they become synonymous with document shredding.

HR departments are using security technology to protect individuals' privacy, and corporations are making certain that all copyrights they encounter are respected. Organizations are becoming exceedingly more diligent in all aspects of their computing environments, ensuring that compliance to laws is strictly adhered to—both to the letter and, increasingly, to the spirit.

User Compliance

User compliance, or more specifically, observance and adherence to company rules, plays a major role in security policy. The concept of "inspect what you expect" means that an organization should follow up on policy compliance and not just assume its users are following the stated rules. Whether the evaluation is log analysis or Internet tracking, the organization must check, or inspect, to ensure that rules are being followed. Note that most rules are not invasive and exist primarily for the safety of both the user and the employer.

Users are tasked with keeping company equipment safe while it is in their possession. For the typical corporate user entrusted with company property, that usually means a laptop computer. Keeping the equipment safe can run the gamut from restricting Internet browsing to appropriate sites and not loading third-party software, to ensuring that the laptop is locked when not in use. When traveling, a laptop and related equipment should be secured in a safe room. If one is not available, equipment should be placed in a locked suitcase. Thieves typically remove items from hotel rooms that are easy to conceal; suitcases are not typically stolen.

Users need to be aware of their surroundings, even when they are traveling within a city. Three employees of a large enterprise had just completed a sales call late one afternoon when they decided to have dinner before returning to their hotel. Traveling together in a nondescript sedan, their laptop computers securely hidden in the trunk, they confidently parked the car in a well-lit area and went into the restaurant for dinner. Potential criminals are everywhere, and the person watching the three clean-cut men in business suits emerge from their car at 5:30 p.m. and walk to the restaurant empty-handed, probably quickly surmised that laptop computers could be in the trunk. After dinner, the three men returned to their car to find the trunk lid damaged—and their computers gone. Security means not merely following the rules but interpreting them so they are relevant for every situation.

While organizations compile comprehensive regulations that are relevant to their mandates when determining rules for user compliance, the following guidelines are applicable to most companies:

- A clearly defined Internet policy must be acknowledged by all users.

- A system policy must be in place that clearly states unacceptable computing behavior, requiring the user to consider the spirit of a policy and not merely its black-and-white rules.

- A process must ensure that company confidential documents are never stored on a user's hard drive. Rather, any documents that are labeled private, or confidential, could only be stored on the company server, as an example.

- Wide use of monitoring tools can aid in identifying misuse. For example, intrusion detection systems (IDSs) look inside a packet to ensure that the payload is what the header claims it to be.

- The organization could provide constant reminders encouraging users to comply with safety rules, for example, pop-up screens that contain warnings, reminding users to log off when they have completed a session. Or, the organization can establish an enforced logoff after a specified period of inactivity.

- Appropriate personnel should know relevant state, local, and federal law enforcement officials.

- Appropriate personnel should be well versed in legal requirements that are germane to the specific industry to which the organization belongs, or the county in which it resides.

- If certain users are responsible for employing third-party service providers, the user responsible needs to ensure that the service provider has adequate, and auditable, security to ensure the corporation's privacy.

Lists can be endless—the challenge lies in delivering the organization's intent without the message becoming stale. By engaging in a practice that promotes continual education, users can be well versed in their employer's mandate, fully comprehending how its security posture is instrumental in helping the organization achieve its goals.

Securing the Future: Business Continuity Planning

Crises will inevitably occur. Whether they are physical, such as an earthquake or a terrorist attack, or cyber, such as a distributed denial of service (DDoS), preparedness is the key to effectively managing a crisis. The difference between falling victim to an event and working through a highly challenging time is planning.

A comprehensive continuity plan is essential in maintaining or restoring business operability. A hospital or public utility, as an example, would require a plan to maintain operations during a crisis. Conversely, a sporting goods distributor might decide to concentrate on a plan that restores its operability after a crisis has passed. The potential lost revenue might not justify the expense of a costly program that attempts to maintain operability regardless of challenges. A hospital or utility would not have a choice.

Continuity plans should consider the following items:

- Knowing the parameters of a given situation that could warrant the use of the plan

- Having a detailed inventory of standby systems, including the length of time required for each one to be fully operational

- Determining what would constitute the completion of a critical period and a return to normal operations

- Selecting an appropriate leader(s) to manage the crisis. While separate leaders could exist for technology and business requirements, one overall leader must be chosen

- Knowing the actions that need to be performed and the persons (or job functions—see next bullet) responsible for performing them

- Assigning job functions rather than specific people to specific continuity tasks so that if a person leaves a firm, the new occupant of the job function is the replacement for the continuity task

- Assigning specific reporting sites if an alarm is sounded

- Ensuring that users know the sites and are confident in their assignments, particularly if the continuity site is in another physical location

- Using the expertise of individuals, particularly the IT staff

- Formally testing the plan, rooting out all weaknesses

- Defining the amount of time needed to bring the continuity plan online

- Most importantly, keeping the continuity plan current, both in its practice and content

Continuity plans are similar to term life insurance policies: One plans for the worst but hopes never to realize the policy's payoff. A detailed and workable plan to maintain operations during trying times can allow a sense of confidence that is only achievable through comprehensive contingency planning.

Ensuring a Successful Security Policy Approach

Comprehensive security policies are tools that employees and management can use to understand how the organization is protecting itself—and what it expects from its users.

One of the main challenges in creating this type of policy is ensuring that it doesn't become overburdened with rules that could become insurmountable barriers. Note that security does remove a certain degree of flexibility. Similar to installing a home security system, the more comprehensive the system becomes, the less mobility one has in the home. A simple perimeter system that places contacts on doors and windows allows full movement within the house. But with the addition of motion detectors and laser beams, a dog's attempt to retrieve food mistakenly left on a kitchen table could conceivably trigger an alarm. The decision to install a comprehensive home system is usually preceded by a discussion centering on the real cost of vulnerability. Deciding on the makeup of the system can only begin after that discussion is concluded, because one cannot effectively mitigate risk until the person knows his level of aversion to it.

In a network environment, if users are routinely bypassing security in their rush to complete work, there could be many possible issues, including, but not limited to:

- Users are ill-informed about vulnerabilities that exist and simply bypass network security measures as a matter of course.

- The systems in place might be overkill for the type of work that needs to be accomplished.

This section attempts to pinpoint key areas where security policies have been known to be vulnerable. Keeping these points in mind when formulating policy can help to ensure its eventual effectiveness. This section examines the following topics:

- Security is a learned behavior
- Inviting the unknown
- Avoiding a fall into the safety trap
- Accounting for the unaccountable
- Workflow considerations
- Striving to make security policies more efficient

Security Is a Learned Behavior

Individuals are not born cautious. Quite the contrary; they are naturally trusting, open, and inviting. Part of the rearing process involves teaching individuals to become suspicious. Cultivating a secure environment in a computing system is not dissimilar to teaching an individual to be wary. Networks are not born cautious, as evidenced by routers that broadcast their location. Security appliances are introduced to shield vulnerable equipment, but they cannot protect users who act recklessly or sloppily; that form of preventive guarding must be learned by users.

Earlier discussions have alluded to the argument that certain organizations are better served by explaining their security posture to users. While it is challenging to fully protect a network from a user who willfully wreaks havoc, the vast majority of users who might cause harm are not doing so maliciously. They usually have no perception of the damage, or potential for damage, they have left in their wake; they simply do not know any better. An organization that openly shares its rationale for security generally finds its users less likely to skirt measures it puts in place, and a corresponding reduction in the amount of inadvertent errors it experiences should result.

Teaching appropriate security techniques takes time. Through the power of conditioning, users can learn how to properly navigate a system without putting it in jeopardy. Repetitively performing tasks and walking through the system with a knowledgeable teacher, users can become skilled at performing safe computing.

Consistent positive reinforcement, whether it is praise or ongoing education, can help to create a corporate culture that is focused on making security a learned behavior.

Inviting the Unknown

Most security systems are designed to deal with known entities, either attacks that have occurred or are feared to occur. Equipment is put in place, and an organization returns to its normal business. A comprehensive network security program dictates that minor vulnerabilities, or seemingly insignificant cracks, should be scanned for constantly, because the most harmful invasions usually come from the most unsuspected places.

Regular security scans should do the following things:

- Identify an organization's most vulnerable points, and assume that attacks could be launched against them

- Identify network areas that the IT department assumes to be highly secure, and determine their weakest links

Even the most secure environments have stress points, and identifying them is the first step in forging a more resilient network. Continually scanning for vulnerabilities in the most unsuspected places can proactively help mitigate the unknown.

Avoiding a Fall into the Safety Trap

Perfectly secure environments do not exist. Purchasing every possible type of equipment doesn't protect an organization if its users are not effectively trained. Furthermore, responsible employees cannot protect a company from a DDoS attack without the help of proper equipment. It is a combination of both that provides the most comprehensive security. Equally important is recognition that implementing security is not a one-time effort. Threats evolve and disappear, only to be replaced by new and more sophisticated ones. Policies must be able to respond quickly, efficiently, and proactively.

A security-minded organization can use a revolving wheel, as shown in Figure 5-1, to underscore its daily practices and to help it create a forward-thinking security posture.

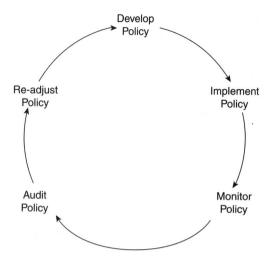

Figure 5-1   *Closing the Loop on Security: Making Policy Review a Constant*

Business environments rarely remain static, and the wheel ensures that an organization can keep pace with an ever-changing world.

Accounting for the Unaccountable

The likelihood of a hacker planning and carrying out a full-scale attack against a random network is remote. But should one occur, its effects could be devastating. Protection equipment, or the act of mitigating threats, is a type of insurance vehicle that organizations use to keep hackers at bay, as discussed in Chapter 3, "Security Technology and Related Equipment."

The most common threats organizations confront are those that come from within. Whether they are premeditated or inadvertent, the end result is usually the same. Human error can result in a nonmalicious DoS attack that, while innocent, can still bring down a network.

Some breaches might appear innocuous on the surface, but they could result in serious damage being inflicted if not immediately addressed. For example, a staffer who routinely borrows the phone line from the fax machine to dial in to his personal ISP opens an unprotected path to the Internet that a hacker could recognize. The staffer might know he is not allowed to do this, but his need to connect to his personal account through the ISP could outweigh his misgivings, particularly if he isn't reprimanded after the first few times. The more he accesses his ISP and gets away with it, the more bravado he will have to continue.

Aberrant activity must be addressed in security policies so that users can understand the spirit of what is expected of them.

Workflow Considerations

Ideally, policy formulation teams should include users who are familiar with an organization's workflow to ensure that a policy reflects the workflow.

Policies that reflect workflow have the added benefit of addressing rules that are too cumbersome for users by avoiding the pitfall that is all too common with restrictive regulations: Users go around them and typically create back doors in the process.

Security policies that take practical considerations into account have a greater potential to effect positive results.

Striving to Make Security Policies More Efficient

Identifying and planning for the natural weaknesses in security policies can be an effective tool to use when creating a comprehensive plan.

Breaches can be avoided when planners model a process before committing it to implementation. For example, a procedure might reasonably dictate that a particular room remain locked during business hours and assign responsibility for the key to one person. But if multiple users require access to the room to carry out their normal course of duties, frustration could ensue if the individual in charge of the key is not always readily available. Users might find a way to circumvent the rule by surreptitiously copying the key. It is understandable that the organization might need to control access to the room, but rather than creating an environment that inadvertently encourages underhanded activity, it could research more reasonable access measures, such as the authentication and authorization tools described in Chapter 3.

Ensure that a process exists to routinely review policies. Even the best-laid plans can require tweaking, and security policies should not be immune from postimplementation analyses. Organizations can also change in size, structure, and equipment that they use; policies should be flexible enough to appropriately reflect any relevant changes to the corporation.

Continue to educate users on the importance of security and on what they can do to help. Most employees have strong positive feelings about their employer and, if possible, they genuinely want to make a difference in their workplace. An environment that encourages its employees to become active participants in the security process will be well structured to deal with threats in the future.

Surveying IT Management

Making the business case for network security requires that a multitude of soft factors be garnered from both the technical and human elements within an organization. While technical elements are relatively straightforward to ascertain, determining human elements can be more challenging, because personal opinion can vary markedly across an organization's senior management team.

To begin the process of determining an organization's tolerance for risk, a series of questions were developed for this book. The questions, presented in the Infosec Management (IM) survey, were created to address a fundamental requirement of most organizations—a company must first acknowledge its aversion to risk before it can begin the process of effectively securing itself. This section discusses the need for determining a consensus on risk and then presents the IM survey.

The discussion centers on the following topics:

- The need for determining a consensus on risk
- Infosec Management survey
- Infosec Management quotient

The Need for Determining a Consensus on Risk

Successful companies typically follow similar paths: A senior-level consensus on goals is established, and then managers work diligently to achieve the stated goals. While individual drive and entrepreneurial spirit are essential factors in every company's success, a firm's senior management team must first reach consensus on the organization's goals and strategies; consensus is simply the surest way to underwrite success. Developing an effective security plan is no different; it requires an organization's senior management team to first reach consensus on its aversion to risk.

It is important to acknowledge that achieving consensus on risk is not a straightforward task. Risk is relative. Every senior manager, unwittingly or not, brings to bear on the organization his or her own personal tolerance level for risk. To achieve effective risk management, every significant senior manager needs his or her opinion to be considered. The IM survey, which is discussed in the next section, was developed to ensure that organizations can achieve consensus for the establishment of their security postures.

Infosec Management Survey

The Infosec Management (IM) survey in this chapter and its sister Infosec Operational (IO) survey, which is presented in Chapter 7, "Engaging the Corporation: Management and Employees," were created for this book to help organizations determine their overall aversion to risk. The IM survey is designed to be completed by IT managers, CIOs, CSOs, and CISOs. The IO survey is designed to be completed by senior managers from every significant department. Material for the surveys reflects issues that are discussed in this book, ranging from policies, processes, and business requirements to equipment and personnel issues. While the survey questions are designed to be applicable to most organizational situations, the manager responsible for disseminating the survey should feel free to change the questions to best reflect his organization's requirements.

The IM survey focuses on policy and the human aspect of risk management; the results can help calculate an IM quotient. The IM quotient is the mean score of all those who participate in the survey. The IO survey in Chapter 7 focuses on technology, equipment loss, and communication; the results can help calculate an IO quotient—the mean score of all those who participate in the survey in Chapter 7. The IM quotient and IO quotient are part of the risk-aversion discussions in Chapter 8, "Risk Aversion and Security Topologies."

Through careful consideration of the results to answers in both surveys, managers can determine whether their current policy does the following things:

- Reflects their immediate needs

- Is flexible enough to adapt to a fluid business environment and a changing security posture

- Reflects the workflow but doesn't attempt to control it

- Has input from every corner of the organization

- Has support of corporate management

- Has an automatic review and readjustment process

- Acts as a business enabler

In addition to establishing an IM quotient and an IO quotient, the surveys aid organizations in highlighting stress points, revealing vulnerabilities that should be addressed in both policy and actions.

Organizations are encouraged to benchmark their results against industry standards, in particular ISO 17799, "Code of Practice for Information Security Management," an auditable standard first published in 2000 by the International Standards Organization (ISO). The ISO (http://www.iso.org/iso/en/ISOOnline .frontpage) is synonymous with quality benchmarking, and its work in the security field addresses similar concerns. It provides a process that deploys security standards that organizations can follow and, ultimately, audit.

The rating scale in Table 5-1 should be used to respond to the Infosec Management (IM) survey questions.

Table 5-1 *IM Survey Rating Scale*

Rating Scale	Rating Explanation
0	Not applicable, firm does not engage in process
1	Meets some requirements
2	Meets most requirements
3	Meets all requirements
4	Overachieves requirements
5	Exceptionally forward-thinking, exceeds all requirements

The survey, shown in Table 5-2, should be distributed to all appropriate IT managers: CIO, CSO, CISO, and so on. It is best to include as many senior IT managers as possible to ensure that consensus can be effectively achieved.

Table 5-2   *IM Survey*

Question or Situation to Be Considered	Rating Schedule
Does the organization have a comprehensive security policy that encompasses all departments, remote offices, and personnel?	5 4 3 2 1 0
Aside from denying access to finance and HR, does individual network access differ markedly by job category?	5 4 3 2 1 0
For recently departed employees, is IT notified, as dictated by policy, either before or within minutes of departure?	5 4 3 2 1 0
For intracompany employee transfers, is IT notified, as dictated by policy, either before or within minutes of transfer?	5 4 3 2 1 0
Are users prevented from reusing passwords?	5 4 3 2 1 0
Are users denied the ability to use either their first or last name as a password?	5 4 3 2 1 0
Are passwords changed, at a minimum, every 30 days?	5 4 3 2 1 0
Are visitors and noncompany personnel accompanied at all times?	5 4 3 2 1 0
Are branch or remote office employees denied the ability to install software on their computers and equipment?	5 4 3 2 1 0
If users are not allowed to load any type of software, is this mandate enforced by policy and practice?	5 4 3 2 1 0
Does IT have the sole responsibility for all software installations on all equipment, regardless of how innocuous the loading might appear?	5 4 3 2 1 0
Are discarded hard drives *sanitized,* a process that overwrites each block of a disk drive and fills it with 0s?	5 4 3 2 1 0
Are comprehensive system logs recorded?	5 4 3 2 1 0

Table 5-2   *IM Survey (Continued)*

Question or Situation to Be Considered	Rating Schedule
Are comprehensive system logs regularly monitored for abnormal behavior?	5 4 3 2 1 0
Does the organization use encryption when forwarding all confidential files and documents?	5 4 3 2 1 0
Does the organization use digital signatures?	5 4 3 2 1 0
Does IT prioritize the patching of pertinent equipment when notified by a patch information service or the vendor?	5 4 3 2 1 0
Does IT apply patches within hours of the patch being released?	5 4 3 2 1 0
Does a backup person exist to monitor and immediately install patches if the appointed person is unexpectedly absent?	5 4 3 2 1 0
Does the organization regularly (at least once per year) survey all departments and remote offices for mandatory equipment logging and tagging?	5 4 3 2 1 0
Do all users unequivocally understand the company's Internet and e-mail policies?	5 4 3 2 1 0
Are the company's e-mail and Internet policies enforced?	5 4 3 2 1 0
Does the organization have a body, or group, that is independent of IT to oversee system security?	5 4 3 2 1 0
Does every process, equipment, and policy have an unequivocal owner?	5 4 3 2 1 0
Does the organization have a policy requiring remote users and travelers to effectively secure their equipment when out of the office?	5 4 3 2 1 0
Does the organization have a formal and continuous security education program that highlights user responsibility?	5 4 3 2 1 0
Does the organization have consistent communication with employees about known security incidents/breaches—particularly how to prevent recurrences?	5 4 3 2 1 0

continues

Table 5-2 *IM Survey (Continued)*

Question or Situation to Be Considered	Rating Schedule
Does the organization have a formal process that comprehensively vets (confirms work history, education, and so on) all employees, including contract workers and temporary staff?	5 4 3 2 1 0
Does the company have a business continuity plan in the event of a crisis?	5 4 3 2 1 0
Is the business continuity plan tested and deployed in a mock trial at least annually?	5 4 3 2 1 0
Does the organization have a process to regularly review security policies and adjust them to reflect any change in equipment, processes, or business requirements?	5 4 3 2 1 0
Is the formal security review process performed by a company-wide group that consists of business and IT managers?	5 4 3 2 1 0
Does the company fully explain its security rationale to employees so that individuals can become active proponents?	5 4 3 2 1 0

Infosec Management Quotient

The Infosec Management (IM) quotient is derived by averaging the scores of those managers who participated in the survey. Extensive IT management participation can help ensure an IM quotient that is truly reflective of the organization's aversion to risk.

The IM quotient (and IO quotient, which is determined in Chapter 7) can be married to a hard-number formulation process that helps quantify security decisions. These formulations are explored in Chapter 8 and form the foundation of the return on prevention (ROP) model.

To establish the IM quotient, determine the average score and convert it to a percentage, as follows:

IM quotient = Average of survey results * (100 / Total possible points)

where Total possible points = 5 * Number of questions

If you use all 33 questions from the survey in this chapter, the formula would be as follows:

IM quotient = Average of survey results * (100/165)

Reserve the result for use in Chapter 8 to aid in determining the organization's risk and risk aversion and to determine the appropriate topologies to avert that risk.

Summary

Policy plays an integral role in security effectiveness. Educating users on their responsibility to enhance security can have a twofold effect: It ensures that deployed equipment can perform tasks with greater effectiveness, and it creates an environment that encourages and supports individual responsibility.

The business case for network security requires that soft elements be acknowledged, considered, and ultimately weighted through adoption of an analytical process. Risk, and aversion to it, must be quantified before effective programs can be developed and put in motion. It is a fundamental step in the process of formulating concrete ROP results.

This chapter focused its discussion of policy on the following topics:

- Outlining steps to secure the physical organization, both equipment and access

- Understanding the importance of operations management of physical and logical equipment

- Safely deploying new software and understanding privacy concerns

- Promoting the need for consistent confidentiality labeling and equipment tagging

- Understanding the need to mobilize the human element within an organization to create a security culture

- Defining policies, detailing pertinent processes, and assigning ownership

- Exploring corporate and user compliance

- Developing a process to work through crises, using business continuity planning

- Acknowledging common vulnerabilities in security policies
- Introducing a fundamental step to quantify soft issues: surveying senior management

The next chapter advances the discussion by focusing on the board and presenting the issues inherent in security governance. Chapter 7 focuses on the IT manager, providing him with an overview of the business side of the organization and equipping him with the necessary tools to effectively lobby his senior-management colleagues on the merits of investing in security. Chapter 7 also introduces the next survey, the Infosec Operational (IO) survey, the results of which are explored in Chapter 8.

CHAPTER 6

A MATTER OF GOVERNANCE: TAKING SECURITY TO THE BOARD

IT security has evolved markedly from its early roots as a tool that perfunctorily protected an organization and its assets. Attacks cause greater collateral damage today, and attackers themselves can just as easily reside within an organization's walls as outside of them. Worse yet, inadvertent attacks caused by sloppy or careless employees can be just as damaging to a company as those perpetrated by persons with ill intent.

The argument for enhancing security in any organization should not stray from basic financial analyses that are fundamental to all investments a company can consider. Return on investment (ROI) modeling is critical to ensure that investments bring value, regardless of how indirect that value might be. The value proposition of enhanced security is that it can aid in ensuring the long-term viability of a business by allowing an organization to concentrate on its core mandate, with fewer unnecessary, and potentially debilitating, distractions.

This book was written to address a number of distinct challenges. IT managers need tools to create a sound business case for security investing, including a process to better understand their organizations, an effective path to garner support, and ultimately, a financial model that could illustrate necessary returns. Senior executives need a forum in which technical terms are presented in an accessible format and in which security issues are discussed in business terms. This chapter has a markedly different mandate; it addresses an organization's senior executives and board members. The discussion explores corporate governance and the softer issues of security deployment by attempting to ascertain the true ROI of investing in security, namely, return on prevention (ROP).

This chapter covers the following topics:

- Security—a governance issue
- Directing security initiatives
- Establishing a secure culture
- Involving the board

Security—A Governance Issue

Proposals of any kind, security investments being no exception, demand the inclusion of certain fundamental components: Cost–benefit analyses need to be performed, metrics need to be put in place, and value propositions need to be clarified to ensure that expenditures are necessary and that returns are both positive and measurable. IT managers must justify all investment proposals appropriately, using the tools in this book to guide them through the process, but that is only part of the equation. After the necessary data has been compiled, the decision to invest in greater levels of security moves beyond sheer financial modeling. The wider implications inherent in return-on-security investing require executives and members of the board to consider the softer and less quantifiable issues that are pertinent to every organization. For ultimately, security investing represents an active business decision that expresses an organization's tolerance for risk, cyber or otherwise.

In a speech at the National Cyber Security Summit in December 2003, Secretary Tom Ridge of the Department for Homeland Security acknowledged that in the first six months of 2003, more than 76,000 incidents had already occurred, many the result of hackers just going about their work. Expanding on that thought, he said, "A few lines of code could ultimately wreak as much havoc as a handful of bombs." The issues are very real; the challenge facing investment proposals is keeping alarmism out of the equation when determining a value for events *not happening*. Governments globally can create measures to protect both hard and soft structures, but much of the cyber-world rests in the private domain.

Secretary Ridge amplified this thought in his address when he stated, "Eighty-five percent of our nation's critical infrastructure, including the cyber-network that controls it, is owned and operated by the private sector. We need businesses . . . to lead the way." He went on to say, the "success of protecting our cyberspace depends on the investment and commitment of each . . . business."[1] Security governance requires organizations to take a broader perspective, understanding that the more successful a security investment is, the less visible and less measurable its results will be.

Directing Security Initiatives

Developing corporate security initiatives that can effectively permeate every sector of an organization requires leaders and members of the board to embrace a culture that leads by example. This section considers the following topics:

- Steering committee
- Leading the way

Steering Committee

The establishment of an executive-level steering committee is discussed in the preceding chapter. Comprising senior managers culled from an organization's varied departments, the steering committee should be responsible for the following items:

- Vet all security-related issues, plans, and proposals
- Determine the necessity and viability of each proposal, including the following:
    - Security requirements addressed
    - Business justification
    - Payback period
    - Softer and less quantifiable sociopolitical concerns
- Guide, implement, review, and renew security initiatives
- Balance system functional requirements against business requirements
- Ensure that measures are consistent with the organization's tolerance for risk
- Be the drivers of a security establishment within their own domains
- Ensure that all departments and all personnel are duly represented by the committee
- Report directly to the CEO, and through him or her, to the board

The establishment of a security steering committee can bring unexpected results, as discussed in Chapter 5, "Policy, Personnel, and Equipment as Security Enablers." Most importantly, it gathers under one umbrella an organization's most senior executives and relies on them to deliver comprehensive security leadership. Serving on the committee ensures each member's acknowledgement, understanding, and acceptance of the policy and the commitment that they can effectively implement the policy within their own departments. Most relevant, the active involvement of senior executives ensures that the ultimate responsibility for the program rests with them.

Steering committee members are in a unique position to appreciate the impact that emerging threats can have on all aspects of an organization. They can determine a response that is commensurate with the corporation's tolerance for risk and, with confidence, advise the CEO and the board on the most prudent course of action.

Leading the Way

Decentralized policy enforcement is critical to the success of many corporate plans, as employees need to feel a sense of entrepreneurship and empowerment to successfully achieve their goals. But specific policies that form the underbelly of an organization typically require a linear top-down approach to ensure successful implementation.

Most employees understand the significance of enhanced security. If pressed, they would probably acknowledge that serious threats could exist almost anywhere, even within their own workplace. But acknowledging threats and performing personal acts to mitigate those threats can be challenging acts to perform in tandem. Newly established directives can command staff to perform certain functions, but human nature suggests that unless employees can bear witness to others actively complying with the rules—in particular, management—it is unlikely that the initiatives will be adhered to over the long term.

Organizations have a number of avenues to ensure that security is a fundamental component of every position in the corporation. At the top of every statement of work or job description, required security activities can be clearly outlined, ensuring that every employee understands and accepts what is expected of him or her upon joining the organization. EVPs should be training VPs, VPs should be training managers, managers should be training supervisors and supervisors should be training direct reports—all the way to the board—ensuring that expectations are created at every level and that there is no misconception as to what is expected. The tone can be established at the outset, beginning at the highest levels of an organization.

Continuous attention to IT security is crucial. Chapter 11, "Security Is a Living Process," discusses the concept of a security wheel, which an organization can use to ensure that its policies are continually monitored, tested, improved, reengineered, and renewed.

Establishing a Secure Culture

The process of developing a secure environment seems relatively straightforward on the surface: The organization establishes a governing security council in the form of a security committee, policy workshops establish rules and procedures, equipment lays the physical foundation for a secure structure, and employees work diligently to implement all that was laid out before them. But the establishment of a secure culture requires select components that are fundamentally more comprehensive than those stated. Senior executives, along with members of the board, must infuse the program into each of the organization's dealings by doing the following things:

- Securing the physical business
- Securing business relationships
- Securing the homeland

Securing the Physical Business

Enhanced security operates preventatively, minimizing potential distractions by proactively addressing potential vulnerabilities. Enhanced security can aid organizations in the following ways:

- Securing against attacks, whether intentional or inadvertent
- Protecting its revenue stream, from loss of unnecessary downtime to loss of revenue
- Safekeeping proprietary and classified information, from trade secrets to databases
- Establishing an equipment implementation road map to address long-term security planning
- Ensuring that independent divisions and remote offices comply with corporate security directives, including the implementation of similar security policies and reporting structures
- Implementing content-managing programs, such as URL filtering, that can control Internet access and manage content flow on a corporate network

- Creating an overall Triple-I program, as follows:
  - *Initiate* a comprehensive security policy program that focuses on continual renewal
  - *Implement* the comprehensive security policy program systematically throughout the organization
  - *Instill* in every executive, department leader, manager, and employee that he or she is an integral component of the security initiative

In essence, developing a structure that incorporates security into the business model can aid the firm in fully acknowledging its reliance on IT, compelling it to address the risks inherent in that reliance while ensuring that it acts in a manner that befits the firm's tolerance for said risk.

Securing Business Relationships

Simply informing staff that precautions must be taken when performing everyday tasks is sometimes not enough. Many employees need to understand the implications of under-security, be it equipment or user related. Similarly, business partners must be aware that enhanced security is in place and, equally important, that security is implicit in all intercompany dealings.

This section explores the following topics:

- Engaging the workforce to better solidify security and build effective relationships
- Creating a sense of security

Engaging the Workforce to Better Solidify Security and Build Effective Relationships

An organization should engage its work force, both managers and individual employees, in fundamental discussions concerning the ever-increasing need for greater security. Depending on an organization's end product, certain staff members might have the misguided impression that an organization could do no wrong in the eyes of its customers or, even if it did, customers had few or limited options.

The reality is that customers, clients, suppliers, partners, and associates typically have a multitude of sources and outlets. Should company A, for example, fail to implement appropriate cyber-security measures, those firms with which company A has business dealings can experience a heightened sense of vulnerability. Concern might stem from the premise that company A's under-security could pose an unacceptable level of risk, or even potential breach of trust, for its partners. The resultant negative implications could necessitate the severing of ties, regardless of how close a business relationship might once have been.

Employees who recognize the role they can play in helping to better secure the organization every day can naturally help to convey a greater sense of security's priority to an organization's customers, partners, suppliers, and associates.

Creating a Sense of Security

If a company uses a DMZ server to accept purchase orders, as an example, its customers should be able to implicitly trust the organization's ability to protect financial data, ordering information, or any other pertinent correspondence between buyer and seller. Customers understand, albeit only fleetingly, when DMZ servers are momentarily unavailable, but their empathy quickly dissipates when the waiting time to reconnect is too long or if they suspect that information they readily shared was compromised. Should the latter have occurred and a customer believes he can substantiate a case for possible negligence, under-security could pose a more serious threat. The issues of jurisprudence and negligence are more thoroughly explored in Chapter 11.

Organizations might initiate formal connections with other firms to efficiently feed a just-in-time production line, using supply-chain methodologies to move product to a line faster while reducing the amount of time raw goods must be maintained as work in progress (WIP). The need for greater efficiency drives most initiatives, but both sides of a partnership must have confidence that minimum acceptable security measures are in effect before trust, however fleeting it might be, is initiated.

Service level agreements (SLAs) can be used to ensure that certain minimum standards are formally in effect among customers, suppliers, and partners. Similarly, an Internet service provider (ISP) can demand that its customers maintain specific security levels before being allowed to connect, to ensure that the ISP and its other customers are not made unnecessarily vulnerable.

The weakest-link scenario is highly prevalent in this arena. Organizations choose to implement security measures that are relevant to their tolerance for risk, but without acknowledging the security practices of those partners and suppliers with whom they connect electronically, their substantial investment in security could be for naught. Business partners who choose to connect electronically with one another, through an extranet as an example, can inherit the other's security posture. Either network is only as strong as the weakest link that exists on either side, because all system aspects, whether positive or negative, are potentially assumed whenever organizations join their systems.

Business transactions over the Internet are increasingly on the rise, resulting in organizations having long since abandoned the practice of operating in the equivalent of hermetically sealed environments. Organizations that can swiftly recognize potential weaknesses in partners with whom they are actively engaged in trust relationships can ensure that security diligence is always at the fore in preventatively addressing potential issues long before they can become true vulnerabilities.

Securing the Homeland

The *homeland* has grown to become synonymous with the country, but at its core, the homeland encompasses every person, partner, customer, supplier, company, policy, program, practice, and even equipment with which an organization comes into contact.

This section explores the following topics:

- Incident reporting
- Equipment path
- Acknowledging vulnerable points

Incident Reporting

It is often thought that the advent of mass media has brought about an increase in the level of urban crime. But the reality is that in many instances, misdeeds were simply getting reported more regularly; the actual numbers of incidents were not necessarily on the rise. While publicizing events can have the effect of stirring other individuals into performing similar acts, more often than not, an increase in raw numbers is simply a representation of people coming forward with their own stories of woe after having read about similar cases in the media. What might appear to be an epidemic are merely silenced victims speaking up. The public justice system might take notice, and certain measures might be enacted to deal with the so-called epidemic. Had individuals not come forward with their personal accounts, an issue might never have been recognized as being so prevalent across a community.

This scenario is analogous to organizations that are contending with cyber-crime today. It is incumbent upon every organization that has been knowingly targeted or infiltrated to report any incident to state, local, and federal officials and to organizations such as CERT. In the CSI/FBI Computer Crime and Security Survey, April 2004, only 34% of respondents admitted reporting cyber-attacks to law enforcement officials. While the number could be significantly higher, it is up markedly from 1996, when the Computer Security Institute started tracking such information. However, the insistence of executive management and the board is required to ensure that these numbers continue to rise.

Debate and policy discussions are occurring in political legislatures around the globe, as politicians attempt to combat the effects of cyber-crime. But every incident needs to be reported so that the epidemic of cyber-crime, should it be an epidemic, is addressed in an effective legislative manner. Without specific knowledge of every incident, governments are at a disadvantage when attempting to fashion legislation that is both viable and relevant.

There is a natural reticence to report cyber-crimes. Companies fear that competitors will sense vulnerability and that customers will fear for their own safety. The reality is that most organizations are equally vulnerable in many respects, and the more that cyber-crimes are publicized, the better it will ultimately be for all corporate users. Should a breach occur, competitors and customers will likely discover the breach at some point anyway, possibly at a most inopportune time. Being forthcoming when it occurs ensures that the company is not only a good net citizen, or *netizen*, but also under the auspices of the term, *if you cannot hide it then feature it*, with certain ingenuity from the marketing department, the negative event could be spun into a long-term positive gain.

In the end, it is incumbent upon executive management and the board to ensure that cyber-crime perpetrated on their organization is effectively reported to appropriate state, local, and federal officials. Delivering that message to all senior managers can ensure that the board's need for cyber-security transparency is always respected.

Equipment Path

Developing a greater security structure is not a one-time expenditure. Even if the potential for attacks were markedly reduced, annual updates and training would still be part of every systems administrator's job function. But the world is continually in flux, and unforeseen cyber-issues could occur at any time. The challenge facing system administrators, and the equipment they are responsible for, is ensuring that both themselves and the equipment are appropriately optimized to deal with any new threats in an effective manner.

An equipment road map, coupled with an organization's desired security posture, as presented in Chapter 4, "Putting It All Together: Threats and Security Equipment," can aid a company in its goal to effectively and preventatively protect itself. Ongoing training of system administrators and their alternates, along with a scheduled program of maintenance, product upgrades, and a path to determine the need for new product implementation, can help to keep organizations proactively protected.

As long as threats continue to exist and the amount of business transactions over the Internet continues to increase, the need to continually revisit security initiatives, both equipment and personnel, remains a top priority for organizations. It is up to executive management and the board to ensure that critical awareness is at the forefront of every user's agenda.

Acknowledging Vulnerable Points

Many believe of late that organizations were becoming increasingly vulnerable to attacks from within their own operations, be they intentional or inadvertent. Organizations responded preventatively, ensuring that potential attackers who might have been residing comfortably within its walls were appropriately addressed. The release of the 2004 CSI/FBI survey[2] reveals that the gap between internal and external intrusions has narrowed and is now fairly split. The UK-PWC survey 2004[3] reveals a marked difference, whereby 64% of large business respondents state that their worst breaches emanated from staff misuse of information systems. The differing experiences show that the issue is still quite fluid, and organizations would be well advised to remain on high alert against both internal and external potential vulnerabilities.

An organization can be well served by using independent security auditors to test and evaluate its security policy and practices. Similar to quality auditors, independent security analyses can check the aptness of internal policies and determine whether remote offices and organizational divisions are implementing the policies in a manner that is consistent with corporate expectation. It is important to note that security initiatives are similar to every other fundamental program in which a company might engage: Activities that must be carried out across an organization require executive and board involvement to ensure that they are effectively and consistently implemented.

Involving the Board

IT security is greater than the sum of its parts, having grown from a tool that proactively protects an organization to a process that involves risk management and corporate accountability. In light of rising levels of disruptive and misanthropic cyber-activity, executive management, along with members of the board, must become actively involved in the governance aspect of this most fundamental of investments.

This section considers the following topics:

- Examining the need for executive involvement
- Elements requiring executive participation

Examining the Need for Executive Involvement

The well-regarded CSI/FBI annual survey draws respondents from a wide cross section of industry and government in an attempt to bring awareness and a sense of urgency to IT and business executives.

The 2004 survey confirms that IT security–related issues are still highly prevalent—90% of respondents experienced breaches the preceding year. Nearly two-thirds of those 90% suffered greater than two attacks, and more than half of those respondents experienced in excess of ten breaches each. Financial losses stemming from the attacks were experienced by 80% of respondents, at an average cost of nearly $2 million per company.

The ground that is used in the formation of sound business arguments for enhanced security has shifted. No longer is the focus solely on what is technically possible and economically optimal. The discussion is now centered on less quantifiable components that include trust relationships, competitive advantage, and the hazards inherent in system unreliability, to mention a few. ROI modeling must still be performed to ensure that alarmism does not constitute the foundation of security business proposals. But the fear looms ever large, as reported judiciously in newspapers around the globe, that a lack of comprehensive security could spell untold disaster for organizations. While business reality is typically far removed from alarmism, the ever-present news coverage illustrates the cyber-security issues that are at play in the media today; it can be a challenge not to overreact—or underreact.

Organizations need to take a wider view of security. They need to fundamentally determine the level of risk they can tolerate and then make security infrastructure investments accordingly. Apportioning a percentage of the overall IT budget to security is no longer a viable option. While that process can be effective in determining the amount an organization might be willing to invest, it does not necessarily ensure the level of security a company might require.

Establishing a secure IT infrastructure requires technical and business executives to evaluate and quantify an organization's critical assets, ascertain the risks to them now and in the future, and ultimately develop a security strategy that is consistent with the organization's business requirements.

Consistent, reliable, and uninterrupted business operability is the root of the discussion. The process of ensuring that an organization is able to concentrate on its core business without suffering undue distractions at best, or critical loss of intangibles at worst, suggests strongly that an organization's executive management must be actively engaged in determining the complete business case for network security.

Elements Requiring Executive Participation

Public companies are required to comply with stringent rules governing regulatory financial filings, making it incumbent upon organizations to ensure the verity of their financial statements. The sanctity of the data behind each entry on a financial statement must be above reproach. Certain ramifications of the Sarbanes-Oxley Act of 2002 (also known as The Public Company Accounting Reform and Investor Protection Act of 2002), including Section 404, the Management Assessment of Internal Controls, and relevant pieces of other legislation are explored in the jurisprudence section of Chapter 11.

It is important to note that legislation in and of itself does not alter an organization's tolerance for risk. But various laws can encourage discussion across a wider range of concerns, including, but not limited to, the following items:

- Ensuring regulatory adherence, including the sanctity of financial reporting
- Addressing specific corporate and national homeland security concerns
- Buffeting business relationships with both customers and suppliers
- Using security to enhance corporate standing by addressing the following issues:
  - Trust
  - Reliability
  - Perceived or potential vulnerability

Executive management can actively address governance concerns in a number of possible ways, including the following:

- Establishing the fundamentals of internal security policy, which are addressed in Chapter 5, "Policy, Personnel, and Equipment as Security Enablers," and Chapter 10, "Essential Elements of Security Policy Development," to ensure that policy is aligned with required expectations.
- Continually checking the pulse of the security program, as follows:
  - Use third-party audits to assess a program's continued relevance.

- Ensure that issues or recommendations reported by security auditors are appropriately handled.
- Determine whether current vulnerabilities are sufficiently recognized.
- Determine whether the program is set to proactively address unforeseen issues.
- Ensure that the company reviews its security posture against industry peers and best in class.
- Mandate that any organization with which the company elects to establish formal IT connections meets a minimum level of security before any information is transmitted.
- Ensure that the board can reasonably state that the organization is effectively and proactively protected.

Possible ramifications from a security breach can be many. Various interest groups have been formed to address the escalating concerns, one of which is the corporate governance task force of the National Cyber Security Partnership (NCSP), composed of executives culled from industry and government. The task force developed a program that businesses could use to effectively integrate IT security into their corporate governance processes. A series of recommendations was published in 2004 that, if implemented, would establish a standard for IT security across domestic organizations. The task force's strongest recommendation, based on the potential negative ramifications of insufficient security, is to bring the discussion of IT security to the board. It would allow directors and executive management to realistically measure their organization's tolerance for risk while correspondingly weighing the need for sustainable corporate and geographical homeland security.

Summary

This book addresses IT security investments from a business management perspective. Upcoming chapters enable the IT manager to build a business case, giving him or her the tools to elicit support across an organization and an ROI model to effectively quantify the investment's required return. While that is fundamentally necessary, it is equally vital that IT security be viewed as an executive management and board-level corporate initiative with far-reaching homeland security implications.

This chapter explored the following topics:

- The role of security as a governance issue
- The need to direct security initiatives
- The process of establishing a secure culture
- The need for active board involvement

End Notes

[1]From the Department of Homeland Security website. Remarks by Secretary Tom Ridge at the National Cyber Security Summit. December 3, 2003. Released from the office of the press secretary. http://www.dhs.gov/dhspublic/display?theme=44&content=3059.

[2]"CSI/FBI Computer Crime and Security Survey 2004." Computer Security Institute and Federal Bureau of Investigation (CSI/FBI). http://i.cmpnet.com/gocsi/db_area/pdfs/fbi/FBI2004.pdf.

[3]"Information Security Breaches Survey 2004, Executive Summary." Pricewaterhouse Coopers UK, Department of Trade and Industry UK. http://www.pwc.com/images/gx/eng/about/svcs/grms/2004Exec_Summ.pdf. April 2004.

CHAPTER 7

CREATING DEMAND FOR THE SECURITY PROPOSAL: IT MANAGEMENT'S ROLE

IT executives and senior-level IT managers can play a pivotal role in their organizations, stretching beyond the fundamental services they provide every day—they can create demand and drive change within their corporations. This chapter focuses on executive and senior-level IT managers by providing them with tools to better understand the business end of their organizations. It further provides a process to proactively engage their senior business management colleagues in security discussions to effectively garner support for their business cases. In view of the growing need to ensure that all users within a system are well versed in security fundamentals, this chapter provides tools that IT managers can use to engage and educate users.

The Infosec Operational (IO) survey at the end of this chapter complements the survey found in Chapter 5, "Policy, Personnel, and Equipment as Security Enablers," by helping to further quantify an organization's return on prevention (ROP). The survey explores the ramifications of system unavailability for both individual users and departments. The results of both the IO and Infosec Management (IM) surveys are used in Chapter 8, "Risk Aversion and Security Topologies."

This chapter covers the following topics:

- Delivering the security message to executive management

- Recognizing the goals of the corporation

- Outlining methods IT managers can use to engage the organization

- Assessing senior business management security requirements

Delivering the Security Message to Executive Management

The ability to discuss ROP without sounding overly alarmist can be challenging. While it is not a compelling way to promote the need for greater security investing, many an IT manager has resorted to alarmism out of sheer exasperation. Living in the trenches every day, they are often witnesses to network carnage. Their immediate work environments, and possibly even their social circles, can help to increase anxiety levels exponentially. By the time an IT manager approaches senior management, his concern regarding the organization's vulnerabilities might be so great that he skips the necessary topic introductions and jumps right into the potential for calamitous attacks. He is possibly so deeply embedded in IT subculture that he assumes everyone knows the perils of insufficient security or, having never before encountered a situation where it was necessary to *sell* concerns to senior management, he could resort to alarmist tactics. While alarmism is never the intended approach, attempting to present a cogent argument without crisp business tools means proposals will most likely be met with resistance and are unlikely to gain acceptance.

While IT managers can find it challenging to deliver this type of message, effective awareness can be created using a process that brings pertinent information directly to influential leaders within an organization. This chapter explores those processes.

Recognizing the Goals of the Corporation

A concise model of cost and return is a fundamental requirement of any investment proposal—both must be wholly quantifiable. But calculating an ROP is not, at first blush, a black-and-white process. Security investment proposals require a thorough knowledge of an organization, including the following items:

- Knowing how the organization can use ROP
- Understanding the organization's mandate and directives
- Acknowledging the organization's imperatives and required deliverables
- Establishing an appropriate security posture

Knowing How the Organization Can Use ROP

Most IT expenditures can be successfully run through a standard ROI model: Invest X in software and an employee can increase her productivity by Y, resulting in concrete staff and cost reductions in Z months. Or an organization might examine the merits of investing in a sales tool that purports to increase associate selling. While not every salesperson will realize a substantive increase in revenues, a compelling argument coupled with conservative projections can typically be modeled. Whether it's an R&D, manufacturing, finance, or HR department, arguments for positive ROI can be put forth in a relatively objective and articulate manner.

While security investments must be presented in a manner that is consistent with standard ROI models, a certain amount of grey area exists and a process that extends beyond basic ROI fundamentals is required. The conundrum in preventive security investing is the more successful the investment, the less successful it will appear to be. With programs that target prevention, as opposed to (postevent) cleanup, it is a greater struggle to prove that monies have been well spent because, on the surface, nothing will have happened—preventive measures will have been successful. ROP addresses this challenge by acknowledging that security infrastructure investments are markedly different from other investments a corporation might consider. ROP incorporates grey-area variables, which have become a major factor in security infrastructure investing.

The discussion in this book centers on the needs of a corporation and is acutely sensitive to its particular revenue and operational demands. The discussion promotes an approach to ROP that is multipronged and organization-wide. It is structured to recognize the unique requirements of vastly different organizations, and it compartmentalizes the subjective and select issues into a comprehensive objective number that can ultimately be used to determine an organization's unique ROP.

Understanding the Organization's Mandate and Directives

A reliable assumption should be that organizations operating in the same field would find common ground in their security postures. But rarely is that the case. Each organization is unique, because each has a distinct tolerance for risk that is relevant only to them. A firm's mandates and directives dictate its priorities, enabling a thorough analysis of what might be required for protection.

A service organization, counting as a prime feature its 24/7 response time, will do everything within its power to keep its system online and fully operational. Its public face demands it. An organization could lose its edge, possibly even its business, if a breach kept it from fulfilling its stated mandate. Conversely, another service organization might not view uninterrupted operability as its core offering, deciding instead to invest monies in ways that could help it better achieve its stated goals.

A financial arm of the federal government that compiles data that could inadvertently impact the stock market will go to extremes to protect its information. The moment the information is legitimately released, its value is effectively worthless, while if the system were to be breached before the official release, the data could be worth untold amounts. But to the breached organization, it is not simply the fact that information might be stolen. The theft might be quickly contained, but the breach itself might render the organization forever weak—who could ever trust the company again? Who could ever rely on its ability to maintain confidences? The organization's mandate might only have been data compilation, and while its integrity to perform the work was never called into question, its ability to secure the data—in essence, its ability to be trusted—was deeply damaged. It might be only be a minor part of the company's mandate, but if not handled properly, the breach could be its undoing.

Acknowledging the Organization's Imperatives and Required Deliverables

Determining an organization's imperatives and required deliverables is instrumental in helping to ascertain security postures. What is important to an organization, and what it must deliver to be successful, is highly individual. An automobile repair operation with a centralized parts warehouse and ten service centers scattered across a metropolitan area has a different set of needs compared to a just-in-time production line, a fast-food chain, or a financial organization. If all its systems were stymied for a full day, the service center, as an example, might find its business grind to a halt because of its inability to order and receive parts into its garages. Equally frustrating for the service center would be its lack of ability to process work orders, which would most likely result in reduced revenues for the day. While it would be debilitating when the system was down, it is unlikely that it would have a significant long-term negative effect on most customer relationships. As the following examples show, issues facing a just-in-time production line, fast-food chain, and financial organization are markedly different.

Organizations that share information on their extranets would also find their operations disrupted should a breakdown in communications occur. If their connections provided just-in-time inventory for a production line, a breakdown in communications could bring operations to a halt. Alternatively, if the affected sites were designed to accept purchase orders, the argument can be made that whenever a system is down, immediate revenue loss occurs. But one widely held view is that revenues are only deferred, as users wait for systems to come back on line. In the former example concerning a just-in-time extranet program, the ground shifts and the issue becomes one of trust and reliability. By sharing confidential information through extranets, organizations allow themselves to be somewhat vulnerable to partners they feel they can trust. If a partner's operations are breached, a company might fear that a trust exploitation attack, as described in Chapter 2, "Crucial Need for Security: Vulnerabilities and Attacks," could be launched against it. Regardless of whether the attack occurs, the implication is that it could, and the inherent, but typically tenuous, trust that might have existed between partnered organizations could be irrevocably damaged.

In some situations, a compromised system would have an immediate, and possibly long-term, detrimental effect on revenues. A multistore pizza chain whose centralized ordering system is breached on Super Bowl Sunday would likely notice the effects rather quickly. From drivers standing around with a lack of orders to deliver to perishables brought in for the big day, the loss of revenues can quickly mount; sales cannot be deferred to another day. While the company can use some of the perishables, the big revenue day will have passed. It's simple enough to calculate losses: food that had to be thrown away, rent on all locations, and associated utilities, insurance, taxes, and payroll costs. More difficult to quantify are future ordering patterns. Consumers were forced to find another restaurant to get their pizza that day. Will they remain with their newfound supplier?

The experience at a financial institution is markedly different. While its internal operations would grind to a halt, management's concerns are not focused on immediate losses. The longer-term ramifications of having been breached are of paramount importance. From loss of data to loss of customer confidence, the company's issues are widespread and potentially quite damaging.

It is difficult to quantify with certainty what might be lost when a system is breached. If e-mail capability is down for half a day, many might argue that productivity goes up. Another argument is that nothing is truly lost, that transactions of any kind, from dialogue between parties to realized revenue, are simply deferred.

Customer responses can range from empathetic and patient to irritated and mistrusting. Human nature dictates that we understand why things happen and can often feel empathy for those that they happen to, but if the problem affects us directly, our patience and understanding typically dissipate speedily.

Establishing an Appropriate Security Posture

An ongoing discussion in many organizations revolves around the question "What is the real cost of vulnerability?" More in-depth than merely drawing a straight line to improved operating results, it attempts to delve into an organization's wider concerns: its soft assets. Beginning with how it is structured internally to external relationships it enjoys with customers and business partners, real cost of vulnerability attempts to construct a profile for risk tolerance. If an R&D department were to be breached, the ramifications would likely be greater than those facing an auto service center. Every event bears relevance to the affected organization only. Even the term *secure environment* is subjective, as organizations attempt to balance the costs of the following items:

- The state of maintaining the status quo

- The state of doing just enough

- The state of doing too much

Each of these three states represents a delicate balancing act with which every organization must contend on a regular basis.

The State of Maintaining the Status Quo

Maintaining the status quo refers to those organizations that neglect to ever alter, in any meaningful way, their current security posture.

Maintaining the status quo becomes an issue, because business environments rarely remain static. Status quo is commonly understood to be maintaining a position, but in reality, it's more closely related to moving backward, because the industry, in its constant push forward, might leave a stagnant organization behind.

An organization that sets high corporate goals might discover that a security posture rooted in status quo could prove detrimental—security threats could get in the way of achieving high performance goals. Many threats already exist, and new ones can appear at any time. Maintaining the status quo on security posture is, in effect, a form of ignoring threats.

The State of Doing Just Enough

The state of *doing just enough* refers to those organizations that acknowledge their aversion to risk, recognize the potential damage certain threats pose, and install equipment that can appropriately mitigate the risks.

The issue inherent in doing just enough is that it can leave an organization overly vulnerable in its battle against unknown and unforeseen threats. While a company might be well fortified to protect itself from historical threats, this type of organization is typically limited in its forward-thinking security posture. In an approach that does not delve far below the surface, the organization might begin to address what it considers to be futuristic security concerns, but its main response system is invariably programmed to deal with existing and known threats.

An organization that does just enough might not realize that its security posture might not be in line with its business goals. By recognizing the issues inherent in merely doing enough, organizations can ensure that their security posture accurately reflects their tolerance for risk.

The State of Doing Too Much

Cautious people often feel that if they were going to make an error, they would prefer to make one on the side of caution. When those same people are charged with developing a corporate security posture, the result can be an organization that is *doing too much*. In essence, the state of doing too much occurs when a company has a level of security that is not proportionate to its type of business.

Doing too much can, remarkably, hamper an organization's productivity, placing controls that are so restrictive that the flow of information slows to a trickle. Protecting an automobile dealership as if it were a biomedical research facility might prove overly restrictive for users, who resort to shortcuts to bypass the heavy hand of the system and unwittingly create back doors for attackers to gain entry.

Accurately assessing an organization's aversion to risk, and then developing a security posture that is in line with its tolerance level and business practices, can help to ensure that users operate effectively within the confines of the system.

The ability to clearly understand the security posture an organization requires represents an important early step in moving the inherent subjectivity of security ROI to the objective side of the ledger.

Outlining Methods IT Managers Can Use to Engage the Organization

The ability to drive an agenda is the mark of a top executive, and while not every individual who strives for a management position embodies this trait, it is a skill that can be honed over time. Executives who deal with external clients are forced to learn these skills early, but many corporate executives can spend an entire career without ever having to interface with an external client. The reality is that internal-facing executives are not precluded from having to sell.

This section explores various strategies IT management can use to effectively lobby support for their business proposals. Internal selling is wholly comparable to external selling, and those executives who recognize this early are usually rewarded with higher budgets and more successful programs. Regardless of their size or scope, organizations typically share one trait in common: They never spend more than they need to, and if an internal requirement is vying for funds, they invariably try to spend even less.

Organizations do not respond to squeaky wheels, nor do they tend to reward alarmist-type scenarios. Concrete proposals supported by influential people within the organization usually carry sufficient weight to, at minimum, get a hearing from senior management. Having a proposal that is warranted and timely might not necessarily be enough to garner approval. Arguments need to be presented in a measurable and concise format, and ideally they should also have the backing of corporate colleagues. If the IT manager can successfully create a groundswell of support, his program has a greater likelihood of achieving success. This section details how a manager can effectively lobby support for his business proposals.

Organizations are fierce protectors of their budgets. If money is not spent, it is earned, and every organization maintains strict control on movement of funds. Profit-generating organizations invest more freely in activities that have a direct correlation to revenue generation and are loathe to increase spending for internal functions. While the need for an investment can be fundamental to the security of an organization, that probably isn't good enough—it needs to have support.

Lobbying Support

An IT manager tasked with improving her organization's security posture has, at first blush, a straightforward assignment. She knows the evils that lurk, but simply detailing them on a business plan is not enough. Organizations have a finite number of budget dollars, and every department head is vying for the lion's share. To be successful, she must go beyond technical analysis and raw data and sell her program long before she attempts to present it. Convincing her coexecutives that the program is good business for their operations is the catalyst for securing the required funds.

It would be ideal if political motions were enacted into laws strictly on the basis that they were beneficial for society. Some of the most thoughtful motions never make it further than preliminary debate. Successful politicians know that enacting laws is more about garnering support than simply having good ideas, and they quietly work backrooms, ensuring that by the time their motion is presented, it already has a bedrock of support.

This section explores the support-building process, from creating support among senior business manager colleagues to establishing a process for achieving employee backing. But supporting a security plan means reaching beyond basic financial considerations; executive management and employees alike must be willing to support a wide array of security initiatives throughout the organization. The discussion in this section explores what is meant by support and offers the following actions to take:

- Consult with senior managers
- Contend with personalities
- Create individualized features and benefits
- Be the glue in the organization

- Drive the agenda
- Be the catalyst for change in the organization
- Acknowledge the responsibility of the IT department
- Consult again

Consult with Senior Managers

Consulting with executives appears to be a straightforward goal, but it is one that eludes many managers. Reaching out to distant peers can pay untold dividends, for both current and future causes. Most people go to their offices, work hard, mingle with their close-proximity colleagues, and leave. It would be challenging to get any proposal approved in that environment, let alone one that might be perceived to be a mundane IT task, yet it is so far-reaching that it touches every aspect of the organization. But unless they are better informed, those managers who are external to the IT group might find it difficult to state why security was fundamental to their operations. The role of the IT security manager is to move beyond his comfort zone and plant those seeds across the corporation.

Soliciting support is an appeal best conducted in person or over the telephone—never by e-mail. The latter can be an impersonal communication medium, and given the amount of daily e-mails, it is far too likely that the receiver will simply delete the message. Begin by identifying the key people within the organization. Depending on the size of the company, it can be prudent to include certain senior individuals who might not have the authority to implement change but have the ear of the following people who do wield that power:

- Vice president (or director or manager) of sales
- VP of marketing
- VP of operations
- VP of research and development
- VP of accounting
- VP of finance
- VP of human resources
- VP of manufacturing

- VP of investor relations
- Those responsible for other key functions, including government compliance, quality auditing programs, 401(k) plans, transportation, warehousing, and ombudsman programs.

When requesting a ten-minute meeting, it is best to keep the preamble on the initial phone call short as well, stating only that IT is facing a challenge and would appreciate counsel. It is the odd person who would turn down such an appeal and, for those who are less agreeable, inform them that a proposal is being written for senior management and that it would be disappointing if he or she were not included.

Immediately following the phone call, it is always good practice to send a short e-mail that summarizes the major points that were discussed and to send thanks to the attendee for his participation. The date for the upcoming meeting should be included, and the day preceding the planned session, it is also prudent to send a follow-up reminder note.

Contend with Personalities

It is often said that individuals derive their uniqueness from their personalities. Remarkably, only a limited number of personality types exist. This makes it far simpler to grasp the character type of an individual with whom one might need to have significant dealings. Whether one is working in a corporate environment or living in a social world, determining personalities so that a plan can be tailored, and ultimately presented in the most favorable light, can prove to be of great benefit.

Modifying discussions for specific personality types is a time-consuming process. It involves an individualized features and benefits plan, to be discussed next in this chapter, and a thorough exploration of the type of person who will be attending the meeting. A particular individual might relish new ideas, and even appreciate being contacted, but if he is not pursued in an appropriate manner, he will find it more difficult to accept the message. Acknowledging personality types can be a useful tool when attempting to establish a base of support. It should begin with the initial phone call to arrange a meeting. Depending on the person, it can range from a breezy discussion that flows into the reason for your call or an immediate brusque request. Most individuals should be amenable to a meeting, given the following points:

- They are approached in an appropriate manner.
- They perceive something is in it for them.
- They are assured that the meeting will be brief.

It isn't always possible to determine an individual's personality type prior to a meeting. If any of the parties are in another location, or are new to the company, obtaining forewarning might not be possible. In those situations, be open for cues that individuals might inadvertently send: shuffling papers, continual crossing and uncrossing of legs, arms crossed tightly against chest, heavy sighs, and other similar distractions. In those cases, attempt to do the following:

- Reach a point quickly
- Make the discussion interactive

Be prepared with a question from the survey at the end of this chapter that can quickly be used—one that has the potential to reignite the discussion.

Table 7-1 can act as a guide when contending with different personalities.

Table 7-1   *Contending with Personalities**

An individual who is swayed by logical analysis and data would respond to	An individual who is swayed by relationships and humanistic concerns would respond to
Data or information	Gaining recognition
Making or saving money	Working for the greater good
Ensuring security	Using power or authority
Gaining control over outcomes	Being creative
Reducing errors and rework	Realizing achievement

*Source: A presentation by Adam Toffoli

The key to a successful meeting is to be prepared. Present pertinent, detailed, and thoughtful data in a manner that is appropriate for the personality types in attendance.

Create Individualized Features and Benefits

Human nature dictates that people are more apt to latch onto ideas, and promote them, if they believe they are the originators of the ideas. Exploiting that notion can help the meeting leader steer conversations, enabling participants to reach their own conclusions.

In creating separate agendas for each meeting, the IT manager should assume the perspective of the executive with whom he is going to meet. He should outline the parameters of enhanced security and present the benefits for his or her group. It is also important to acknowledge what impact, if any, a change might have on the executive's operation.

The VP of sales might be focused solely on revenue generation, but she might harbor a concern that enhanced security will ultimately slow the system, resulting in poor response time to her clients. If data could be presented that identified a marked increase in trust between firms whose computer networks were connected, as well as evidence that system speed would not be substantially affected, she might recognize that improving trust could generate more revenue from existing clients without a substantive decrease in system speed. One sales axiom states that it is easier to get more business from existing clients than to bring on, and nurture, new clients. While the VP of sales is typically focused on the latter, she is still preoccupied with getting more out of what she already has. Specifically, the sales group has the potential to become IT's staunchest ally.

The IT manager can also benefit from understanding, and addressing, significant changes that have occurred in the sales process over the last generation. Most salespeople today are relationship builders, investing their time creating synergies between clients and their employer. Salespeople present value propositions and promote value-added services in their quest to create demand for an end product. Rarely do they attempt to sell a product directly. An enhanced security posture is a valuable tool that salespeople can use to better position their firm. Clients need more than mere products; they also require the following items:

- Reliability of content
- Surety of delivery
- Safety of construction
- Excellence in service
- Fairness in price

In essence, clients need trust. A firm that establishes an enhanced security program helps to provide that requisite trust. It is also a tool that salespeople can use to sell tangible value to their customers.

Most other managers have similar concerns, which are expressed as follows:

- The VP of marketing might recognize that enhanced security could provide a new angle with which to promote the company. Regardless of the end product or function of the organization, trust is at the core of all significant relationships. Marketing staff can find value in the program as a tool that can promote the firm as a trustworthy just-in-time partner, supply-chain provider, and financial partner and in the promoting of a business segment where value can be marketed. Enhanced security provides multiple opportunities for self-promotion, and remarkably, it is also what clients, partners, and suppliers want to hear.

- An executive in charge of production is always concerned that his just-in-time factory is never compromised. An uninterrupted flow of product could only be ensured when his suppliers are protecting themselves and their distribution channel.

- The CFO wants appropriate security to protect the company, but she also demands high-level security between her department and the rest of the organization.

- The head of HR is deeply concerned about protecting the sanctity of individual salaries, benefits, personal data, pensions, and 401(k) information.

- The Investor Relations director wants to ensure that the organization's public face is kept untainted at all times.

While each executive arrives at the table wanting to discuss the corporation as a whole, each invariably has a major concern that centers on his or her own department. Discussing the needs of the organization and outlining how security could benefit the executive's specific business unit help to acknowledge the goals that each executive must accomplish, while noting that certain goals could potentially be realized by enhancing security. Conclusions will be reached, and a new advocate could be the outcome. The executive's help might be indirect. A request might be made to enlist her as a supporter to approach senior management and to present her own argument for the importance of enhanced security.

The IT manager's time commitment is not to be underestimated. Compiling the meeting list, constructing a specific plan for each group, and then making individual pitches is an involved process. But it remains the optimal forum in which to garner support.

Be the Glue in the Organization

Most people do not venture far from their comfort zones, and in office environments, that typically results in individuals not straying far from their close-proximity workgroups. Whether they are from accounting, finance, research, human resources, marketing, or production, most people walk through corridors looking at the floor and the walls rather than engaging in eye contact. An IT manager trying to garner support across an organization has the opportunity to bring disparate groups together. Sales and financial services might be at odds with each other, along with marketing and production. They have separate agendas, and each typically conflicts markedly with the other. Sales groups need every client to have unlimited credit, and marketing people typically project such optimistic forecasts that production is pressured to ramp up long before end-customer purchase orders are placed. While many departments seemingly operate in direct contrast with one another, one underlying thread runs through an organization: its IT group. Virtually every employee needs access to a computer to perform certain duties. Some people within a company might find IT somewhat distant, or set apart. The challenge for organizations is to harness IT's unique position in an effort to bring all operations closer together.

When reaching out to other department heads, the IT manager has an enormous advantage—no one assumes that a hidden agenda exists. It is not the finance manager trying to reduce her risk on certain accounts or the production manager trying to unburden himself from a warehouse full of unsold product. The IT manager's scope covers each department and every individual; by working to ensure that the most important elements of the organization are secured, he brings integrity to the table.

Maintaining a high degree of openness in the meetings ultimately pays dividends. The IT manager should let it be known that he is consulting with every other significant executive in the organization. It is not necessary to state whether other executives ratified the plan, but it is prudent to say that they could agree with the reasoning.

Organizations require *glue*, and reaching out to department heads to build support for enhanced security can result in the IT manager being that glue. In discussing specific benefits, each executive will naturally share unrelated issues he might be facing, particularly if he feels that IT can be part of the solution. Working with the executive to resolve his issues inevitably garners goodwill and can even result in a new advocate for the program.

Regardless of support, the IT manager will have reached out to senior individuals that he might only have uttered morning greetings to before, and the avenue to contact the person about future programs now exists.

Drive the Agenda

Enhanced security is not just a budgeting issue. Long after monies have been committed and new appliances are in place, situations can still exist that result in unnecessary vulnerability for a corporation.

Unless directed otherwise, the typical user in an organization does not generally possess a high awareness of security. This is not to imply a disregard for the corporation, it is simply reflective of insufficient communication. Most employees have a high degree of pride in themselves, their chosen careers, and by extension, for whom they work. But if they are not directly and continually informed about potential security hazards, their personal sense of responsibility could diminish.

Remote offices of a large enterprise can prove to be a greater challenge to security than those departments that are housed in close proximity to a head office. Remote branch management is always aligned with company direction, but remote staff can typically take a dimmer view of the corporate office, often viewing it as a hindrance to daily activities rather than a partner. When staff is informed that extra steps are required to enter sales orders, or that processes can take somewhat longer than before enhanced security measures were introduced, a certain amount of resistance might become evident. Branch staff will probably not view enhanced security as a benefit for their clients; they can also feel that greater security measures imply a lack of trust in remote staff. A typical branch user is focused on the end customer: delivering product on time, expanding business with existing clients, and developing new accounts. Security is not necessarily at the forefront of the user's mind.

Similar situations are played out in most departments across organizations; it is human nature to be wholly centered on one's own functions. But it is possible to alter thought processes and educate users on individual responsibility. The IT manager can approach his newly developed senior management contacts and request 20-minute blocks of time to speak with their groups. Meetings can be held over coffee breaks or at the beginning of a workday. It is best to avoid mass audiences, opting instead to speak with small groups, preferably no more than ten at a time. This not only allows interactivity, but small groups also typically ensure better audience attention, because it is more difficult for a limited-sized group to dismiss a speaker. Concise security presentations can include the following items:

- Cost of recent breaches in the country
- Cost of breaches within the industry, if available
- Cost of breaches within the organization, if relevant
- A quick overview of the company's internal security infrastructure
- An overview of key areas that need to be protected
- Highlighted benefits for each specific audience and department, as follows:
  - Production: A discussion of secure *tunnels* to supply-chain partners.
  - Accounting: A discussion surrounding the ability to perform secure credit analyses and similar functions online.
  - Finance: A discussion regarding enhanced security for banking, financial reporting, and regulatory filings.
  - Investor Relations: A discussion concerning how security can mitigate a possible tarnished public face and a discussion to address potential corporate governance issues.
  - Sales: A discussion surrounding how enhanced security can safeguard just-in-time tunnels with customers who, not unexpectedly, might have concerns about allowing suppliers access, even if it is only to their extranet. Companies do business with organizations they trust.
  - Marketing: A discussion of how enhanced security becomes another marketing vehicle for them (or one less negative public relations issue with which they might need to contend).

- A discussion regarding the weakest-link scenario: how one person circumventing procedures can open an organization to a potential litany of issues. Chart the following items, which users can do to help:

  - Don't use the same password for every application, and never share accounts.

  - Be inventive, and choose a password that a hacker can't easily guess.

  - Never use a password of 1234, 1qaz, QWERTY, or any combination that simply runs across or down a keyboard.

  - Never write a password on a scrap of paper and tape it under a keyboard or, even worse, tape it to a monitor. Extend a password the same respect as a personal banking PIN.

  - Question strangers walking in corridors. If a person is uncomfortable approaching them, call security or immediately report them to a manager.

  - When traveling, store laptops in room safes, secure them with a steel cable lock, or place them in a locked suitcase.

  - Avoid leaving laptop cases visible in an automobile. Always store them in the vehicle's trunk, and if you are unsure of parking safety, carry the bag.

  - When flying, never check a laptop case as luggage; maintain it as a carry-on.

  - A computer's first line of defense is its antivirus software. Don't disable it, and avoid canceling any update or scanning process. If scans are not running on a regular schedule, notify the system administrator immediately.

  - Refrain from installing noncorporate-issued software.

  - Consult with IT to learn how to encrypt company-sensitive documents.

  - Do not download pirated music or similar applications. Not only is it illegal, but those imports are frequently the source of virus infections.

  - Do not open e-mails of unknown source, particularly their attachments. The Mydoom virus started the trend that made aberrant attachments remarkably difficult to differentiate from legitimate ones, but standard operating procedure remains the same: If the source of an e-mail is unknown, regardless of how innocent or important an attachment might appear, do not open it. Double-delete the e-mail: Delete it normally, and then delete it from your Recycle Bin. When in doubt, contact IT.

- When using a wireless connection, ensure that Wired Equivalent Privacy (WEP) encryption is activated.

- Security is everyone's business, and poor security habits can make each employee vulnerable. If an employee witnesses a possible issue, he should report it to a manager.

- Do not venture to questionable sites on the Internet. Most sites have cookies, and every workstation keeps a trail of where it has been. If a user is uncomfortable with the trail, it is likely for good reason, and it is also probably against company policy to visit that website.

- Refrain from participating in newsgroups using a corporate e-mail account.

- If you have a question about security, contact a security consultant in IT or a manager.

• A discussion centering on the most important element: Every individual in the corporation is instrumental in enhancing security; it needs to be part of a user's daily routine.

Presentations should not run longer than 20 minutes. Most executives are reticent to agree to open-ended amounts of time, and audience attention typically strays if presentations are much longer than 20 minutes. Keeping audiences interested, making presentations punchy, omitting technical jargon, inviting user involvement, and not lingering on a single point give you the potential to create a company full of security advocates.

Be the Catalyst for Change in the Organization

Organizations are perpetually in flux, and as they grow ever larger, their various departments become seemingly more disparate. Individuals want involvement, and even more importantly, they want to feel that they matter and that everything they do counts. Delivering that message to every department creates a significant opportunity for an IT manager to guide change in an organization. It can also serve to boost user morale by making staffers active participants in an important process. Informing each person that everything he does matters is highly significant; it illustrates that each person is an integral part of a company. It is not just about sales, marketing, production, R&D, or finance; it is about individual respect, for the end customer, colleagues, the organization, and themselves. Fostering corporate spirit by encouraging a sense of personal responsibility can go a long way toward helping an organization achieve its goals. An involved work force, regardless of its size, has a greater chance for success when it pulls together as a team.

Human nature suggests that a catalyst is required for change to occur, and reaching out to members of an organization and informing them that everything they do makes a difference is simply an excellent way to create a catalyst.

Acknowledge the Responsibility of the IT Department

Users play a significant role in protecting the organization, but it is strategic to underscore the role of IT in the process; otherwise, users and the company's executives might feel that too much of the burden is theirs. The IT manager should reassure both users and executives that the bulk of security work remains in his department, but unless users practice safe computing, the manager's work will all be for naught. Users should know the five main issues that could inadvertently attract a security breach. They are as follows:

- Insufficient monitoring, both user and network
- Weak application-level security
- Weak network security
- Weak patch management
- Uninformed or careless users

Consult Again

Security is a process rather than a one-time action. Creating new behaviors and forming new habits require commitment, leadership, and continual positive reinforcement.

The presentations allow a positive forum for initial feedback, and the proceeding four weeks can determine whether reforms are being implemented. The IT manager should ideally publish a short newsletter that summarizes the major points and actions that are required from the security seminars. The manager can further reinforce his presentations by issuing follow-up notes every six to eight weeks, sharing current highlights from the security industry and including new tips that can be used to further protect the organization. Equally important, the notes should be short and breezy, but long on substance.

Enhanced security awareness can help to mitigate higher levels of threat and work to better protect an organization and its components, as follows:

- Its individuals
- Its financial concerns
- Its production flow
- Its sales efforts
- Its client and supplier partners
- Its revenue
- Its image
- Its integrity

Security continues to be a living challenge, and it requires constant attention both on the technical end and the people side. Continual consultation and positive reinforcement can maintain interest and support of the program and can help to ensure greater relevance over the long term.

Assessing Senior Business Management Security Requirements

The line that divides needs and wants can be somewhat blurry, making it vital that true needs be established early in the development stage of a business proposal. After it has been established, a need must be further defined, allowing a distinction to be drawn between whether a need is fundamentally required or simply very useful for an organization. The Infosec Operational (IO) survey was created for this book to aid IT executives and IT managers in defining fundamental needs for a corporation, and in so doing, establishing a framework to begin assessing tolerance for risk.

The IO survey is married to the IM survey of Chapter 5; combining the results of both surveys begins the process of establishing an organization's tolerance for risk. The respondents to the IO survey in this chapter are senior-level business managers; the respondents to the IM survey in Chapter 5 are IT executives and IT managers. The results for both surveys, reserved for use in Chapter 8, are designed to aid organizations in determining risk tolerance. A company must acknowledge its aversion to risk before it can begin the process of effectively securing itself, and these surveys serve as a vehicle to begin that process.

IT executives are asked to deliver the IO survey to their senior-level business management colleagues in an attempt to ascertain each manager's aversion to a particular situation. Questions are repeated, with certain variables altered, to determine whether needs change when a particular situation changes. For example, if e-mail were down for four hours, the VP of sales might find the circumstances disturbing, but not necessarily detrimental to her long-term business. Posing the same question, but changing the parameter to 72 hours without e-mail, would likely elicit a very different response. Through this process, true needs can begin to be established across an organization.

The IT executive can use the results of the survey to gain the following benefits:

- Establish a senior-level business management consensus for greater security needs

- Create a baseline of support among senior-level business management colleagues

- Address the specific needs of particular departments, which will undoubtedly be highlighted through the IO survey process

- Be the catalyst for high-level discussions among senior business managers

The IO survey, created for this book, is applicable for a wide array of corporations. But if required, IT executives can adjust questions to better reflect their individual needs. Because the survey results are used in Chapter 8, it is best to ensure that the quantity of questions remains unchanged.

Every Question Counts: Delivering the Survey to Respondents

When delivering the survey, the IT manager must acknowledge that business-minded respondents might deem certain questions as not being particularly relevant to his or her operation. The survey is designed to be an organization-wide awareness tool, recognizing that one issue could have negative implications for a multitude of departments, some of which could be indirect. In that sense, each question should bear relevance to virtually every senior business manager who answers the survey. An attack against an organization's extranet whose primary function is to feed a just-in-time production line could, for example, have cascading effects across the corporation. The following departments and personnel can be affected by a security incident:

- **Production**—Productivity can be curtailed because its just-in-time production line runs out of product.

- **Logistics**—This department can be reduced to people standing around aimlessly, with no orders to pick, no boxes to fill, no skids to stack, and no trucks to load.

- **Sales**—A department could miss its revenue target for a given month or quarter, because the warehouse cannot ship what production has not built. Worse yet, the department will likely need to contend with upset customers. Missed delivery dates would also likely have negative cascading effects at the customer's end.

- **Marketing**—The department might have to contend with a potential public relations issue should customer anger grow to a fever pitch.

- **Finance**—This department could miss its financial projections, resulting in inaccurate current and forward-reaching forecasts.

- **Investor Relations**—This department, responsible for direct dealings with shareholders, would need to deal with the fallout from missed financial targets and potentially missed profit targets.

- **Senior executives**—Depending on how pervasive the issue might be, senior executives might need to contend with the issue on its quarterly conference call with securities analysts.

In this context, each question in the survey should bear, at minimum, some relevance to the respondent. Considering a similar example, if the server belonging to the sales department were stolen, significant repercussions would eventually be felt in every department in the organization.

Infosec Operational Survey

This section presents the IO survey. The rating scale in Table 7-2 should be used to complete the survey found in Table 7-3.

Table 7-2   *Rating Scale for the Infosec Operational Survey*

Rating Scale	Rating Explanation
0	Not applicable
1	Would have little impact
2	Would have some impact
3	Would impact the organization as a whole
4	Would have a significant impact on operations and client expectation of the organization
5	Would have grave effects on the organization's ability to operate and possible negative implications regarding its long-term reputation

The Infosec Operational survey, shown in Table 7-3, should be distributed to all appropriate senior managers. While every organization is different, it is best to include senior business managers from a wide cross section of the corporation to ensure that consensus can be effectively achieved.

Table 7-3   *Infosec Operational Survey*

Question or Situation to Be Considered	Rating Schedule
Should e-mail be inaccessible for 8 continuous hours, how would this impact the organization?	5 4 3 2 1 0
Should e-mail be inaccessible for 48 continuous hours, how would this impact the organization?	5 4 3 2 1 0

continues

Table 7-3 *Infosec Operational Survey (Continued)*

Question or Situation to Be Considered	Rating Schedule
Personal calendars and contact lists are routinely used within e-mail programs. If all were unavailable for 4 hours, would the organization be limited in its ability to be productive or to generate revenue?	5 4 3 2 1 0
Personal calendars and contact lists are routinely used within e-mail programs. If all were unavailable for 30 hours, would the organization be limited in its ability to be productive or to generate revenue?	5 4 3 2 1 0
Should the public web server be inoperative for 2 hours, resulting in customers not being able to perform stock checks, place purchase orders, or request PO changes, what would be the impact?	5 4 3 2 1 0
Should the public web server be inoperative for 8 hours, resulting in customers not being able to perform stock checks, place purchase orders, or request PO changes, what would be the impact?	5 4 3 2 1 0
If an incident brought down an organization's IP telephony system for 4 hours, what would be its impact to operations?	5 4 3 2 1 0
If an incident brought down an organization's IP telephony system for 24 hours, what would be its impact to operations?	5 4 3 2 1 0
Should extranet connections be severed for 8 hours, what would be the implication for just-in-time production lines? What would be the implication for automated replenishment programs for clients?	5 4 3 2 1 0
Should extranet connections be severed for 48 hours, what would be the implication for just-in-time production lines? What would be the implication for automated replenishment programs for clients?	5 4 3 2 1 0
Companies use field salespeople to visit clients, perform stock checks, and enter sales orders remotely to ensure that stockouts do not occur. How would losing the ability to connect and enter orders, for 8 hours, impact the business?	5 4 3 2 1 0
Further to the previous question, what would the affect be if the ability to connect remotely were unavailable for 36 hours?	5 4 3 2 1 0

Table 7-3   *Infosec Operational Survey (Continued)*

Question or Situation to Be Considered	Rating Schedule
If the firm uses real-time databases, whether they are hand-held devices to pick orders in a warehouse, track product-build status on a production line, or in the field to interact directly with customers to provide real-time data, how would a 4-hour loss of wireless contact affect service levels?	5 4 3 2 1 0
Further to the previous question, how would a 24-hour loss of wireless contact affect service levels?	5 4 3 2 1 0
Acknowledging the possibility that a database could become corrupted, a firm might rely on its daily data backup to ensure security of its information. Are senior executives confident that backups are always picked up daily and stored in geographically secure locations?	5 4 3 2 1 0
A DDoS (distributed denial of service) attack will not necessarily bring a system down but can bottleneck it so severely that the system becomes exceedingly slow. For those firms that rely on its IP telephony for quick response to clients or next-day delivery to customers, would the system being down, or severely slowed, for 6 hours impact the business?	5 4 3 2 1 0
Further to the previous question, would 30 hours of severe slowness impact the business to a great degree?	5 4 3 2 1 0
While businesses can revert to maintaining paper records for a short time, multiple users or locations that access the same data can be quickly stymied. Would 8 hours of paper recordkeeping impact the organization's ability to effectively run its business?	5 4 3 2 1 0
Further to the previous question, could product be sold that was no longer available? As an example, could registrants be signed up for courses that no longer had room?	5 4 3 2 1 0
Is product information time sensitive, such as in hospitals or public utilities, whose inventories might have specific timespans? Would 6 hours of a slowed or stopped system affect the organization's ability to function effectively?	5 4 3 2 1 0
Should the power be down for 2 continuous hours, how would this impact the organization?	5 4 3 2 1 0
Should the power be down for 8 continuous hours, how would this impact the organization?	5 4 3 2 1 0

continues

Table 7-3   *Infosec Operational Survey (Continued)*

Question or Situation to Be Considered	Rating Schedule
Should fraud affect the financial database, rendering it inaccessible for 8 continuous hours, how would this impact the organization?	5 4 3 2 1 0
Should fraud affect the financial database, rendering it inaccessible for 30 continuous hours, how would this impact the organization?	5 4 3 2 1 0
Should a strategic R&D document be leaked to a competitor, what impact would this have on the organization?	5 4 3 2 1 0
Should a strategic marketing document be leaked to a competitor, what impact would this have on the organization?	5 4 3 2 1 0
Should a strategic financial document be leaked to a competitor, what impact would this have on the organization?	5 4 3 2 1 0
Should your departmental server be stolen, what impact would it have on the organization?	5 4 3 2 1 0
Should the CEO's laptop computer be stolen, what impact would it have on the organization?	5 4 3 2 1 0
Should the CFO's laptop computer be stolen, what impact would it have on the organization?	5 4 3 2 1 0
How would a lawsuit regarding the security systems (or lack thereof) impact your organization?	5 4 3 2 1 0

Infosec Operational Quotient

The Infosec Operational (IO) quotient is derived by averaging the scores of those managers who participated in the IO survey. Extensive business management participation can help to ensure an IO quotient that is truly reflective of the organization's aversion to risk.

Using the results from the IO survey, the IO quotient can be determined by performing the following mathematical operation:

IO quotient = Average of survey results * (100 / Total possible points)

where Total possible points = 5 * Number of questions

If you use all 31 questions from the survey in this chapter, the formula would be as follows:

IO quotient = Average of survey results * (100 / 155)

The IO quotient (and the IM quotient established in Chapter 5) are brought together in Chapter 8 for a formal process that can begin to quantify security decisions. Together, these two sets of results form the foundation of the ROP model.

Summary

The IT manager can drive change within an organization by proactively engaging senior management colleagues in security discussions and by directly reaching out to employees.

Using these processes allows the IT manager to construct a concrete platform for his network security business case. Understanding the organization, garnering support, creating a groundswell, and educating users are fundamental components of any business proposal. Developing a survey that explores the ramifications of system unavailability is the next step in creating a process that produces an objective figure from a series of intensely subjective situations.

This chapter guided the IT manager in the following areas:

- Exploring an understanding of the organization's mandate and goals
- Acknowledging the need to engage the corporation
- Understanding the process to effectively lobby organization-wide support
- Assessing senior management security requirements

The next chapter uses the IM and IO quotients to begin a discussion of establishing an ROP model.

CHAPTER 8

RISK AVERSION AND SECURITY TOPOLOGIES

This chapter uses information that was presented in Chapter 4, "Putting It All Together: Threats and Security Equipment," along with the results from surveys completed in both Chapter 5, "Policy, Personnel, and Equipment as Security Enablers," and Chapter 7, "Engaging the Corporation: Management and Employees." The surveys from both chapters can aid organizations in deriving a security topology model that is both relevant and viable.

This chapter covers the following topics:

- Risk aversion
- Risk-aversion quotient
- Security modeling
- Diminishing returns

Risk Aversion

Using explanations and examples, this section explores the following topics:

- The notion of risk aversion
- Determining risk tolerance
- What assets to protect
- Short-term and long-term risks

The Notion of Risk Aversion

Risk aversion is highly subjective. One person's high-risk situation is another's light adventure. For example, driving slowly through a tough inner-city neighborhood late at night with the car windows down and the stereo pumping out classical music might appear to be foolhardy, but depending on the viewpoint of those assessing the situation, it could be seen as intensely risky or simply engaging in light comedic adventure. Whether the discussion embodies an individual or an organization, the ability to tolerate risk is wholly personal to that one entity.

Certain organizations are greater targets than others. Companies that engage in activities that might be construed as being less than beneficial to every group in society could find themselves the victims of targeted attacks, whereas smaller, less visible companies might only need to defend against random attacks and potentially disgruntled associates. Regardless of a corporation's visibility, or lack thereof, the potential randomness of attacks implies that every organization is, at certain levels, equally vulnerable.

The ability of corporations to tolerate risk can never be assumed. Whichever route an organization takes to determine its level of tolerance, risk aversion will continue to be an intensely subjective matter.

Why Risk Tolerance Is Inherently Individual

Logic would state that a research and development (R&D)–oriented company, as an example, would have a lower tolerance for risk than a chain of convenience stores. The R&D house needs to guard its current research along with its legacy research; losing either could result in significant long-term issues. In comparison, most people might view the risk tolerance of a large chain of convenience stores as relatively high: a large distribution center with a fleet of trucks on the road and a chain of stores that all operate in the same manner, cash in the till, food on the shelves, milk in the cooling unit, and lotto tickets at the register.

Many readers might feel that these two examples are at opposite ends of the spectrum for risk tolerance. And they are, unless you happen to run one of the companies. The convenience store operator is dealing with a different set of issues than the R&D house. Convenience stores are typically quick turns, cash-driven businesses that require speed of cash flow to deliver consistent profitability. Should a server be rendered inoperable, the ability to run products through the till is gone, because bar coding is used extensively in convenience stores. If the till is out of commission, revenue cannot be effectively collected. The store cannot sell its fragile refrigerated items or any of its other time-sensitive products, such as lottery tickets, which are typically a high-volume revenue generator.

continues

Why Risk Tolerance Is Inherently Individual (Continued)

The bar coding provides current inventory levels, allowing for reordering on a quick and continual basis. Assuming that the corporate server has suffered a similar fate, the ability to move product through the distribution center and out to the stores is stymied. Consumers, particularly in the convenience sector, are typically fickle. Consistency and reliability are what they are searching for, and should they walk into a store and discover that services are not available, they might not continue frequenting that store in the future. Giving consumers what they want in a quick and efficient manner is at the crux of a convenience store's offering—from the product they want to purchase to the ease, consistency, and reliability of the environment in which they purchase it.

These are two very different examples, reflecting two vastly different requirements for enhanced IT security, yet both illustrate compelling arguments—issues for their executive managers to decide. The ability to tolerate risk is relevant to the type of business in which an organization is involved. But ultimately, no single type of business is unequivocally more vulnerable than any other, because the ability and willingness to tolerate risk is highly personal. Organizations do not invest in higher levels of security because of the business in which they are engaged; they invest in greater levels because their tolerance for risk is low.

Determining Risk Tolerance

Whether it concerns an individual or a corporation, risk tolerance is highly personal. One argument says that size, or even type, of business does not necessarily have a bearing on the level of risk a corporation is willing to tolerate. To resolve this argument, an organization attempts to determine its logical risk tolerance level. It can conduct studies to establish the amount of risk it can afford to take on and then logically structure the company based on the findings of the analytical report. But in the end, studies can only make suggestions; logical analyses can only focus on black-and-white issues.

Surveys found at the end of Chapters 5 and 7 can aid executive managers in developing a greater awareness of their true aversion to threats. The surveys use a process that combines logical situational analysis with a subjective read of the corporation's needs. While the tool leads the respondent to a model that can be implemented, it also attempts to engage executive management in a discussion that can help to succinctly assess the organization's tolerance for risk.

Organizations should take a long-term perspective of risk tolerance and develop a formal review process to ensure that risk tolerance reviews are mandated—and occur at prescribed times. While reviews should ensure that risk tolerance levels are not changed too frequently, or even needlessly, any review process should allow for situational reviews to occur quickly in the event of major structural events, such as change of ownership or other significant happenings.

Which Assets to Protect

Assets are typically viewed as constituting physical goods or intellectual property. But depending on the organization, an asset can also be its operations or, more specifically, its undisturbed operability. An organization, such as a selling forum website whose business is conducted almost completely in the open, could be damaged if its services were severely disrupted. While the website must retain and effectively secure private data, its customers demand reliability, requiring a market that is always open for business. Uninterrupted operability is at the crux of its business.

Short-Term and Long-Term Risks

Risk can be viewed in the near term, as organizations attempt to ascertain damage that could occur if preventative measures were not put in place. Some examples of short-term risks are as follows:

- Damaged and unavailable equipment

- Interrupted sales and service revenue

- Bottlenecked supply chains and production lines

- IT overtime payroll costs to mend immediate situations

When a long-term approach is assumed, security initiative risks consider the following items:

- New equipment and its corresponding upgrade path

- Preliminary and ongoing training

- Damaged customer relationships

- Lessened revenue stream

- Loss of trust

- Reliability

- Pertinent other intangible components

Tables 8-1 and 8-2 show how low-risk-tolerant and high-risk-tolerant organizations, respectively, can determine how short- and long-term events could affect a corporation's tolerance for risk. Because events that could occur are inherently individual, every corporation should determine its own list of relevant events. Each table has one sample line and a few of the possible risks to show an example of how to get started. An organization could list all the risks in such a table to determine how short- and long-term events could affect a corporation's tolerance for risk.

Table 8-1 *Awareness Chart Example for Low-Tolerance Organization*

Risk	Impact	Risk Tolerance	Risk-Aversion Decision
Damaged/unavailable equipment	Very high	Not tolerant	Complete redundancy system
Interrupted sales and service revenue	. . .	. . .	. . .

Table 8-2 *Awareness Chart Example for High-Tolerance Organization*

Risk	Impact	Risk Tolerance	Risk-Aversion Decision
Damaged/unavailable equipment	Varies	Tolerant	Backup system is manual
Interrupted sales and service revenue	. . .	. . .	. . .

Risk-Aversion Quotient

The surveys presented in Chapters 5 and 7 are designed to quantify the subjective elements that are an inescapable component of business structures and operating systems. These surveys produce an Infosec management (IM) quotient and an Infosec operational (IO) quotient that are referenced in this section covering the risk-aversion quotient.

This section explores the following topics:

- Calculating the risk-aversion quotient
- Risk-aversion quotient and risk tolerance
- Using the charts

Calculating the Risk-Aversion Quotient

Use the following formula to calculate the risk-aversion (RA) quotient:

$$\text{RA quotient} = \frac{\text{(IM quotient + IO quotient)}}{2}$$

To calculate the RA quotient, populate the Results column in Table 8-3 with the reserved results from the surveys found in Chapters 5 and 7.

Table 8-3   *Calculating the Risk-Aversion Quotient*

Measurement	Components	Results
Chapter 5 survey: Infosec management quotient[1]	IM quotient	_____ (from Chapter 5 survey)
Chapter 7 survey: Infosec operational quotient[1]	IO quotient	_____ (from Chapter 7 survey)
Risk-aversion quotient[2]	(IM quotient + IO quotient) / 2	_____ (Risk-aversion quotient)

The following is an example of survey results from a hypothetical organization. Because individual results can vary, average figures were used in the following example to determine a company's risk-aversion quotient:

IM quotient (from Chapter 5 survey): 74%

IO quotient (from Chapter 7 survey): 67%

RA quotient = (IM quotient + IO quotient) / 2

RA quotient = (74 + 67) / 2

RA quotient $\cong 71\%$

Risk-Aversion Quotient and Risk Tolerance

When the risk-aversion quotient has been determined, the level of risk tolerance can be identified, as illustrated in Table 8-4.

Table 8-4   *Risk-Aversion Quotient and Risk Tolerance Equivalency Scale*

Risk-Aversion Quotient	Risk Tolerance
1–20	High
21–40	Medium-high
41–60	Medium
61–80	Medium-low
81–100	Low

In the previous example, the risk-aversion quotient was determined to be 71%. Using Table 8-4, the company is shown to have a medium-low risk tolerance.

Using the Charts

Similar to all charts, the risk-aversion quotient and risk tolerance equivalency scale should be used as guides rather than an unequivocal path that an organization should follow. While a company can use the IM and IO surveys to determine its own tolerance level, as shown in Table 8-4, survey respondents will likely be executives and managers culled from a wide cross section of an organization. While one hopes for independent responses, a certain percentage of respondents can respond with particular agendas in mind. The security steering committee or executive management must take the information derived from the surveys into consideration and, if necessary, choose a model that best reflects its tolerance for, or aversion to, risk.

The surveys build consensus and can serve a multitude of purposes, including the ability to shed necessary light on oft-forgotten or overlooked areas of an operation that can leave an organization unduly vulnerable. The mean scores should help to serve as a guide in representing the needs of an organization's managers, but the scores should not necessarily be the determining factor in an organization's required security posture.

Security Modeling

The task of determining which topology to implement on a network can be challenging, even after IM and IO surveys have been completed. While the surveys can aid organizations in determining their risk tolerance level, as shown earlier in Table 8-4, this section advances the process by using the ranking to offer various equipment choices. But one size rarely fits all, and a range of possible options is presented for each of the varying category types.

This section discusses the following topics:

- Topology standards
- One size rarely fits all
- Security throughout the network

Topology Standards

The discussion in Chapter 4 centered on the following three topology standards:

- Basic
- Modest
- Comprehensive

Table 8-5 illustrates how the risk-aversion quotient translates to a security model that can be adopted. Note that for some tolerance categories, a range of models apply.

Table 8-5 *Risk Tolerance and Security Model Mapping*

Risk Tolerance	Security Model		
	Basic	Modest	Comprehensive
High	x		
Medium-high	x	x	

continues

Table 8-5 *Risk Tolerance and Security Model Mapping (Continued)*

	Security Model		
Risk Tolerance	**Basic**	**Modest**	**Comprehensive**
Medium	x	x	x
Medium-low		x	x
Low			x

The security models are covered in more detail in Chapter 4. In the previous example in this chapter, the risk-aversion quotient was determined to be 71% and the risk tolerance was medium-low. Using the risk tolerance level, the security model could be determined as being comprehensive or modest.

One Size Rarely Fits All

Blending security requirements and specific models is not an exact science. As evidenced earlier, subjective influences can be incorporated into the process to ensure that an organization's needs are fully met.

Table 8-5 reflects the individual nature of security posture requirements. One size cannot fit all; two companies operating in the same field, with like structures and similar databases, can require different security postures. Whether it is the strategic value of information that is being protected or the physical operability of a company that is of paramount importance, security requirements will inevitably be singularly unique.

A modest model does not necessarily come in one size. It can be basic or comprehensive, or a blend of both. The equipment that is required should be wholly dependent on the needs of the organization, rather than a predetermined model. Cost is fully explored in Chapter 9, "Return on Prevention: Investing in Capital Assets," when the analysis considers total cost of ownership (TCO) and return on prevention (ROP). At this point in the discussion, the most logical level—basic, modest, or comprehensive—should be chosen.

Also, within organizations, markedly different perspectives can exist. An alarmist might state that a fully redundant system is needed to ensure that an organization is as secure as possible. But depending on the business or the industry in which an organization is involved, a fully redundant system might not be necessary. It might be desired, but after a thorough cost analysis, the relative cost of protection might outweigh the risk.

The mandate of this chapter and the next is to help determine the suitability of a chosen security level and to ensure that equipment specific to that model delivers the requisite protection within a sound TCO and ROP analysis.

Security Throughout the Network

Security has been traditionally focused on protecting the organization at the perimeter by keeping out potential intruders, whether they are cyber or physical. The term *crunchy on the outside* refers to strong perimeter protection. As explored in Chapter 3, "Security Technology and Related Equipment," however, firms are beginning to become crunchy on the inside as well, with firewalls and similar protective devices becoming more frequently installed between departments. A finance department, as an example, can only ensure the verity of its documentation when it can assure the board of the sanctity of its data. The need for individual departmental protection, possibly only at a basic level, should not be underestimated, particularly as an organization grows.

Modest Security Scenario for an SMB

When a model has been chosen, as explained in Chapter 4, the system administrator or IT manager can choose from a list of components to develop the required infrastructure. The art of developing network topology can be challenging. Most IT managers acknowledge the subjective nature of their craft— what might be considered a fundamental piece of equipment to one IT manager could be viewed as extravagant to another. For the purposes of continuity, Table 8-6 represents an SMB's shopping list for the modest model, and the shaded items are considered essential components.

Table 8-6 *Shopping List for Modest Security for a Medium-Sized Business*

Module	Function	Equipment
Campus	Network management	HIDS
	Corporate users	Core switch
		Virus scanning
	Corporate servers	Switch
		HIDS

continues

Table 8-6 *Shopping List for Modest Security for a Medium-Sized Business (Continued)*

Module	Function	Equipment
Edge	Corporate internet (DMZ)	Edge router
		Firewall*
		DNS server
		HTTP/FTP server
		Layer 2 switches
		NIDS appliance
		SMTP server
		HIDS
	VPN and remote access	Dial-in server
		VPN concentrator
	WAN	WAN router

*To be considered basic, a perimeter firewall should come with additional features such as basic IDS and basic VPN capabilities, which are available from vendors such as Cisco on its PIX Firewalls.

The security topology for an SMB is formally represented by Figure 8-1.

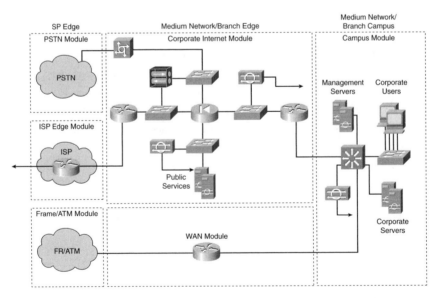

Figure 8-1 *SMB Security Topology (Source: "SAFE: Extending the Security Blueprint to Small, Midsize, and Remote-User Networks")*

Note that in Table 8-6, equipment for the service provider (SP) edge module was not provided, because the SP typically provides required equipment.

Managing Requirements

In an ideal world, network layouts are finalized, investment capital is readily available, and infrastructure is fully provisioned. The reality is that most organizations need to build networks over time, as requirements increase and funding attempts to keep in step.

When a model has been chosen, an organization might discover that certain components of the model are already deployed on its network. But regardless of whether equipment is readily available, it is important not to be intimidated by large topology shopping lists. The lists can be adapted to account for a variety of situations, including the recognition that an organization could be in one of three phases: early adoption, growth, or mature phase.

An organization does not need to acquire all equipment at one time; some can be more immediate than others. The life cycle can also vary for different pieces of hardware and software. Typically, the more costly a component, the longer its life cycle, although upgrades will be a continual expense over the life of most products.

Modest Security Scenario for an Enterprise

Table 8-7 provides a topology shopping list for a modest security model, as shown in Figure 8-2, on an enterprise-size network.

Table 8-7 *Shopping List for a Modest Security Model in an Enterprise-Size Network*

Module	Function	Equipment
Campus	Network management	HIDS
		Virus scanning
		OTP server
		AAA services
		SNMP server (read-only)
		Network log server
		Switch

continues

Table 8-7 *Shopping List for a Modest Security Model in an Enterprise-Size Network (Continued)*

Module	Function	Equipment
Campus	Building distribution	Switch
	Building access	Switch
		Host virus scanning
	Corporate users	Core switch
		Virus scanning
	Corporate servers	Switch
		HIDS
Edge	Edge distribution	Switch
	E-commerce	Router (FW)
		NIDS
		HIDS on servers
		Firewall
		Switch
	Corporate internet (DMZ)	Edge router
		Firewall
		DNS server
		http/FTP server
		Layer 2 switches
		NIDS appliance
		SMTP server
		HIDS
	WAN	Router
	Remote access and VPN module	NIDS
		VPN concentrator
		NIDS
		Firewall
		Router

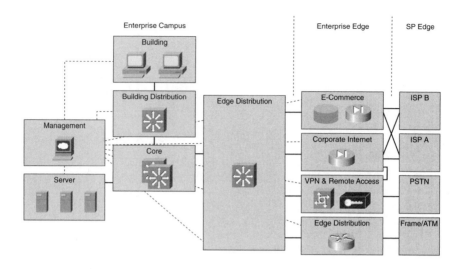

Figure 8-2   *Modest Security Topology for an Enterprise (Source: "SAFE: A*
Security Blueprint for Enterprise Networks")

Diminishing Returns

The three security models (basic, modest, and comprehensive) differ markedly in level of protection, but the law of diminishing returns recognizes that as an organization moves from one level to the next, its ability to extract equal value from each significant move begins to diminish. While the organization's level of protection increases, its most dramatic change occurs when it goes from no security to incorporating a basic model.

Figure 8-3 illustrates the law of diminishing returns as it applies to the security models and expenditures.

A comprehensive model can be desired by many organizations, but depending on the type of business in which a corporation is engaged, this type of model might not be wholly necessary.

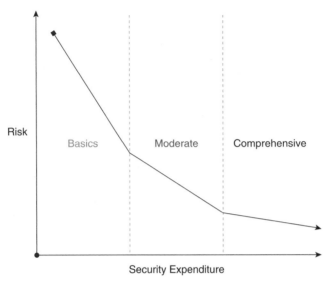

Figure 8-3   *Law of Diminishing Returns*

The graph line starts to flatten out between moderate and comprehensive, because the functionality that an organization would obtain from an ultra-specialized dedicated appliance might already have been partially addressed by a product that was previously used in the modest or basic model. Another reason for the flattened graph line is that the comprehensive model calls for redundancy, namely, hot-standby equipment that begins to work should the primary equipment fail; it does not necessarily imply that a raft of new functionality will be incorporated onto a network. For example, a comprehensive model would likely call for a virtual carbon copy firewall, identical to the one at the network's perimeter, to be available should a situation ever render the primary firewall ineffective. While an organization would not realize an immediate benefit from investing in an alternate firewall, should the primary unit fail, the hot standby would be ready to go live. By addressing a company's fundamental need for uninterrupted operability, the financial benefit of a comprehensive security installation can begin to be derived.

The result is that the comprehensive model requires that a certain level of funding be allocated to hardware-operational contingency planning.

Summary

Risk aversion is unique to every organization, requiring those involved in assessing a corporation's level of tolerance acknowledge the implications inherent in each security model type.

The topology models presented in Chapter 4, along with the Infosec management quotient from Chapter 5 and the Infosec operational quotient determined in Chapter 7, are brought together in this chapter to aid the reader in determining a security topology for his or her network.

Representative shopping lists are presented for two model types, and the law of diminishing returns is explored as it relates to security investments.

This chapter discussed the following topics:

- Significance of risk aversion
- Developing a risk-aversion quotient
- Security modeling examples
- Relevance of diminishing returns

CHAPTER 9

RETURN ON PREVENTION: INVESTING IN CAPITAL ASSETS

Financial modeling is a fundamental component of all business investment cases. IT security investment proposals have unique qualities that can pose expenditure justification challenges. This chapter is designed to explore various financial models and to develop one that IT managers can effectively use to support their business cases.

This chapter covers the following topics:

- Examining cost of attacks

- Budgeting for security equipment

- Analyzing returns on security capital investments

- Acknowledging nonmathematical security fundamentals

Examining Cost of Attacks

Determining costs incurred as a result of specific attacks should seem simple enough to do, but typically many intangibles are involved and costing analyses can prove somewhat challenging.

This section considers the following topics:

- Determining a baseline

- Providing alternatives

Determining a Baseline

In 2003, the Computer Security Institute and Federal Bureau of Investigation (CSI/FBI) survey reported that while 75% of its respondents reported financial losses from having been attacked, only 47% of them were able to quantify the amounts.[1]

Corporations and individuals can use information from organizations such as the CSI/FBI, along with other equally reliable sources, when attempting to put a dollar figure on events, or they can determine their own costs. Regardless of the route taken, an IT manager who is charged with developing a business case for network security is strongly encouraged to use measurable financial figures to ensure that the proposal presented to executive management is based on credible fundamentals.

Should an IT manager want to develop his own costing analysis for a virus attack, as an example, some of the important business elements to consider are as follows:

- Cleanup costs, specifically the following:
  - Number of workstations and servers affected
  - Typical amount of hours it took to clean the affected equipment
  - Average labor rate of those performing the cleanup operation
  - Cost of external help
  - Costs as a result of the system, or certain equipment, being down, as follows:

    Number of hours employees were without workstations and servers

    Productivity per employee lost because of system, or specific equipment, being unavailable
- Lost revenues
- Loss of integrity, in the eyes of customers, suppliers, employees, and the general public
- Potential loss of goodwill
- Potential exposure of intellectual property
- Possible damage to customer relationships
- Possibility for legal ramifications

The process of calculating the costs of an attack can be rather involved. The CSI/FBI information is culled from a wide cross section of industry, and it can serve as a reliable alternative to calculating costs in-house. Looking at major business categories by industry type, respondents of the survey are identified as emanating from the following areas:

- High-tech sector, 17%
- Financial sector, 15%
- Governmental agencies, 15%
- Manufacturing sector, 11%
- Medical sector, 8%

Breaking down survey responses by organization size and considering only major categories, respondents were culled from the following groups:

- Organizations with more than 10,000 employees, 28%

- Organizations with 1000 to 5000 employees, 22%

- Organizations with less than 100 employees, 18%

For the purposes of this chapter, data collected by the CSI/FBI survey is used to ensure a certain objectivity and uniformity to the models presented throughout. Note that while the figures listed are considered conservative in nature, it is acknowledged that the act of collecting data in this manner is not scientific and is not representative of an empirical analysis.

The CSI/FBI survey does not, nor can it, qualify respondents' policies and practices. But those issues notwithstanding, it can serve as reliable tool that organizations can use to establish a baseline of general costs.

Providing Alternatives

The CSI/FBI statistics can provide reliable measuring points, but IT managers can use alternative methods when developing a business case for network security. Single-loss expectancy (SLE), annualized rate of occurrence (ARO), and annual-loss expectancy (ALE) can be effectively used when attempting to place value on an event that *did not* occur.

This section considers the following topics:

- Single-loss expectancy

- Annualized rate of occurrence

- Annual-loss expectancy

Single-Loss Expectancy

The single-loss expectancy (SLE) is the cost associated with a single attack on a specific asset. SLE is typically determined by multiplying an asset's value (for example, the value of a server) by its exposure factor. The formula for calculating SLE is shown in Equation 9-1.

$$\text{SLE} = \text{Asset value} * \text{Exposure factor}$$

Equation 9-1 *Single-Loss Expectancy Calculations*

Both asset value and exposure factor are examined in the following subsections.

Asset Value

Asset value can be challenging to estimate. In the example of a web server, you must determine whether the asset value represents the data or simply the media in which it resides.

The asset value could be represented by the formula shown in Equation 9-2.

Cost of replacing information
+ cost of replacing software and hardware and reconfiguration
+ lost availability
+ associated costs (loss of data confidentiality and integrity)

Total Asset Value

Equation 9-2   *Asset Value Calculations*

The asset value cost would vary depending on the kind of attack that had occurred. A DoS attack, as an example, would typically not involve hardware replacement, whereas an outright theft of a server would include many possible variables, such as costs associated with loss of confidentiality and integrity.

Table 9-1 illustrates representative figures that an IT manager can use to estimate the value of a stolen web server.

Table 9-1   *Example of Valuing a Web Server*

Component	Value
Server hardware	$20,000
Server software and reconfiguration[1]	$3,000
Information contained on server	$75,000
Loss of availability[2]	$60,000
Loss of confidentiality and integrity[3]	$40,000
Total loss of corporate web server	$198,000

[1]Should events result in a web server needing to be replaced, software replacement should not incur additional expense. Software licenses are owned by the organization, so IT need only reinstall the software.

[2]This number represents the loss in productivity and future sales.

[3]This number is an estimate of soft, or less easily quantifiable, damages.

Exposure Factor

An exposure factor illustrates an asset's vulnerability to a given threat. It measures the magnitude of a threat's impact on a particular asset and determines a percentage of the asset that would be lost should a particular type of threat occur. Table 9-2 contains values in which an IT manager has estimated the exposure factor of a web server for two possible events.

Table 9-2 *Examples of Exposure Factor Estimates for a Web Server*

Event/Attack	Exposure Factor	Comments
Denial of service	0.80	During a DoS, a web server's operations would be crippled by 80%.
Physical theft of server	0.95	Should a web server be stolen, it would be considered inoperable, or represented as having a factor of 100%. But assuming that an administrator had a complete backup of the system, information contained on the server would not be lost for more than a few hours or days.

SLE Example

Using the SLE formula, you can plug in the total asset value calculated in Table 9-1 and the exposure factors illustrated in Table 9-2 to calculate the SLE of a DoS attack or a physical theft of the server. The results for each of these events are shown in Equation 9-3.

SLE = Asset Value * Exposure factor

SLE of DoS = $198,000 * 0.80 = **$158,400**

SLE of web server physical theft = $198,000 * 0.95 = **$188,100**

Equation 9-3 *Web Server SLE: DoS Versus Theft*

An IT manager can attempt to estimate the total costs surrounding a single attack, or she can instead choose to pull information from an array of different sources. The CSI/FBI information has been discussed, but other governmental and institutional agencies gather information as well, including the UK Department of

Trade and Industry (DTI) Information Security Breaches Survey 2004, published by Pricewaterhouse Coopers (PWC) and the DTI.

Depending on system resources and time availability, using third-party data can ensure greater credibility and speedier compilation when developing a business case. For example, the CSI/FBI report states that in 2003, the average loss due to a system penetration attack was $56,212. The ability to determine similar numbers internally can be challenging.

Annualized Rate of Occurrence

The annualized rate of occurrence (ARO) is the probability, or rate, that an attack might happen over a one-year period.

Table 9-3 illustrates two probabilities of attacks, likely estimated by an IT manager.

Table 9-3   *ARO of Potential Attacks*

Attack/Event	Probability That the Event Will Occur over a One-Year Period
DoS	40%
Physical theft of server	2%

Statistics can be excellent tools, provided that sources are reliable. The CSI/FBI determined, as an example, that 36% of its respondents had been victims of system penetration attacks in 2003.

Note that at times, statistics from different sources can appear to be conflicting. In organizational environments that are focused on prevention, it is prudent to err on the side of caution while continuing to study the trending.

NOTE   Exposure factor is often represented as a decimal value, whereas ARO is usually represented as a percentage.

Annual-Loss Expectancy

With SLE estimates and ARO statistics completed, the annual-loss expectancy (ALE) can be calculated. The formula used is shown in Equation 9-4.

$$\frac{\text{Single Loss Expectancy (SLE)}}{* \text{ Annualized Rate of Occurrence (ARO)}}$$

Annual Loss Expectancy

Equation 9-4 *Annual-Loss Expectancy Calculations*

Equation 9-5 illustrates DoS and theft ALE when the estimated numbers are used.

$$\text{ALE} = \text{SLE} * \text{ARO}$$

ALE DoS = SLE DoS * ARO DoS
ALE DoS = \$158,400 * 40% = **\$63,360**

ALE Theft = SLE Theft * ARO Theft
ALE Theft = \$188,100 * 2% = **\$3,762**

Equation 9-5 *ALE Example*

Equation 9-6 represents the ALE from a system penetration attack when figures are sourced from the CSI/FBI statistics.

$$\text{ALE penetration attack} = \$56,212 * 36\% = \underline{\underline{\textbf{\$20,236}}}$$

Equation 9-6 *Calculating ALE Using Available Statistics*

The ALE can be used in a capital-budgeting process whenever an organization is considering an equipment investment proposal. Relevant attack costs can be determined in-house, or organizations can comfortably use external information culled from a wide cross section of industry and government on the North American and European continents.

Budgeting for Security Equipment

The next step in the business case is to develop a cost model for the equipment that is designed to protect an organization from attack.

This section explores the cost of equipment, as follows:

- Total cost of ownership
- Present value

Total Cost of Ownership

The total cost of ownership (TCO) includes all associated equipment costs, whether recurring or nonrecurring, including all aspects of hardware, installation, maintenance, and upgrades.

The following model, presented in Tables 9-4, 9-5, and 9-6, provides an example for assessing costs, but it does not purport to be exhaustive. If other costs are pertinent to an organization, such as ongoing training, as an example, they should be included in the final model. Note that the costs shown in Tables 9-4 and 9-5 are incurred only in the first year of ownership.

Table 9-4 *Procurement Costs*

Equipment	Procurement Cost
Security appliance	P

Table 9-5 *Nonrecurring Associated Costs*

Equipment	Installation Costs: Labor, per Diem, and so on	Training	Associated Equipment[1]	Total of Associated Nonrecurring Costs
Security appliance	I	T	A	$I + T + A = N$

[1]For example, a 19-inch rack and cables

Table 9-6 *Recurring Associated Costs*

Equipment	Labor Cost to Operate, Maintain, and Upgrade	Software/Hardware Upgrade Cost	Total of Recurring Associated Costs
Security appliance	L	U	$L + U = R$

NOTE	Depending on the organization and the level of analysis expected from those who prepare the metrics, additional TCO variables could include the cost of floor space, insurance, utilities, and so on.
	The following TCO calculation uses a model that restricts cash outlay to the first year. Because many factors can affect overall calculations, including, but not limited to, amortization period or whether the equipment is being rented or leased, you are encouraged to gather as much data as possible before compiling this portion of the model.

From Table 9-4 through Table 9-6, TCO can be calculated as shown in Equation 9-7.

TCO = Procurement Costs + Non-Recurring Associated Costs + (y * Recurring Associated costs)

$$TCO = P + N + (y * R)$$

Where:
P = Procurement Cost
N = Non-Recurring Costs
R = Recurring Costs
y = useful life of the equipment in years

Equation 9-7 *Total Cost of Ownership*

Later in this chapter, the model is more rigorously held to financial analysis standards by bringing all elements to present value. But for the following TCO example, a firewall that is expected to be in production for three years is examined.

Table 9-7 shows the procurement costs (P), Table 9-8 shows the nonrecurring associated costs (N), and Table 9-9 shows the recurring associated costs (R) for this example. Note that the costs shown in Tables 9-7 and 9-8 are incurred only at the beginning of ownership.

Table 9-7 *Procurement Costs*

Equipment	Procurement Cost
Firewall	$18,000

Table 9-8   *Nonrecurring Associated Costs*

Equipment	Installation Cost	Training	Associated Equipment	Total of Associated Nonrecurring Costs
Firewall	$3,000	$2,000	$800	$5,800

Table 9-9   *Recurring Associated Costs*

Equipment	Labor Cost to Operate, Maintain, and Upgrade	Software/Hardware Upgrade Cost	Total of Recurring Associated Costs
Firewall	$3,000	$2,000	$5,000

Equation 9-8 calculates the total cost of ownership for this firewall, which is expected to be in production for three years.

$$TCO = P + N + (y * R)$$

TCO of Firewall = $18,000 + $ 5,800 + (3 * $5,000) = $38,800

Where:
P = Procurement Cost
N = Non-Recurring Costs
R = Recurring Costs
y = useful life of the equipment in years

Equation 9-8   *Firewall Total Cost of Ownership Example*

Every business proposal can require a different level of analysis, and acknowledging that an executive audience might require an in-depth examination of total costs for proposals under consideration, the following section explores the concept of present value.

Present Value

Present value is the process of valuing a future payment, or cash flow, in current or present-day dollars.

To analyze future cash flow in its present time value, future expenses need to be applied to a discount rate—a particular interest rate that brings future cash flow to its present value, allowing it to be stated in current dollars. A discount rate eliminates the time value of money from future cash flows.

The discount rate is also referred to as cost of funds or cost of capital. It is the rate used for adjusting the present economic value of a resource, for example, the cash flow needed to purchase a firewall. Because equipment typically has a useful life of three years, present value takes into account the declining value of money. The discount rate approximates a calculated rate that is typically higher than a central bank's lending rate, or similar standard financial metric, such as lease rate, cost of (borrowing) money, or the potential opportunity cost of funds no longer available for other investments. The discount rate is used in capital-budgeting tools, such as return on investment (ROI), net present value (NPV), and internal rate of return (IRR), to calculate future cash flows back to present dollars. It equalizes various investment options, in particular those with varied useful lives.

By removing the time value of money from future cash flows, a discount rate attempts to account for the declining value of money.

The IT manager can estimate the discount rate or consult with the finance department to determine the capitalization rate typically used by the organization.

Use Equation 9-9 to calculate the present value of TCO.

TCO Present Value = Procurement Costs + Non-Recurring Costs + (Time-Adjusted Recurring Costs)

TCO Present Value = P + N + (Time-Adjusted R)

Equation 9-9 *Present Value of Total Cost of Ownership*

Using the previous firewall TCO example, and assuming a three-year useful life for a firewall, the following example illustrates the three-year period by using a discount rate, or cost of capital, set at 10%.

Table 9-10 shows the values for the TCO present value calculation before accounting for the time-adjusted recurring associated costs.

Table 9-11 shows the TCO present value calculations for this example using a discount rate, or cost of capital, set at 10% using the formula shown in Equation 9-9. The Cash Flow Present Value column of Table 9-11 shows the time-adjusted recurring associated costs (Time-adjusted R) by multiplying the Discount Factor by the Cash Flow.

Table 9-10   *TCO Prior to Time Adjustments*

Firewall Cost	Symbol	Cost
Procurement cost (incurred only at the beginning of ownership, year 0)	P	$18,000
Nonrecurring associated costs (incurred usually at the beginning of ownership, year 0)	N	$5,800
Recurring associated costs (incurred every year for 3 years)	R	$5,000

Table 9-11   *Firewall TCO Present Value Example*

Year	Discount Factor When Discount Rate Is 10%	Cash Flow Out	Cash Flow Present Value
0 = (P + N)	1.000	$23,800	$23,800
1 = (Time-adjusted R)	0.909	$5,000	$4,545
2 = (Time-adjusted R)	0.826	$5,000	$4,130
3 = (Time-adjusted R)	0.751	$5,000	$3,755
Total	—	$38,800 (TCO)	$36,230 (TCO present value)

Discount Factor

The discount factor is derived from the discount rate by using the formulas shown in Equation 9-10.

$$\text{Discount Factor} = \frac{1}{(1 + d)^y} \quad \text{where } d = \text{discount rate and } y = \text{year}$$

Discount factor or year 2 with a discount rate of 10% would be $= \dfrac{1}{(1 + .10)^2} = 0.826$

Discount factor or year 3 with a discount rate of 10% would be $= \dfrac{1}{(1 + .10)^3} = 0.751$

Equation 9-10   *Discount Factor Calculation*

The adjusted time value of money illustrates that in today's dollars, the firewall would cost $36,230 for a 3-year useful life.

Value of Present Value

Present value can be particularly useful for comparing investments with varying useful lives.

Analyzing Returns on Security Capital Investments

When compiling data for an IT security investment proposal, it can be challenging to deliver one of the most basic capital-budgeting requirements: quantifying returns of events *not happening,* while using objective figures to support the business case. Fortunately, information collected in the annual CSI/FBI survey can serve as independent, impartial, and reliable data that can effectively illustrate potential costs and associated vulnerabilities inherent in under-security.

Choosing an acceptable and representative evaluation tool is the next challenge the IT executive faces, and this section aids in the search of an appropriate analysis tool by exploring the merits of the following topics:

- Net present value
- Internal rate of return
- Return on investment
- Payback period
- The bottom line

It is important to note that while other models can be used, such as economic value-added and option models, the discussion in this book is best served by focusing the analysis on the four methods covered in this section.

Net Present Value

Net present value (NPV) provides a dollar value for a future return brought back to present time. It is calculated by adding the present value of benefits, for every year over a specified time period, and then subtracting the initial recurring and nonrecurring costs of the investment. A positive NPV represents a profit, while a negative NPV signifies a loss.

To calculate the NPV of a security equipment acquisition proposal, the formula shown in Equation 9-11 is used.

$$NPV = \text{Present Value Savings} - \text{Present Value TCO}$$

Equation 9-11 *Net Present Value*

The following example continues the firewall example from earlier in this chapter to show the NPV:

Step 1. Calculate the present value of TCO—Table 9-11 illustrates that the present value of TCO over three years would be $36,230.

Step 2. Calculate the present value of money saved by having avoided attacks—Table 9-12 illustrates that the present value of money saved over three years would be $39,776. This value is based on yearly upgrades to software to provide constant protection.

Table 9-12 *Present Value of Money Saved for Departmental Firewall[1]*

Year	Discount Factor When Discount Rate Is 10%	Cost Not Incurred (Money Saved by Not Being Attacked)[2]	Present Value of Money Saved
1	0.909	$16,000	$14,544
2	0.826	$16,000	$13,216
3	0.751	$16,000	$12,016
Total savings	—	$48,000	$39,776

[1]If the firewall were not consistently upgraded, the year-over-year savings would likely be less, because a firewall must be current to protect efficiently. For example, while the savings in year 1 would be $16,000, the potential savings could drop by a third each subsequent year, because lack of updates implies less potential protection.

[2]Cash flow represents estimated savings—costs not incurred. It is estimated that without a departmental firewall, the company could have experienced information theft averaging $16,000. The company determined this figure by estimating that the average theft would cost $80,000 and that the probability of theft occurring was 20%. It is recognized that objective numbers can be difficult to find, let alone support; the authors recommend that business proposals use the data published in the CSI/FBI annual report.

Step 3. Calculate the net present value of cash flow when investing in a firewall—Apply the values to the NPV formula shown in Equation 9-12.

NPV = Present Value Saving – Present Value TCO

NPV = $39,776 – $36,230 = **$3,546**

Equation 9-12 *Example of NPV Calculations of a Firewall*

NPV Example Bringing All the Elements Together (Alternate Method)

Table 9-13, which arrives at the same results as the previous NPV example, illustrates the NPV of the investment where TCO and savings are included in present value.

Table 9-13 *Net Present Value of Investing in a Firewall*

Year	Discount Factor When Discount Rate Is 10%	Cash Flow (Without Present Value Considered)	Present Value of Cash Flow
Year 0–3 TCO	—	∠$38,800	∠$36,230
Year 1 savings	0.909	+$16,000	+$14,544
Year 2 savings	0.826	+$16,000	+$13,216
Year 3 savings	0.751	+$16,000	+$12,016
Total	—	$9,200	$3,546 (NPV)

Both examples demonstrate that the NPV of the investment is positive, and therefore the recommendation is to invest in a firewall.

In the previous examples, the NPV calculations were determined using costs savings culled from the CSI/FBI statistics.

In a new example, Equation 9-13 presents annual costs savings (ALE) from purchasing an intrusion detection system (IDS) for a web server segment to prevent DoS attacks (from figures calculated earlier in the chapter).

ALE = single loss expectancy (SLE) x annualized rate of occurrence (ARO)
ALE DoS = SLE DoS X ARO DoS
ALE DoS = $158,400 X 40% = $63,360

Equation 9-13   *Annual Savings for IDS on Web Server Segment Example*

Table 9-14 shows the NPV using this ALE, considering a DoS attack on this web server segment.

Table 9-14   *Net Present Value of Investing in an IDS*

Year	Discount Factor When Discount Rate Is 10%	Cash Flow	Present Value of Cash Flow
Year 0–3 TCO	—	∠$32,000*	∠$32,000*
Year 1 savings	0.909	+$63,360	+$57,594
Year 2 savings	0.826	+$63,360	+$52,335
Year 3 savings	0.751	+$63,360	+$47,583
Total	—	$158,080	$125,512 (NPV)

*For the purpose of this example, the present value TCO of a network-based IDS was estimated at $32,000.

Calculating NPV provides a view of the required cash flow that is stated in current, or today's, dollars. When the present value of the savings is not considered, the value of an IDS system appears to be $158,080. By using present value to calculate the TCO and potential savings, the net present value becomes $125,512.

Internal Rate of Return

Internal rate of return (IRR) can be viewed as a sort of go/no-go decision level for an investment proposal. IRR is often used to analyze investments that span over many years. IRR is similar to NPV in that IRR equals the discount rate by which the net benefits must be discounted, over the time period, until the point that they equal the initial costs. Table 9-15 provides a simplistic example of IRR.

Table 9-15   *Internal Rate of Return: Firewall with a 3-Year Useful Life*

| Year | Cash Flow | 10% Discount Rate | | 12% Discount Rate | | 15% Discount Rate | |
		Discount Factor	Present Value	Discount Factor	Present Value	Discount Factor	Present Value
Year 0–3 TCO	∠$38,800	—	∠$36,230	—	∠$36,230	—	∠$36,230
Year 1 savings	+$16,000	0.909	+$14,544	0.893	+$14,288	0.870	$13,920
Year 2 savings	+$16,000	0.826	+$13,216	0.797	+$12,752	0.756	$12,096
Year 3 savings	+$16,000	0.751	+$12,016	0.712	+$11,392	0.658	$10,528
Total	$9,200	—	$3,546 (NPV)	—	$2,202 (NPV)	—	$314 (NPV)

Table 9-15 illustrates that the cost of capital would have to be less than about 15% to make the financial investment in a firewall feasible over a three-year period, which is typically considered the useful life of corporate networking equipment. That assumes losses would be no greater than $16,000 per year. (Estimating that an attack would cost $80,000, and that chances of falling victim to such an attack were 20% per year, derived savings of $16,000.) The CSI/FBI reports figures that are higher; therefore, firewalls, particularly at the perimeter of a network, can be a wise investment.

Return on Investment

Return on investment (ROI) is a reliable tool that is widely used to compare the attractiveness of various business investments. ROI equals the present value of the net benefits over the useful life of the proposed equipment, divided by the TCO of the equipment. It is usually expressed as a percentage over a specific amount of time; three years is a common timespan for IT equipment. The ROI formula is shown in Equation 9-14.

$$ROI = \frac{PV\ Savings - PV\ TCO}{PV\ TCO}$$

Equation 9-14   ROI Calculation

The following example illustrates the ROI for the firewall from previous examples. All savings and costs are shown in present values in Equation 9-15.

$$ROI = \frac{PV\ Savings - PV\ TCO}{PV\ TCO}$$

PV Savings = $39,776 (from Table 9-12)
PV TCO = $36,230 (from Table 9-11)

$$ROI = \frac{\$39,776 - \$36,230}{\$36,230} = \mathbf{9.79\%}$$

Equation 9-15   Example of ROI Calculations for a Firewall

While ROI relates the percent return expected from a particular project, it does not specify the magnitude of the project. This begs the question "Would a 20% return on a $10,000 project be better than a 10% return on a $50,000 project?" NPV would be a superior source for that type of comparison criteria.

Payback Period

Payback period states how long it will take an investment to recoup initial funds and show a profit, a significant element when time and cash flow are an issue. The payback period formula is shown in Equation 9-16.

$$Payback\ Period = \frac{PV\ TCO}{Annual\ Net\ Savings}$$

Where Annual Net Savings = Total PV Savings/years

Equation 9-16   Payback Period Formula

Equation 9-17 illustrates the payback period of a firewall.

(251)

Premises:
PV TCO = $36,230
Total PV savings = $39,766
Years = 3
Annual Net Savings = $13,259

Payback Calculations:
Payback Period = $\dfrac{\text{PV TCO}}{\text{Annual Net Savings}}$

Payback Period = $\dfrac{\$36,230}{\$13,259}$

Payback Period = **2.73 years (2 years 9 months)**

Equation 9-17   *Example of Payback Period Calculations of a Firewall*

While payback is simple to calculate, its drawback is that it does not sufficiently illustrate the magnitude of the savings, nor does it highlight any benefits the investment could provide after the break-even point.

The Bottom Line

This chapter presents a number of financial methods IT managers can use to fiscally rationalize their security investment proposals. Each process has its own unique limitations, not the least of which is the challenge of attempting to derive a return, a discount rate, or a present value from an event not occurring.

IT security is a relatively young industry. Most established industries have a wealth of actuarial data that has been amassed over decades. The security field relies on recent data, culled from concerned IT and business professionals who cut a wide swath across industry and government and whose common goal is to create a forum for sharing this pertinent data.

IRR and NPV bring unequalled value to financial modeling, but given the specific nature of IT security investing, it is the view of the authors that ROI, or return on security investment (ROSI), is the most appropriate vehicle to ensure the effective development of an informed and substantive business case for network security. But no single method is perfect for assessing security capital budgeting.

What cannot be disputed, whether the source is CSI/FBI, PWC-UK, or any other well-regarded resource, is that cyber-crime is on the rise, and the risk to industry, both in dollars and reputation, must be measured by every organization before any long-term plan can be put in place.

Acknowledging Nonmathematical Security Fundamentals

Much of the discussion in this book has centered on why, how, where, and what to secure. But the question of when to secure is somewhat more elusive. Financial modeling can dictate that the time for security is when it is financially feasible. Managers might say that the time for greater security in when something is relevant to secure. But much of what is protected in IT security is not always tangible, for example, customer relationships, trust, goodwill, and the sanctity of data that supports each entry on a financial statement.

Organizations are highly exposed to the vulnerabilities inherent in Internet connectivity, and the exposure increases every day as viruses become more virulent and users neglect to exercise ever-greater caution. Moving away from the Internet is not an option for most organizations. Competitiveness demands an ever-increasing presence, and therefore reliance, on all things electronic. But many organizations have grown much larger by using their reliance on the Internet, as the face of business transactions has changed dramatically over the last generation. In her article in *iQ magazine*, Kathy Harris identifies ten categories of potential value that businesses can realize by virtue of being connected to the Internet: from quick time to market, new revenue streams, improved customer service, and greater process effectiveness to the creation of intellectual capital, greater asset utilization, and better connectivity with partners and vendors. The argument is made that softer benefits resulting from the newfound reliance on the Internet are difficult to quantify, yet going backward cannot be an option. She goes on to state that, ". . . creating value propositions always requires a certain amount of qualitative judgment."[2]

The financial modeling in this chapter should be fully used and effectively presented. But in the end, IT security is far greater than the mere sum of its parts.

Summary

This chapter explored various options IT managers can use when developing a business case for network security. Certain financial tools, such as IRR and NPV, are appropriate for situations that can deliver tangible results, for example, the benefits derived from installing a new customer relations management software system. The benefits resulting from the new software can be reflected in a multitude of ways, from an increased level of calls handled in a call center to fewer people required to perform the same amount of work.

But given the intangible elements that are inherent in IT security investing, ROSI is presented as the most apt vehicle to deliver measurable results.

Comprehensive metrics are not yet available to perform empirical financial analyses for IT security. But items in the public domain, such as the CSI/FBI annual surveys and the PWC UK biannual surveys, serve to provide a compelling argument for the need for greater security. Chances of attack are no longer negligible and, should one strike, the ramifications can be potentially severe. But moving away from Internet connectivity is not an option for most organizations, because the benefits realized from online interactivity far outweigh the downside risks.

This chapter explored the following topics:

- An examination of the cost of attacks

- A process of budgeting for security equipment

- An analysis of security capital investments returns

- An exploration of nonmathematical security fundamentals

End Notes

[1]"Computer Crime and Security Survey 2003." Computer Security Institute and Federal Bureau of Investigation (CSI/FBI). www.gocsi.com/forms/fbi/pdf.jhtml.

[2]Harris, K. "Eye on results, a renewed focus on metrics helps companies invest more strategically—and wisely." *Cisco iQ magazine.* November/December 2002.

PART III

POLICIES AND FUTURE

CHAPTER 10

ESSENTIAL ELEMENTS OF SECURITY POLICY DEVELOPMENT

Security policies ensure that effective security measures are implemented correctly and consistently across an organization. Security policies determine which hard, soft, tangible, and intangible assets need to be protected—and how to protect them.

They further ensure that monies invested in equipment and training personnel are properly used and aptly deployed.

Effective security policy formulation provides a comprehensive framework that employees can use to reduce inadvertent errors that could compromise a system. The establishment of rules can aid organizations in their attempt to protect against poor software configuration, weak password formation, careless users, inadequate system monitoring, unapplied patches, and a raft of other similarly harmful conditions. In addition, security policies can be very effective when paired with business continuity, or continuity of operations (CoOP), plans. These policies can be used to address an array of potential issues ranging from security threats to natural disasters.

Effective security should act as a business enabler, allowing a corporation to pursue its mandate in a secure environment. When formulating security policies, it is important to acknowledge that organizations, even those operating in the same field, are rarely alike. Structure, network, risk tolerance, and general approach to commerce always differ markedly, necessitating the construction of unique procedures for every firm.

All policies, whether they govern security or direct an accounting process, need to represent the natural flow of work rather than attempt to direct it. If a policy is overly restrictive, it can become counterintuitive, as users blatantly work around the policy to perform functions as they see fit.

This chapter considers the following topics:

- Determining required policies
- Constructing reliable and sound policies
- Using policy tools and policy implementation considerations
- Performing comprehensive monitoring
- Knowing policy types
- Handling incidents

Determining Required Policies

While the type of business an organization is engaged in can influence its required security posture, the equipment it uses is typically the determining factor that governs policy content. An organization that is solely hard-wired throughout its operation, and does not allow remote access, can find policy formulation to be relatively straightforward. Organizations that are using some form of wireless technology, along with remote access, VPNs, DMZ servers, and a variety of associated equipment, need wider-ranging policies to address each specific technology and major appliance.

When developing policies, efficiency can be gained by incorporating future system expansion into existing procedures. For example, if a company does not currently use VPNs but is considering implementing them within the next 24 months, including a generic policy on VPNs might avoid having to return to the task of policy formulation after new equipment is installed.

Whether policy is developed for existing equipment or the organization has integrated its future expansion plans into current procedures, developing separate policies for major equipment is the most comprehensive way to protect the organization. Every piece of equipment is unique; certain appliances allow users specific access, while others keep users at bay. Regardless of the device or process function, determining procedures for each device or process ensures that parameters are respected and rules enforced.

Constructing Reliable and Sound Policies

Policies should be a logical representation of practices that are inherent in an organization. They should also hold users to a high standard, ensuring that company property and resources are appropriately respected. Policies should consider the following areas:

- Reliability
- Access
- Constancy
- Answerability

Reliability

Policies should provide reliability, ensuring that, as an example, no person or equipment can tamper with a database. Individuals must be able to trust data that is sent or presented and not have to question its reliability. Alternately, when examining a bank balance, the reader must be assured that the data reflected on a ledger is wholly accurate and not be concerned that 0s might have been added or deleted.

Reliability dictates a process whereby users can be assured of content.

Access

Controlling access ensures that only those users specifically authorized for certain functions can access them. It also ensures that data is protected during transmission and that it cannot be read or manipulated while en route.

When data is received at its destination, access ensures that it can only be read or accessed by the authorized recipient.

Constancy

Constancy ensures that data is available when it is needed. Should a system be brought down by a security threat, constancy ensures both backup reliability and data integrity. For example, if a primary server were to fail, a secondary server would step in immediately and resume service, without concern for loss of data or databases.

Answerability

Log analyses must be maintained and checked regularly to uncover irregularities as early as possible. While it can be an enormous task to manually check logs, systems can be programmed to highlight significant events, such as file deletions or modifications, resulting in users being accountable for the actions they take. It also ensures that a system administrator can be quickly directed to examine a potential problem area.

Answerability ensures that a system can do the following:

- Point to the user or PC that accessed a file

- Pinpoint the time of day the target was accessed

- Detail any actions that might have been carried out

Using Policy Tools and Policy Implementation Considerations

Tools are available on the market that can aid in policy formulation. Equally fundamental is proper implementation of new policies. This section considers the following topics:

- Useful policy tools

- Policy implementation

Useful Policy Tools

It is always beneficial to deconstruct an organization to get a thorough understanding of what might be required to protect both its equipment and personnel.

The advent of user-friendly policy development tools can aid organizations in the development of security polices, or the tools can simply serve as a basis for discussion, ensuring that a security committee has not overlooked significant areas. While a number of such tools are available on the market, one example is *Information Security Policies Made Easy* (http://www.informationshield.com/ ispmemain.htm). The tools can prompt the policy formulators to describe the company network in the following terms:

- State the number of users

- State the type of equipment currently residing on the network

- Describe the password process in place

- State whether the company has a DMZ server

- List remote offices or other remote users

- State the type of remote access currently used, such as VPN

- State whether wireless technology is being used

- List external connections to partners

- State whether the company is using IP telephony

- Determine further pertinent questions to ascertain the current situation

After questions are answered, policies appropriate to the organization's current posture are presented. The policies can be implemented, or a security steering committee could use them as tools to initiate pertinent discussion among committee members.

Policy Implementation

If a policy reflects a new technology, sufficient training must be conducted prior to implementation. For example, if a VPN is being installed, users require effective training prior to installation to avoid unnecessary downtime. Relevant IT staff must be pretrained as well.

Prior to a policy being formalized, offline testing should ensure that it fully addresses the situation for which it was created. White-hat hackers, which are independent auditors trained to look for vulnerabilities, can be used to perform an assessment of the test environment. They create a situation and then record how the process played out, asking the following questions:

- Did IT discover the white-hat hacking?

- How long did it take IT to realize the system was under attack?

- How far into the system did the white-hat hackers get before being noticed?

- Were the security holes plugged?

A report can quickly summarize areas that need to be addressed. For example, if certain staff members were not immediately notified of an attack, the report might highlight a number of potential issues, as follows:

- A file containing pertinent names and phone numbers is not readily available.

- CD-ROMs with OSs and patches are not readily available.

- Pertinent staff are not comfortable with the battle stations they are expected to assume when in crisis mode.

These items can be quickly remedied, but sometimes they need to be highlighted and rectified before wide-scale implementation.

The following additional processes are worth considering when developing policies:

- **Maintain checks and balances**—For example, the individual responsible for unearthing irregularities in logs should not also have access, or modification rights, to data-sensitive files such as payroll, R&D, or finance.

- **Limit access**—Users should not be granted any greater system or physical access than necessary to perform their jobs. Access should be granted on an as-needed basis and should be revoked when no longer required.

- **Keep users abreast of changes**—If a new policy is implemented, but users are not fully informed, issues could result. For example, if a new policy states that passwords must change every 30 days but users are not informed, they will log on the 31st day and be unable to access their accounts without creating a new password. With notice, and an explanation of the policy, users can become active participants in the process, ensuring that they construct secure passwords as scheduled.

  As another example, a new policy might dictate that backup tapes are stored by a third party, and through formal negotiation, it has been arranged that the tapes will be collected every morning at 9 a.m. But if reception personnel are not duly informed, they are unlikely to release the tapes to a courier.

Performing Comprehensive Monitoring

Security policies need to reflect the confidential nature of data and databases, along with ensuring protected access to networks and equipment. Security could be as simple as requiring a password for specific database access, or it could require two-factor authentication to use certain equipment, as described in Chapter 3, "Security Technology and Related Equipment." Regardless of the methods used, a consistent monitoring process must be established and reviewed on a continual basis, to ensure that any new equipment or measure is incorporated into procedures without delay.

The following list represents examples of key areas that can be monitored but is not meant to represent an exhaustive listing:

- **Internet access control**—Users can visit sites that can spell trouble for an organization. Alternately, the Internet can act as a magnet, diverting users' attention from their primary work responsibilities. URL filtering, as described in Chapter 3, can be used to restrict Internet access.

- **Encryption use for mobile employees**—Laptop-equipped users should ensure that stored data is encrypted, to protect the company against data theft.

- **Comprehensive virus scans**—Virus scans must be performed on all pertinent equipment, including CD-ROMs, DVDs, floppy disks, e-mail, USB keys, and so on.

- **Password sanctity**—Passwords should not only be highly protected, but they should also be changed regularly, preferably at the forced prompting of a system. They should also contain at least six characters, which can include any combination of numbers and letters. Passwords are expanded upon in the "Password Creation" Tech Tip, later in this chapter.

- **Software and hardware installation**—Software or hardware installation on workstations, laptops, servers, and other equipment should only be performed by IT staff, by IT-sanctioned employees, or by using fully automated installation tools distributed by the IT department. Because remote offices might require immediate attention, assigning one individual from every department to act as an IT advocate should ensure that users do not try to circumvent this policy.

- **Software authorization and licenses**—Only authorized and licensed software can be installed on company equipment. This policy ensures that copyrights are respected and unwanted software is not loaded onto networks. Similar to the previous point, software can only be loaded by IT personnel or their sanctioned advocates.

- **Physical security**—Physical security of equipment should conform to insurance requirements and user common sense. When traveling, equipment should be locked in a hotel room safe, placed in a locked suitcase, secured with a steel cable, stored in the trunk of a vehicle, or when in doubt, be carried.

- **Comprehensive backup data handling**—To avoid loss of data, systems should be backed up regularly and their tapes stored off-site, preferably in geographically secure locations. Third-party organizations can provide pickup and storage services.

Knowing Policy Types

Every major appliance and process should ideally have a dedicated policy. The following list is provided as an example of the types of policies an organization might have and an abbreviated accounting of what they might contain:

- Physical security policies
- Access-control policies
- Dialup and analog policies
- Remote-access policies
- Remote configuration policies
- VPN and encryption policies
- Network policies
- Data sensitivity, retention, and ethics policies
- Software policies

Physical Security Policies

These policies cover both perimeter and equipment, ensuring that physical access is limited to authorized persons.

While traveling has been discussed in both this chapter and in Chapter 5, "Policy, Personnel, and Equipment as Security Enablers," it is worthwhile to note that user common sense should ultimately prevail. When a remote user travels to the head office, as an example, equipment such as laptops should not be left unattended unless secured in a locked meeting room. When flying, laptops should always be regarded as carry-on luggage, and when parking an automobile, if the user is unsure about leaving a laptop bag in the vehicle's trunk, it should be carried with the user.

Perimeter security includes alarms on doors and windows, controlled parking facilities, fenced property, and similar types of physical deterrents. Certain hotels and prominent office towers have instituted preparking authorization. Security personnel stop users on their way into a parking facility and confirm that the driver is a registered guest of the hotel or an expected visitor to an office tower. After the visitor is approved, she can park her vehicle.

Server rooms should be locked at all times, and access to the room must be severely restricted. If a company's offices are located within an office building, the server room should be established within the office premises. If communications facilities and wiring closets are not housed within the server room, they should be treated in a similar fashion.

Access-Control Policies

Passwords are a fundamental component of access control. Encouraging users to develop passwords that are creative, thoughtful, and difficult to predict can aid in fortifying a network.

System-level passwords are typically found on administrator accounts, such as those required to configure routers. These passwords should be changed at least quarterly, although the ideal situation would be every 30 days.

User-level passwords, such as those found on desktop computers, e-mails, web access, and databases should be changed at least quarterly. But similar to system-level passwords, they are ideally changed every 30 days.

Password distribution is critical to security. It is the responsibility of each user to safely guard his or her password. But before users can be prompted to enter a password, equipment must be delivered and installed, and users must log on for the first time. At times, an initial logon password, assigned by IT when new equipment is issued to remote offices, can represent the weakest link. The initial password might be too easy to deduce: It can often be as basic as a user's name or even the month a unit was shipped to the remote office. A seemingly simple task can ultimately pose a great challenge, particularly because it is ill-advised to e-mail new passwords or to use other electronic methods for communicating them. It would be similar to leaving house keys and alarm shutoff information in full view for anyone to see; the aim of home security is to safeguard private codes so that they cannot be used for unlawful and unauthorized entry. Ensuring that passwords or password distribution is not compromised can take certain effort, and organizations that can implement an effective process to disseminate passwords can potentially avoid creating one of the weakest links in the security chain.

Tech Tip: Password Creation

Poor or weak passwords can allow effortless entry into equipment or networks. Informing users about the sanctity of passwords, both in the formation and safeguarding of them, can help to protect an organization's overall system.

Weak passwords can have the following characteristics:

- Contain less than six characters
- Contain words found in any dictionary, either foreign or English
- Use common words, such as names of pets, friends, siblings, coworkers, film characters, computer terms, computer names, Internet sites, company names, and hardware or software names.
- Use birthdays or other personal information
- Contain words or number patterns, such as aaabbb, qwerty, zyxwvuts, 123321, and so on
- Be stored online or written down

Strong passwords have the following characteristics:

- Contain words that are not found in any dictionary
- Contain no jargon
- Are not based on any type of personal information
- Have at least eight characters, consisting of numbers, letters, and punctuation
- Use uppercase and lowercase characters
- Are committed to memory

continues

Tech Tip: Password Creation (Continued)

Strong passwords can be used poorly. In particular, users should avoid the following tactics:

- Reusing an internal company password as another password for personal use, such as a personal ISP account, stock trading, 401(k) benefits access, and similar situations where personal passwords are required.

- Using personal passwords for company access.

- Using the same password for various levels of access. Each higher level of access typically requires a unique password; do not use a password for more than one application.

- Using the same password for different equipment. An IT person might have responsibility for multiple pieces of equipment, each requiring its own password. Similar to the previous point, all equipment should have unique passwords. Alternatively, if equipment supports central authentication, such as AAA that was discussed in Chapter 3, a single password that is changed frequently could be used to administer devices connected to the network.

- Sharing user passwords with anyone, including a manager.

- Revealing a password, even if prompted on official-looking forms.

- Revealing a password in an e-mail or in front of others.

- Sharing passwords with coworkers, even if a user is going to be on vacation or away from the office for an extended period.

Programs are available to validate user password choices to ensure that they are in line with company policy, prohibiting those that are deemed to be weak.

In essence, reliable password policies should stress length and character requirements, strict expiration dates, and dictionary checks and should disallow reuse of passwords.

Dialup and Analog Policies

Remote access for users should be viewed as an exception rather than a rule. While many users require remote logon capabilities, most employees do not need this type of access; it should only be granted on an as-needed basis. Reminding users that remote access can render an organization vulnerable can serve to make users far more diligent when accessing a network.

Organizations should restrict the amount of time and the type of users who are granted remote access. After access is granted, activity should be routinely checked to ensure that continued access is required. Periodic activity monitoring would also ensure that inappropriate third parties do not gain system access.

This section considers the following topics:

- War dialers
- One-time passwords
- Outgoing traffic monitoring
- Fax line use
- Dialup workstations
- Inbound dialing
- Password storing
- Strong authentication

War Dialers

War dialers are hackers who are external to a company. They use analog telephone lines in an attempt to connect to a system that has an attached modem. Automated programs continuously dial numbers until a potential target is found; when the telephone is answered, the modem-handshake signal is heard. It typically takes two to three rings before call display features reveals a caller's ID, so war dialers preset their systems to disconnect if the target has not picked up by the second ring. By disconnecting early, a hacker hopes to evade a log analysis that would reveal his identity. Alternatively, a hacker might use a caller ID block that would prevent his identity from being revealed.

A plausible protection remedy is to configure a modem so that it does not answer until the fourth ring. But this also requires that users be effectively trained, ensuring that all parties understand that the latency being built into the system is for security purposes.

One-Time Passwords

One-time passwords (OTPs) are covered extensively in Chapter 3. Establishing a rotation of OTPs can help to ensure that access is limited to authorized users.

Outgoing Traffic Monitoring

A system that logs or monitors outgoing traffic can reveal inappropriate activity. It can protect against users who might attempt to send or remove confidential data. For example, a user in an office might choose to connect a laptop to a fax line to surreptitiously send out data. Or the user might connect to the fax line, leave work, and, after being off the premises, dial into the fax line and pull confidential data out of the connected computer.

A policy that prohibits users from seeking an alternative mode to either sending or receiving data and restricts users to assigned network connections can aid in resolving this issue. Consistent log checking can handily reveal a breach of this policy.

Fax Line Use

Further to the policy that regulates monitoring of outgoing calls, a policy stating that fax lines can only be used by fax machines and never be used, for example, by networked workstations, can ensure that users do not use fax lines for dialing out and that administrators will be on the lookout for any such transgressions.

Dialup Workstations

Although less common today, dialup desktop workstations are still used by some organizations. Where they are still in use, policy must address the need to ensure that these workstations are never connected to a network.

Inbound Dialing

While not as common anymore, certain organizations still allow users to dial into the network and retrieve e-mails. When inbound calls are no longer desired, a remote-access server (RAS) can be configured to ignore incoming calls.

Password Storing

Certain systems are programmed to encourage users to store passwords in the automated logon sequence, releasing users from needing to remember the password the next time they log on. Users should refrain from the practice of saving passwords and should be instructed to bypass all prompts that might encourage them to commit passwords to the memory of the equipment. Should a laptop be stolen or an unauthorized person were to sit at a user's workstation, the unauthorized party would be able to gain immediate access to a company network, replete with all rights and privileges accorded to that user.

Strong Authentication

Two-factor authentication, often referred to as strong authentication, can help to ensure that only rightful users gain entry to a system or facility. A user is prompted to provide a username and then possibly a fob-generated password and PIN, as an example. The process, described in detail in Chapter 3, ensures that a stolen fob or smart card would be rendered useless without an accompanying PIN.

Remote-Access Policies

Users working from a remote office branch office (ROBO) or a small office home office (SOHO) can communicate using dedicated or nondedicated connections from their workplace. Access of this kind must be controlled to ensure that unauthorized persons cannot also gain entry to the company network.

Remote-access policies cover the following equipment:

- T1
- Frame Relay
- VPN access

Dedicated T1 lines and Frame Relay technologies can be used to, as an example, interconnect offices such as branch offices to head offices. Individual users connecting from hotel rooms and homes would typically use xDSL or cable technology to build a VPN tunnel, which is discussed in greater detail in the section "VPN and Encryption Policies," later in this chapter. A VPN connection builds a secure encrypted tunnel between a user and her corporate network, allowing the same access as if she were in the office.

OTP authentication, or public/private keys, as discussed in Chapter 3, should be used to ensure utmost security.

Remote Configuration Policies

System administrators require a secure environment whenever the need arises to configure or manage remote devices. They typically have the following two options:

- Secure Sockets Layer (SSL)
- Secure Shell (SSH)

Secure Sockets Layer

SSL provides point-to-point security and, as described in Chapter 3, is commonly used in financially based web transactions. SSL encrypts a session. As an example, if a financial transaction is being conducted, everything that is resident on that page is encrypted, regardless of whether it requires encrypting intensive graphics or music. A system administrator can use SSL whenever the need arises to configure devices remotely. While SSL is prudent for many applications, it does inject a certain amount of *latency,* or slowness, into a transmission.

Secure Shell

SSH also provides encryption, but rather than securing an entire session, it offers greater specificity by operating at the command line, narrowing its focus to specific applications.

In general, communication performed at the command line is typically done in a clear-text session, usually on port 23. SSH allows a particular *Telnet* stream to be encrypted; Telnet is a protocol that issues instructions at the command-line interface of a system. A secure Telnet done on port 22 allows exchanges to be encrypted, reducing the need to encrypt an entire session.

VPN and Encryption Policies

Virtual Private Networks (VPNs) allow a remote user to create a secure connection to a corporate network by forcing all traffic to and from the user's PC to go through the dedicated VPN tunnel, as opposed to going through a split tunnel.

When a VPN is in place, organizations must do the following:

- Determine users who require remote access

- Determine encryption requirements

- Determine encryption standards

- Adjust expectation levels and educate users

Determine Users Who Require Remote Access

Limiting remote access to only those users who truly require it always constitutes good policy. Local field salespeople might feel they need access, but depending on a host of variables, including the type of business an organization is engaged in, the physical location of the office, and the speed with which product or services need to be delivered, salespeople might be able to work offline to enter orders without loss of efficiency. They can download pertinent data as soon as they reach the office or e-mail the information from the client's location. Though often desired by many users, direct access is not required in all remote situations.

Determine the Maximum Time Length of Encrypted Sessions

Ideally, VPN connections should be disconnected after ten minutes of inactivity. In addition, it is prudent to predetermine a maximum amount of minutes or hours a user can be continuously connected. Limiting connections to three hours would require users to log off and reauthenticate to create a new VPN tunnel for an additional three-hour maximum.

Determine Encryption Standards

Specific protocols can be used to build a VPN tunnel, and IPSec is one of the more common ones.

When a systems administrator uses IPSec, he must decide on the strength of encryption that is required. As an example, DES (56-bit key) and 3DES (triple 56-bit key) are various strengths of encryption. 3DES is slower than DES, which results in a latency tradeoff for superior encryption. 3DES has greater encryption capability but a somewhat slower system speed. Advanced Encryption Standard (AES) is an emerging standard that is available in 128-, 192-, or 256-bit encryption.

The strength of the encryption key should be reviewed at least annually, because something better might be available or an organization might decide that it requires stronger encryption over time.

MD5 and SHA are both hash mechanisms. Hash is explained in the sidebar "Example of a Secure Data Exchange" in Chapter 3. The system administrator must also decide whether a strong, or stronger, hash is required. MD5 is strong, and SHA is stronger.

Adjust Expectation Levels and Educate Users

Users should be briefed on appropriate VPN use, ensuring that passwords or sessions are never shared and that secure connections are used only for individual requirements. Ideally, password construction should use the following:

- OTPs stored on a fob, as an example

- Two-factor authentication

Users should understand that *split tunneling* is not allowed. Split tunneling can occur when a remote user connects through a VPN to the corporate network and, while still connected, initiates a direct Internet session, which would be in clear text. Should a hacker notice the Internet communication, he might be able to access the remote laptop and secure an encrypted direct tunnel to the user's corporate network. To counter this possibility, organizations typically restrict users from opening another tunnel or deny direct communication to Internet websites when they are already connected on a VPN tunnel.

Network Policies

Establishing rules and procedures for each major appliance and network segment is prudent for an organization. Every piece of equipment is unique, and tailoring individual policies can help to ensure that critical elements are not overlooked.

This section considers the following topics:

- Router policy
- Firewall policy
- DMZ policy
- Extranet policy
- World Wide Web policy
- Wireless policy
- Server policy

Router Policy

Router policies comprise many aspects; two of the more prevalent ones are as follows:

- Access warning
- Traffic efficacy

Access Warning

Routers should post a welcome banner, sometimes referred to as an *unwelcome* banner, because it advises visitors that unauthorized entry is not allowed and that violators will be pursued and prosecuted. Most security requirements, whether physical or online, clearly state that potential violators need to be forewarned that certain actions might constitute trespassing or violation of private property. After he has been warned, the potential invader is subject to all possible ramifications should he pursue an unauthorized path.

Traffic Efficacy

A router can be used to filter incoming and outgoing traffic. Users leaving a network, for example, exiting a corporate network and going to the Internet, can be prompted to authenticate to ensure that they are allowed to leave. Because the router is usually not the preferred appliance on which to store user account and password information, the router can confirm status with the authentication server, the appliance that typically stores access-control lists, as described in Chapter 3. After authentication has occurred and approval has been granted to the router, the traffic is allowed to exit.

Firewall Policy

By default, a firewall blocks traffic that emanates from outside its network. Should a request be made to change the default behavior on a firewall, those users desiring the change should be required to seek approval from a firewall committee, who should in turn obtain approval from the security steering committee. Any change that requires a *hole* to be punched in a firewall, a process that allows certain traffic to flow in, can naturally result in the system being exposed to certain vulnerabilities.

Action of that kind should have multiple layers of approval before it can proceed.

DMZ Policy

DMZ servers, as described in Chapter 3, reside outside corporate networks. They typically act as way stations for a company's public website.

DMZ policies consider the following items:

- Working parameters
- Ownership and evolution
- Security configuration and activity requirements

Working Parameters

DMZ servers must be highly secured, but they should not be so overly protective that users struggle to gain access. Should accessing a company's public website prove to be an issue, routers or firewalls can be used to strategically control incoming DMZ server traffic.

Ownership and Evolution

Ownership of equipment and processes, as discussed in Chapter 5, plays a key role in effectively managing an organization's assets. For example, responsibility for the DMZ server must be determined. The sales department is typically the largest user of the DMZ server, and its personnel might consider the server their responsibility. But if they are not actively installing patches and inspecting the server's logs for abnormal activity, the DMZ server can represent a potential vulnerability for the organization.

All equipment, regardless of where it might reside on a network, must be assigned a rightful, responsible, and responsive owner.

An organization might find that its DMZ server evolves from its early beginnings as a simple lookup tool to one that now includes a database that accepts purchase orders and sends out confirmations. The more an appliance does, in particular a DMZ server, the greater is its exposure and potential vulnerability.

Security Configuration and Activity Requirements

Equipment needs to be configured appropriately to ensure that it achieves its optimal security level. The programming can be done directly on the appliance, or it can be done remotely. Detailed information on DMZ servers must be kept at the ready in case urgent situations arise. DMZ servers face greater exposure, and the ability to act quickly and decisively is of utmost importance.

Certain other information should also be readily available to ensure ease and speed of operability, including host contacts and location, hardware, operating system and its respective version, and any departmental users that might have privileged or department-wide passwords.

A system that either checks for patches or automatically notifies the system administrator and her alternate regarding pertinent equipment patches should be established. Equally important, patches should be applied as soon as they become available.

Extranet Policy

Organizations use extranets to share information with clients, suppliers, and other pertinent parties. This method can permit real-time sharing of data that can aid, for example, in keeping production lines running smoothly on just-in-time programs. While third parties are not allowed direct access to corporate networks, organizations need to address certain vulnerabilities. Trust exploitation, as described in Chapter 2, "Crucial Need for Security: Vulnerabilities and Attacks," represents an example of a possible infiltration point.

Extranet policy includes the following topics:

- Business justification
- Security approval review
- Extranet connectivity

Business Justification

Users desire any function that can create an environment where it might be easier to do business. From using an extranet that systematically feeds a just-in-time production-line program to using one as a simple tool to effortlessly connect a company with its suppliers and customers, a multitude of programs can be successfully deployed. Using these programs and needing them can represent two distinct arguments, neither of which necessarily constitutes business justification.

Proposals should clearly illustrate cost savings, inventory reduction, and productivity improvements that can be realized by the introduction of a particular extranet. A strong business case must exist for a company to increase its exposure and devote IT resources to creating additional extranets.

Security Approval Review

Security reviews should be conducted prior to an extranet being approved. While an extranet might prove highly productive for a sales department or production facility, the inherent vulnerability in making an extranet available might prove too great for a particular network. Other options might be explored. Passing every proposal before a security review committee ensures that an organization can measure its risk and, where appropriate, offer alternate solutions.

Extranet Connectivity

An extranet security policy needs to address how independent organizations connect with one another. While dedicated links continue to be the preferred mode of connection, VPN tunnels, as discussed in the section "Adjust Expectation Levels and Educate Users," earlier in this chapter, can help organizations communicate safely. Regardless of the connection mode that might be used by companies, minimum levels of protection must be agreed upon before any connection is initiated. Similar levels of protection can help to ensure that hackers cannot easily use the connection as a springboard to hack any of the participating networks.

World Wide Web Policy

URL filtering, described in detail in Chapter 3, can aid an organization in limiting its users' access to the Internet, along with limiting its potential for legal liabilities. Whether an organization invests in access-filtering tools or trusts that its users will not visit particular types of sites, users must know, in formal policy, what constitutes unacceptable Internet browsing.

Stock market trading, retail, pornography, gambling, and a variety of other sites might be unacceptable for an organization. Users should be told to use their judgment, and when in doubt, they should not venture onto unknown sites.

With or without URL filtering, user common sense, backed by clear policy, should always prevail.

Wireless Policy

A wireless policy should cover the following points:

- Installation of wireless access points
- Wireless testing
- Encryption between computers and access points
- Preconfigured MAC addresses
- Cryptic SSID usage
- Wireless end user authentication

Installation of Wireless Access Points

Access points (APs), also referred to as wireless hubs, need to be strictly controlled so that users cannot install their own hubs. Wireless APs are widely available, and certain users might be tempted to install a hub so that they can roam the office and maintain a network connection. Completely oblivious to the potential back doors that could be created, users look to install retail-type hubs to increase personal productivity.

Ensuring that unlawful hub installation is strictly forbidden and that the message is widely disseminated to all users by policy can help to ensure that rogue access points cannot be created and penetrated.

Wireless Testing

A policy stipulating the periodic testing of wireless APs is critical to ensure that unauthorized hubs have not been installed on a network or that existing ones have not been unlawfully penetrated.

White-hat hackers can be used to perform these independent tests.

Encryption Between Computers and Access Points

Wireless communication, by default, occurs in clear text. Wired Equivalent Privacy (WEP) is the most common encryption standard for wireless communication. WEP provides wireless point-to-point encryption between access points and computers, or from access point to access point.

Preconfigured MAC Addresses

A concern in wireless environments is that a hacker could station himself outside a window and connect to the corporate network, as described in Chapter 2. Traffic would flow from a hub in the building to the hacker's laptop, located outside the building.

System administrators can incorporate solutions into the policy to mitigate this type of threat. As an example, by storing directly on the wireless hub the MAC address of each NIC that is allowed to communicate with it, the hub cannot allow an unknown NIC to enter the network, effectively negating the efforts of the wily hacker—notwithstanding the hacker having been able to snoop the MAC address of a valid workstation and impersonate it when it was offline. NIC and MAC addresses are described in detail in Chapter 3.

Cryptic SSID Usage

Wireless hubs operate in assigned areas, and any wireless appliances residing in a hub's vicinity, typically laptops and wireless accessories, connect to that AP. A hub can be configured to accept wireless connections from equipment or MAC addresses that it recognizes. Service set identifier (SSID) provides a unique name to identify an access point.

Systems administrators typically prefer to configure a wireless hub by geographic location. For example, if the marketing department were located in building 2 on the fourth floor, a hub's unique name might be 4thFloorB2-XYCorp. All wireless cards that want to connect exclusively on that access point would need to be configured with that SSID information.

The issue with naming such explicit geographic locations is that a hub broadcasts its availability every few seconds. Wanting to avoid any chance of giving a hacker such detailed information, system administrators can name APs using a cryptic mode. The earlier example of 4thFloorB2-XYCorp could follow a policy requiring it to be named in a more explicit fashion that is even less revealing: 4thFloorSBNE. The fourth floor would remain the same; building 2 is (building) site B, with B representing the number 2, and NE represents the northeast corner of the fourth floor of building 2. Its location has been made even more precise, while the company's name has been excluded from the hub's SSID.

Wireless End User Authentication

To effectively limit access to a corporate network, a wireless policy should include rules regarding the authentication specifics that are required from users who connect wirelessly. The policy should address the authentication standard, such as Extensible Authentication Protocol (EAP), implementation, and maintenance requirements. The policy should specify the authentication that is required to thoroughly address the following:

- Who is allowed entry
- When they are allowed to enter
- What network resources they should be able to access

Server Policy

Server policy procedures contain the following strict guidelines for use and handling:

- Contact and location
- Operational data
- Patches
- Trust relationship between systems
- Physical access
- Activities and events

Contact and Location

Preparing for unknown and unforeseen circumstances requires an IT department to follow a policy of compiling a comprehensive listing of all equipment under its command, with an emphasis on its various servers. Included on each list should be the following items:

- Server type
- Server location
- Person responsible for the server (its owner)
- Alternate person responsible for the server

Should an issue ever arise, early moments will not be lost trying to determine the best person to call.

Operational Data

All components related to the successful operation of a server should be kept at the ready, ensuring that any upgrades or patches can be implemented easily and that any possible changes in staffing will not have an adverse effect on maintenance and servicing of equipment.

Pertinent information for each server can be documented in its own binder. The information contained can run from the benign (for example, informing a new systems administrator that regular maintenance is performed in the overnight hours) to the more complex, by developing a set of strict guidelines to ensure business continuity, such as a provision for bringing a backup server online. The binder can include the following items:

- Software loaded on the server
- Pertinent appliances attached to the server
- Hardware version
- Operating system version
- Main functions and applications, where applicable
- Configuration restrictions, if applicable
- CD-ROMs of operating system
- CD-ROMs of patches
- CD-ROMs of all applications

Any updates or changes to the corporate enterprise management system should be kept current in the binder.

Patches

Security patches should be installed within a set time frame after the company has been notified of their availability. Notifications can be automatic and are available from a variety of service vendors or organizations, such as CERT and SANS (http://www.sans.org).

It can be difficult to know which patches might be vitally important and which ones can wait. Too often, the most benign-looking patches can be the most important ones. A policy that ensures that all available patches are responded to in a predetermined timely fashion continues to be the most prudent course to follow.

Should demands on a systems administrator's work load prove too great, numerous third-party services specialize in servicing patches for organizations.

Trust Relationship Between Systems

Trust relationships that exist between various pieces of equipment must be periodically inspected to ensure not only that a trust has not been violated but also that the relationship is still required. For example, an organization might use two servers to handle its sales functions. One server stores customer names, and the other processes new purchase orders, customer returns, and customer rescheduling. A routine check can ensure that a trust that exists between the two servers has not been breached. Just as importantly, it can determine whether some degree of the relationship is still required. In an attempt to improve service levels, the second server might have been preloaded with all pertinent customer information, negating the need for it to retrieve any information from the first server.

A periodic system review, in addition to using host-based IDSs, can serve as a check and balance, ensuring that unneeded vulnerabilities are routinely revealed and that potential security risks are limited to those that are truly required.

Physical Access

Servers should be located in secure environments, preferably locked rooms that guarantee highly restricted access. Should an unauthorized person ever gain entry, the ability to wreak havoc by bringing down a web server, as an example, is quite real.

Server room security is so great for certain organizations that air vents leading to a server room are secured; air is allowed to flow, but a person cannot maneuver undetected in the venting system.

Securing servers and restricting access are prudent points to pursue.

Activities and Events

Server activity should be monitored to ensure that any untoward behavior is summarily uncovered. Logs should be reviewed to examine which files have been deleted and by whom. If an activity appears unusual, it can be quickly investigated, and if a problem exists, it can be remedied early, before even greater damage can be inflicted.

All security-related events should be reported immediately, and depending on the nature of the supposed breach, an escalation path should be predetermined to deal with every type of incident.

Data Sensitivity, Retention, and Ethics Policies

A policy that addresses the inherent responsibilities of employees and considers an organization's handling of confidential data, e-file retention, and employee conduct would take into account the following items:

- Employee vigilance
- Public and confidential information
- E-mail maintenance
- Employee conduct

Employee Vigilance

Staff members are required to act responsibly at all times, whether they are carrying out their required job functions or ensuring that passwords are always kept private and protected.

Security requires vigilance on the part of users; confidential documents used as part of a presentation, as an example, should never be left unattended in a conference room. Laptops should always be safely secured when not in use, and if a secure place does not exist to store a laptop, the user should carry it with her. Thorough security requires that users employ common sense in their daily activities, affording company assets the same respect as they would their own property.

Public and Confidential Information

Information typically falls into one of two categories: public or confidential. Rules for accessing, distributing, and storing both types should be clearly defined. This policy, typically called data classification, should state how an organization determines the following items:

- Public information
- Confidential information
- Accessing information
- Distributing information
- Storing and disposing of information
- Disclosing confidential information

Public Information

Public information is typically defined as information that can be freely given to anyone, without the giver incurring any possible repercussions. The information might include company literature, pamphlets, sales and marketing tools, public financial reports, and similar widely disseminated offerings.

Confidential Information

Confidential information is usually labeled accordingly, but it also requires users' common sense to realize when particular information might be considered private. An internal telephone directory might not be labeled confidential, but it is generally understood that it should never be disseminated outside an office.

Persons who are privy to private conversations instinctively know never to reveal information that is integral to a company's success, such as trade secrets, private financial data, future plans, and similar pertinent data.

While common sense and respect are key elements when maintaining confidences, organizations can include a statement in their policy indicating that any persons who knowingly breach company confidential information can be prosecuted to the full extent of the law in the jurisdiction in which they are employed.

Accessing Information

The ability to access confidential information should be clearly defined. If material is meant for specific individuals, e-mailing it can ensure that a user would require a network password to access, at minimum, his or her e-mail account. A file attached to an e-mail can be secured with an additional password, ensuring that only the rightful owner could open the document. Encryption, another option, is discussed in the section "VPN and Encryption Policies," earlier in this chapter.

If information is *company-wide confidential*, meaning that it is company confidential but meant for all users, an organization might post it on its intranet, ensuring that a user would need to sign on with a network password to access the information.

Information that is deemed public could be posted on a company's public Internet site.

The confidential policy should also stipulate who in the organization has the authority to change security classifications, such as downgrading a document from confidential to public.

Distributing Information

Sensitive documents distributed through interoffice mail can be well served with a process similar to that used by registered mail, ensuring that the recipient, or his or her agent, signs for the envelope and that the sender receives acknowledgment of said acceptance.

Private documents forwarded by e-mail could use encryption, ensuring that only the intended receiver could decipher it, as described in the section "File Encryption" in Chapter 3.

Storing and Disposing of Information

Confidential documents can be stored in a password-protected e-mail account or a password-protected server. Hard-copy documents can be stored in a locked file cabinet that, depending on the nature of the confidential note, can be located in a locked access-controlled room.

Disposal of documents should be handled appropriately. Physical documents need to be shredded by equipment that renders material unreadable, ensuring that it is impossible to reconstruct a document. Hard drives should be sanitized before they are disposed of, ensuring that private information is unrecoverable.

Disclosing Confidential Information

Users should be fully cognizant of the ramifications that could ensue should confidential documents be exposed, regardless of whether it is intentional or inadvertent. Should a corporation identify specific documents to be confidential, the organization must inform its users of the following:

- What are the confidential classifications
- What each classification demands
- What is required of each user
- What consequences might ensue should confidentiality be breached

By recognizing the fundamental importance of company confidentiality, employees can understand the underlying logic that supports the labeling and be in a better position to ensure that confidentiality remains intact.

E-Mail Maintenance

E-mail messages should be assigned classifications, enabling users to prioritize them appropriately. Low, normal, high, private, confidential, and other similar terms connote the sender's intent, but they should be applied within the strict guidelines of corporate policy to ensure consistency and respect for content.

When confidential information is sent through e-mail, it should be signed and encrypted using a standard such as Signed Multipurpose Internet Mail Extensions (S/MIME), a protocol that was initially developed by a private consortium of vendors. Later versions are available today. S/MIME allows users to send almost any type of file or document in an e-mail message, including text, images, audio, video, and so on.

Many guides are available that suggest the length of time a company should retain e-mails. The Sysadmin, Audit, Network, and Security (SANS) Institute makes the following recommendations:

- Administrative correspondence: 4 years

- Fiscal correspondence: 4 years

- General correspondence: 1 year

- Informational correspondence: Discard after reading

When in doubt, or if dictated by law, policies can span longer periods of time to ensure that comprehensive recordkeeping is maintained.

Employee Conduct

Ethics play a major role in every organization. Policies regarding ethics enable users to know what constitutes acceptable behavior on their part and, just as importantly, how they should expect to be treated.

Most organizations seek to create dynamic cultures that are steeped in the following:

- Respect for others, including fellow employees, management, clients, and stakeholders

- Openness, providing a forum for candid dialogue

- Empowerment, allowing employees to achieve their potentials

- Trust, ensuring that employees share in the most sacred of trusts: respect for company property, both intellectual and physical, and organization-wide focus, knowing that the entire team is pulling in the same direction

- Integrity, in achieving both individual targets and company-wide goals, by acting and excelling within the spirit of company policy

Setting expectations can aid individuals in achieving their best.

Software Policies

Software policy can be further divided into the following three subgroups:

- Operating system policy
- Virus protection policy
- User software policy

Operating System Policy

An organization must strive to have a similar operating system across its entire structure. In an urgent situation, IT must be able to service the network as a whole, and if network segments are radically different from one another, or if IT is not aware of various installations, the ability to combat a given issue can be slowed.

An organization might decide, for example, that all workstations need to be equipped with the same operating system and that all software copies need to be of the same version. Servicing, particularly if performed under any type of duress, would be infinitely more efficient in that type of environment.

Virus Protection Policy

Safe computing requires that every user exercise common sense and thoughtfulness in his daily routine. A presentation outlining particular actions that could potentially compromise a system might help users act more thoughtfully and responsibly.

Virus protection policy could include the following rules for users:

- Never block a virus update that is attempting to run.
- Always follow the preventative procedures set forth by the antivirus provider.
- Never open e-mails from unknown sources.
- Always double-delete suspect e-mails (see the "Double Delete" Tech Tip).
- Never open attachments that are remotely suspect.
- Never respond to junk mail or chain mail.

- Never unsubscribe to an e-mail service that you never subscribed to initially.

- Never download files from suspicious sources.

- Always scan files pulled from floppy disks, CD-ROMs, USB keys, and other similar media.

Tech Tip: Double Delete

Double delete refers to a process that a user can employ to permanently delete an e-mail that he had previously deleted from the Inbox folder of his e-mail software. Specifically, when a user deletes an e-mail from his Inbox folder, he has only moved it to the Delete folder of his e-mail software. To truly delete an e-mail, the user must first locate his Delete folder, select the particular e-mail, and then delete the e-mail from the Delete folder.

By thoughtfully using known policy procedures and responsible common sense in their daily routines, users can ensure that unknown and potentially unsafe files and attachments containing hidden viruses are not allowed to inadvertently infiltrate a company network. It would be challenging to list every possible action that could potentially make a system needlessly vulnerable to attack, which is why the term *common sense* has been used throughout this chapter. Similar to citizens who are required to act within the spirit of a particular law, common sense makes it incumbent upon users to act within the spirit of a company's security policy, regardless of whether a rule is specifically stated.

User Software Policy

User software policy considers the following items:

- Installation policy
- Database policy
- E-mail policy

Installation Policy

Much has been discussed about rogue equipment being installed on networks. Installing rogue software on operating systems is also not acceptable. A policy that ensures that only IT, or IT-sanctioned, staff are permitted to install software is highly advised.

Database Policy

An organization typically applies certain rules to its processes. For example, a rule might state that databases are stored on separate or dedicated servers and that each server requires multiple authentication processes to be accessed. If one server were ever compromised, a hacker wouldn't necessarily have access to its information if he didn't possess all the requisite passwords. If user accounts must be stored on the same server as the database, the user and password file should be either password protected or better encrypted.

Passwords should always conform to corporate policy rather than relying on what might be suggested in a software manual.

E-Mail Policy

E-mail policies should convey acceptable and unacceptable user behavior. They are subdivided into the following categories:

- Access
- Vigilance
- Content
- Confidentiality

Access A policy that addresses e-mail access from hand-held devices and other remote methods, such as webmail, should be developed. Many organizations consider this type of access to be lacking in security and are loathe to allow it.

Vigilance E-mail usage has become an issue in many organizations. Users are continually bombarded with spam e-mails that attempt to sell everything from sports equipment to pornography and everything in between. While much of it is a nuisance, and some of it rather objectionable, certain e-mail attachments can contain viruses. The hapless e-mail reader is often so bombarded with e-mails that he just rifles through his inbox, clicking on each one in an effort to get through them quickly. Many network issues could be avoided with a certain amount of vigilant policy enforcement on the part of users. Stopping viruses at the gate and refusing them entry onto a corporate network would go a long way in helping to forge a security posture that is increasingly more secure.

Content An organization needs to ensure that its users understand its philosophy on e-mail etiquette. Distributing the formal policy to users the moment they join a company can ensure that each user is fully cognizant of the firm's expectations. A policy should consider addressing the firm's stance on the following issues:

- Sexual matters, from orientation to pornography
- Religious matters
- Proper use of language, in particular, undesirable slang words
- Political messages
- Gender and race messages
- Disability comments
- Anything that could be construed to be offensive to another individual

While organizations might want to acknowledge that a certain amount of personal e-mail use is acceptable, it should make clear that the system is monitored and that users should have no expectation of privacy. Should privacy be required, users should send and receive e-mails from their homes.

Confidentiality A confidentiality notice should be included in every e-mail emanating from an organization. It can resemble the following notice:

> CONFIDENTIALITY NOTICE: This communication and any attachments and/or enclosures can contain information that is (legally) privileged or confidential and is intended only for the use of the individual or entity to whom it is addressed. If you are not the intended recipient, you are hereby notified that any use, dissemination, distribution, copying, or disclosure of this communication and any attachments and/or enclosures is strictly prohibited. If you have received this communication in error, please notify us immediately and then permanently destroy this communication without making a copy. Thank you for your cooperation.

Summary of Policy Types

Table 10-1 displays sample content for each of the policy types covered in this section.

Table 10-1   *Sample Content for a Network Security Policy*

Policy Name	Examples of Content
Physical security	Building perimeter, server room
Access control	Authentication, Authorization, and Accounting
Dialup and analog	Fax lines, passwords, authentication
Remote access	Connectivity from remote offices (SOHO, ROBO)
Remote configuration	SSL, SSH
VPN and encryption	Requirements and standards
Network	Router, firewall, DMZ, servers, extranet, Internet, wireless
Data sensitivity, retention, ethics	Public, confidential, and distribution of information; e-mail maintenance; employee conduct
Software	OS, virus protection, database, e-mail usage

Some interesting sources for examples of security policy formation are The SANS Security Policy Project (http://www.sans.org/resources/policies/#template) and the Site Security Handbook (http://www.ietf.org/rfc/rfc2196.txt?number=2196).

Handling Incidents

Planning for difficult situations is highly advisable, and a policy to address security incident handling could prove invaluable. A contact person responsible for every major piece of equipment or network segment should always be at the ready, along with the person's backup. An enterprise might require certain IT staff to carry pagers, guaranteeing the availability of personnel to contend with issues as they arise. Because of illness, vacation, or termination, alternate personnel should also have alternate resources to ensure the highest degree of business continuity possible, even in times of intense system stress. Equally important, key personnel need to know where to report should an alarm sound, and they should be comfortable with the tasks that are required of them.

Appropriate authorities should be notified, including state, local, and federal law enforcement officials. Organizations such as CERT and other pertinent security awareness groups can provide invaluable support. Fighting computer crimes requires vigilance on the part of users and systems administrators. It also relies on corporations who are victims of computer crimes to create an environment that publicizes said crimes. Creating greater public awareness can serve to evoke vigilance on the part of users and corporations everywhere and can help to curtail the needless spreading of malicious content.

The act of advising law enforcement officials and independent security industry groups can represent a major step forward in helping to thwart the seemingly insatiable appetites of those individuals who want to inflict mindless damage.

Summary

Organizations invest untold amounts to fortify their systems, but equipment alone does not embody a solution. A security system is only as strong as its weakest link, and company internal human error, be it intentional or inadvertent, can represent a system's greatest vulnerability. A combination of equipment and positive user involvement is the concrete platform organizations can use to build a sound, security-rich environment.

Employees naturally seek direction, and the creation of effective security policies can provide that necessary guidance. Ensuring that policies are enforceable and measurable can result in the development of an environment that proactively works to secure itself.

This chapter discussed the following topics:

- The need to determine appropriate policies
- The process of constructing reliable and sound policies
- Acknowledging tools and implementation considerations
- Establishing a process for comprehensive monitoring
- An array of policy types
- The importance of incident handling

CHAPTER 11

SECURITY IS A LIVING PROCESS

Individuals charged with developing a business case for network security quickly understand that security is a living challenge that must be continually reviewed. Potential threats lurk everywhere and include hackers external to a company, hackers internal to a company, sloppy or ill-informed users, and extranet-partnered customers or suppliers. All have the ability to pose threats that can go beyond computing systems, potentially resulting in legal implications for certain organizations.

Making the business case for network security requires a thorough analysis of an organization's fundamentals. It should attempt to solidify strengths, root out weaknesses, uncover opportunities, and confront threats. The process complements the security wheel, which is discussed in this chapter, by highlighting organizational assets and challenges that can serve to advance the corporation.

Relentless need for greater technology, coupled with an ever-increasing dependence on the Internet, has created an environment that is rife with potential vulnerabilities. But many of the greatest threats can be significantly reduced when users exercise vigilance in their everyday activities. This book has shown that the solution is not just equipment. It asks users to become aware and get involved. But mostly, it implores leaders to share security concerns with staff members and then ask for their help. Not surprisingly, staff response is usually highly positive. People want to be involved; quite often, they just need a reason. The ripple effects of positive morale can never be underestimated.

This chapter covers the following topics:

- Security wheel
- Scalability
- Jurisprudence
- SWOT: Strengths, Weaknesses, Opportunities, and Threats

Security Wheel

Making the business case for network security is not a one-time event. Long after monies have been approved and equipment installed, an organization's macro and micro worlds retain the potential to change at any time. Whether the changes are the result of global terror threats, domestic malfeasance, or inadvertent user mishaps, computing systems are highly vulnerable to ever-fluid situations and the potential for significant damage.

Policies are never constructed in a vacuum, and after being constructed and deployed, they should not be left to wither in a void either. Constant review, renewal, rejuvenation, and regeneration can keep policies current, relevant, and viable.

The Cisco security wheel,[1] constructed with policy at its core, as shown in Figure 11-1, has the following components in continual motion:

- Secure

- Monitor

- Test

- Improve

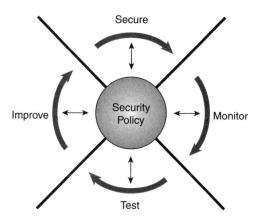

Figure 11-1   Security Wheel

Secure

Secure, residing at the top of the wheel, as shown in Figure 11-2, is the implementation stage. Whether new programs are being initiated or the wheel has been fully rotated and long-standing programs are being improved upon, the entry point for any implementation begins at secure.

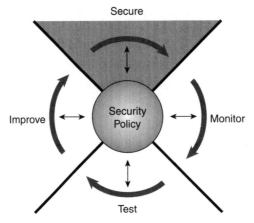

Figure 11-2 *Security Wheel: Secure*

This section considers the following topics:

- Authentication
- Encryption
- Firewalls
- Vulnerability patching

Authentication

Every user has a personal identifier that includes his or her username, password, PIN, digital certificates, or other similar coded tool that can be used to establish identity. Before a system can grant access to a user, it must first verify that a user is truly who or what he claims to be, and that he has a legitimate right to come in. The system would most likely use strong authentication, using a two-factor identification and verification process, for example, something a user has, such as an access card, and something a user knows, such as a PIN.

Upon request to gain access to the network or equipment, the user's identity is mapped and the user's authorization level is confirmed. The process of authentication, authorization, and accounting (AAA) is described in Chapter 3, "Security Technology and Related Equipment." The process ensures that only legitimate users are allowed to enter and, when they are inside, access is limited to pre-established levels, typically tied to user job functions.

Encryption

Encryption turns data into a format that is unintelligible to unauthorized parties.

An overview of encryption, presented in Chapter 3, includes a discussion about public and private keys, data encryption standards, and assorted other mechanisms that are widely used to ensure that important information is kept away from unauthorized eyes.

Encryption protocols can offer the additional options of integrity and authenticity, in addition to confidentiality.

Firewalls

A firewall prevents intruders from gaining access to internal systems. As discussed in Chapter 3, a firewall usually allows a single point of delivery from an organization to the Internet, as well as allows controlled access from the Internet to DMZ hosts. Rules for access are established, and any transaction that falls outside the prescribed rules is blocked.

Firewalls were originally tasked with protecting the perimeter of a network. As security needs grew, interdepartmental firewalls were added to provide protection for organizations that needed to proactively protect data-sensitive divisions, such as finance, R&D, HR, and other pertinent departments.

Firewalls were once considered the domain of corporate networks, but they are starting to be used on home networks as hackers sense the vulnerability with which many home users leave themselves exposed through dedicated high-speed DSL or cable connections.

Vulnerability Patching

Networks typically contain a wide array of equipment sourced from a variety of vendors. While every supplier takes measures to ensure that equipment is fully functional upon delivery, issues invariably surface that require patches, or fixes.

After the vendor recognizes the vulnerability, a patch is created and published to rectify the newly discovered issue.

A systems administrator charged with ensuring that patches are current has a number of issues with which he must contend, including finding out about the existence of any new and applicable patches. As explained in Chapter 3, organizations such as CERT and SANS regularly publish patches. Other services can provide patch alerts for all equipment an organization might have on its network. The systems administrator would need to detail pertinent equipment and respective operating versions, and the service would notify the administrator whenever a patch was published and available.

The challenge next moves to determining a reasonable time frame for installing the newly available patches. The moment a systems administrator is notified about a potential vulnerability, the assumption must be made that a hacker has also been made aware of the same information. Hackers could subscribe to the same patch informational services as systems administrator. Depending on the severity of the vulnerability, hackers might attempt to cause damage right away. The safest course of action is to ensure that patches are applied within a predetermined time frame after notification. Given that patching must be accomplished as part of a systems administrator daily routine, finding the time to implement necessary fixes is not always a simple task. Automated patch-management systems centrally deploy patches to devices across an organization. Systems administrator can use these systems to ensure timely installations.

When organizations are faced with the need to apply many patches within a short time frame, prioritization ensures that the most vital patches are applied first. The severity of a particular threat is relative to the equipment an organization has in place, and prioritizing patching for those threats where the company is not yet sufficiently protected can aid in minimizing potential damage.

Monitor

Network monitoring is somewhat comparable to a peace officer walking his daily beat. The officer observes the ebb and flow of the community as he strolls his familiar path, his eyes alert and his demeanor calm. Similarly, network monitoring, as shown in Figure 11-3, is a process that monitors normal course network activities. It observes and reports.

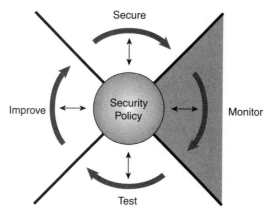

Figure 11-3 *Security Wheel: Monitor*

This section considers the following topics:

- Intrusion-detection systems (IDSs) and intrusion-prevention systems (IPSs)
- Data collection and retention

Intrusion-Detection Systems (IDSs) and Intrusion-Prevention Systems (IPSs)

IDSs capture network data and examine it to ensure that a network is secure. Because an IDS scrutinizes the data as it passes through, the IDS is relegated to being a reactive tool. Conversely, an IPS takes action to protect against an ongoing attack.

In essence, the IDS is passive—it detects and reports, whereas the IPS is active—it detects, reports, and intervenes.

Data Collection and Retention

Monitoring procedures likely result in a great deal of data being collected. The issue then turns to deciding the type of data an organization desires to collect. Does each action that occurs within every network segment need to be logged, or should the system be designed to flag and record only specific activities, such as file deletions or unsuccessful network logon attempts?

Equally important is deciding how long to retain the collected data. Certain file retention is legally required, and time frames can differ by state and specific statute. While those statutes need to be strictly observed, deciding how long to retain other data is individual to each organization. Regardless of the time frame chosen, instructions must be disseminated across the organization to ensure that rules are being enforced consistently.

Test

Network testing, as shown in Figure 11-4, is critical to ensuring optimal network preparedness. After equipment has been purchased and installed, testing both equipment and administrator knowledge of the equipment can reveal any possible holes in an organization's security posture.

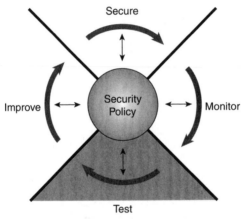

Figure 11-4 *Security Wheel: Test*

Testing considers the following areas:

- Determining responsibility for testing
- Network vulnerability scanners
- Audit and review

Determining Responsibility for Testing

Other than the process of testing itself, the most important elements of testing are performing the elements consistently. An individual might be assigned to the process, but should employment be terminated or the employee is out sick, on vacation, or simply too occupied with other required tasks, necessary testing can be missed.

An organization can construct a formal procedure that defines a process to follow, or it can pursue an outsourcing path, contracting formal testing to a vendor that specializes in this type of service. Certain challenges are associated with outsourcing, namely, cost and the acceptance that a third party has access to the workings of the corporate network. After it is accepted, outsourcing has far-reaching benefits. Not only can required testing be done consistently and continually, but also the vendor will likely be aware of any new vulnerabilities long before a heavily tasked internal systems administrator would discover them; this is the vendor's business.

Data collected for testing purposes should be retained for the audit and review process.

Network Vulnerability Scanners

It is prudent to monitor the state of security preparedness, and network vulnerability scanners can probe a network to ensure that security issues are handily addressed.

Audit and Review

The process of log auditing was not designed so that a systems administrator could witness an attack. Rather, log auditing was designed to be a preventative tool. It can be used to pinpoint patterns that might not be easily discernible through standard log checking. It might reveal that a series of reconnaissance attacks have occurred, as described in Chapter 2, "Crucial Need for Security: Vulnerabilities and Attacks." In and of themselves, reconnaissance attacks might not cause harm, but to a systems administrator performing a thorough log audit, the attacks should represent a possible foreshadowing of future events.

Reviewing test logs can determine the strength of an organization's security posture. It can also determine whether a system can recognize when it is under attack and, assuming it does, whether the system noticed the attack in time to protect itself.

Improve

Interpreting results from the audit and review process and deciding which, if any, should be implemented constitute the improvement stage, as shown in Figure 11-5. In addition, many organizations can use the improvement stage as a springboard for continuous learning. Managers can be assigned the task of ensuring that they are well informed of recent security happenings, whether they concern innovative new products or pertinent current events. By habitually sifting through the vast array of available market data in search of relevant information, an organization can ensure that it is perpetually operating in a preventive and proactive mode.

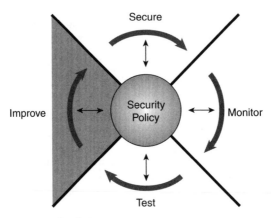

Figure 11-5   *Security Wheel: Improve*

This section considers the following topics:

- Security policy adjustments
- Implementing changes

Security Policy Adjustments

The steering committee, or similar corporate body, should review all recommendations that were revealed through the initial three phases of the security wheel to decide what changes, if any, are required to solidify the organization's security posture. Should the company elect to make improvements, those changes must immediately be reflected in the security policy manual.

Users need to know what is expected of them at all times, and without hesitation, they should be able to inherently trust the rules that are detailed in a firm's security policy. The situation is analogous to an individual who decides to alter his last will and testament. He might decide to change a beneficiary, but should he neglect to have the amendment appropriately witnessed before he dies, his final will and testament will not be valid. A security policy that does not immediately reflect all rule changes can suffer the same fate. Should an attack ever occur, no one would ever want to hear a user say, "I was following the security policy; I didn't know the rules had changed."

Implementing Changes

Updating security policies to reflect changes is a prudent practice, but simply including new rules in departmental manuals might not be sufficient. Training is usually required and can run from the complex, sending personnel to extensive professional training programs, to the simple, explaining to users new actions they must follow.

Awareness is fundamental to the success of any program. Informing users of significant threats, and advising them about steps that can be taken to help the organization mitigate potential issues, can ensure that recent changes are implemented in the way in which they were originally conceived.

Scalability

An organization might assume a particular security posture, but through a regular rotation of its security wheel, the organization might discover that it has unwittingly altered its posture.

Organizations can view security postures as falling into one of the following camps:

- Basic
- Modest
- Comprehensive

An organization might have chosen a modest plan when it originally wrote its security policy, structuring its posture on the equipment and processes inherent in a modest level, as described in Chapter 4, "Putting It All Together: Threats and Security

Equipment." Plans get set in motion, and normal-course business is conducted. Situations can occur, whether they involve malicious attacks by outsiders, inadvertent errors by insiders, or potential vulnerabilities that are recognized and plugged before they can become issues. An organization must respond quickly and effectively to every situation by ensuring that concerns are addressed directly, and any resultant change is promptly reflected in its security posture.

This process works well in theory, but it can be challenging to implement on a daily basis. When situations do occur, changes are made expeditiously, so the organization can quickly resume doing business. Making the security wheel a fundamental component of an organization's process ensures that changes made on the fly are always reflected in policy and, most importantly, that changes respect the posture the company already has in place.

Changes rarely occur in a vacuum; typically, one change begets another. For example, an organization faced with a particular situation might implement a variety of solutions to combat the problem, possibly resulting in the company moving markedly away from its modest security posture. If the newly implemented changes reveal that the organization is pursuing a posture that is fundamentally more comprehensive, the organization should ensure that related policies are changed to reflect a similar comprehensive structure. The concern is that an unplanned mix of modest and comprehensive security postures might leave the company with a sense that it is more secure than it actually is, and a false sense of security can be worse than no security. Firms with acknowledged low levels of security can ensure that users are particularly diligent in their dealings; those firms who think they have a high degree of security installed on their systems might be less concerned with employee activity. And that is where the seeds for great vulnerability are typically planted.

A continual rotation of the security wheel can ensure that a firm's physical and logical structure is created, implemented, and reviewed in a fashion that is commensurate with its desired security posture.

Jurisprudence

The law is a living organism. It is a series of rules, regulations, conventions, precedents, and structures that are created, maintained, and improved upon to reflect societal needs for both current and future generations. Laws govern a society's people, organizations, institutions, and structures, and they impose a system of order encompassing the foregoing entities and the relationships among them.

Political legislators are working to design legislation that accurately reflects the ever-changing technological landscape while substantively protecting both organizations and individuals.

This section considers the following topics:

- Hacking
- Internal issues
- Negligence
- Privacy
- Integrity
- Good netizen conduct

Hacking

It has been a long while since hackers were viewed as mere nuisances. Today, the proliferation of attacks is widespread, encompassing targets that include vast enterprises, home users, and every conceivable system in between. The menace posed by hackers continues relatively unabated; attacks are increasingly more virulent, forcing organizations and users to become more diligent in their daily activities.

Attacks were historically viewed as acts perpetrated by individuals intent on inflicting vandalism, but they are quickly becoming recognized for what they truly are: intensely malicious acts of a grievous nature intended to cause harm. Attacks can cripple systems and result in untold damages, some of which can never be quantified. Whether attacks are premeditated, carried out for personal gain, or have some link to cyber-terrorism, politicians around the globe are striving to enact legislation that serves to deter individuals from attempting to inflict damage, and punish those who wreak havoc.

Internal Issues

Acts carried out by company insiders can be just as damaging as those inflicted by hackers. Company-internal errors, whether intentioned or not, can bring down a system or cause a business to be unnecessarily vulnerable. Users can inadvertently create a distributed denial of service (DDoS) attack, as described in Chapter 2, or with premeditated intent, they could access company-confidential information for their own purposes.

Limiting Internet access, whether by implementing URL filtering, as described in Chapter 3, or by continually elaborating on the company's Internet-use stance can help to restrain certain activities. An organization might be logging heavy activity at gaming sites if some of its users enjoy participating in gambling during the course of their workday. Other users might choose to collect illegal pornography, putting not only the company at risk for harboring individuals that perform illegal activities but also putting the company's reputation at risk in the frequently more damaging forum of public opinion.

Developing a system that encourages strict controls and maintains a process for checks and balances can ensure that an organization is in a position to act proactively, and user actions are less likely to put the company at harm.

Negligence

Security infrastructure is relative to an organization's tolerance for risk. While one person's high risk might be another's light adventure, the outcome that results from a particular activity would be the same in either scenario. Negligence is defined as a failure to take prudent care and, for organizations, it can be the difference between acting responsibly and failing to adequately protect the company against known vulnerabilities. If a company employed a third party to perform certain work and, while in possession of client data, the third party was easily broken into by an external hacker, the third party could potentially be found negligent if it did not use practices or equipment to adequately protect itself. *Adequate protection* could be considered a relative term, but a company could be looked upon as having been negligent if it did not take fundamental precautions to proactively deal with potential threats.

Hackers have been able to infiltrate well-known websites to launch multiple attacks, making it increasingly incumbent upon companies to ensure that their systems cannot be used as launch pads for further attacks. While attack scenarios are typically more complex, for explanation purposes, an attack example could be as simple as the following scenario.

A hacker launches an attack against a well-known website, victim A. The virus implanted in victim A automatically launches its own attack against another well-known website, victim B, effectively bringing down both A and B. B might incur untold loss of revenue or reputation and, in an attempt to reclaim certain losses, might seek to prove negligence on the part of A. While the guilty party is clearly the hacker, seeking damages from the hacker would probably not serve any monetary purpose. Should B be able to prove that A was negligent in not protecting its own system from an attack and, further, that A should have been able to ensure that its system could not unwittingly become involved in launching further attacks, B might be able to prove negligence on the part of A. While this example grossly oversimplifies a complex issue, Figure 11-6 illustrates how simple it could be for an innocent bystander to unwittingly participate in a DDoS attack, and possibly be viewed as potentially negligent.

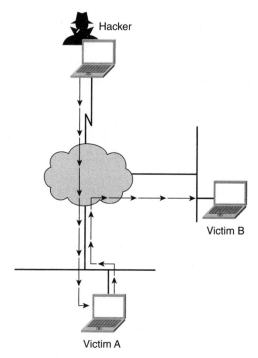

Figure 11-6   *Victim and Perpetrator at the Same Time*

Privacy

Respecting individual and corporate privacy has become an increasingly sensitive issue over the last generation. Legislation is beginning to dictate parameters for organizations in the collection, use, and disclosure of information and, in certain cases, creating guidelines for how these tasks must be accomplished. Specifically, consent is required, and in many instances, such consent must be implicit. Even when consent has been granted, it is incumbent upon the collecting organization to ensure that information is only used and disclosed for the purposes for which the information was originally collected, particularly if the information could be deemed highly sensitive. This is relevant whether the data collector is a commercial or a nonprofit organization.

The Health Insurance Portability and Accountability Act (HIPAA) of 1996 presents standards for the maintenance and transmission of personal information regarding individuals. Every organization in possession, or potentially in possession, of information must be able to protect the security and confidentiality of electronic personal information. The act ensures that the interchange of said electronic data is standardized and that privacy is ensured.

The Gramm-Leach-Bliley Act, or The Financial Modernization Act of 1999, includes provisions to protect individuals' personal financial information. The act extends protection beyond formal financial institutions to include all organizations that handle personal financial relations, from firms that provide income tax services to those that provide credit counseling. In essence, the act requires all financial institutions to design, implement, and maintain safeguards to protect consumer information.

To effectively comply with privacy guidelines in certain existing and proposed legislation, organizations are developing privacy policies to operate in conjunction with security policies. These new policies work to ensure that data is protected from external attacks and internal inadvertent errors, as well as protected against possible internal disregard for the sanctity of the information with which an organization has been entrusted.

Integrity

Long gone are the days when officers of a public company could sign their name to official financial information and feel confident that the figures were wholly accurate. Today, all parties must ensure that proper security exists and appropriate methodology is used in the compilation and calculation of financial documents. Strict scrutiny and a high degree of security are now fundamental to ensure the integrity of internal financial statements.

The Sarbanes-Oxley Act of 2002, or The Public Company Accounting Reform and Investor Protection Act of 2002, outlines procedures with which public companies must comply to ensure that their financial statements are wholly accurate and that senior executives must attest to said accuracy in sworn statements.

In May 2003, the U.S. Securities and Exchange Commission adopted rules pertaining to Section 404 of the Sarbanes-Oxley Act, the Management Assessment of Internal Controls, to include the following items:

- Management is responsible for establishing and maintaining adequate internal controls for financial reporting.

- Management must present the framework it used for assessing and evaluating the internal control model.

- Management must provide its assessment of the effectiveness of the internal control structure.

Internal control is further defined as follows:

- Thorough maintenance of records

- Transactions being safely recorded

- Timely detection of any breach that could have a material effect on financial statements

Ensuring that strict security controls are in place is becoming increasingly more fundamental for organizations today. Guaranteeing the sanctity of financial statements, including the calculations behind every entry on a balance sheet, such as booking and timing of payables, requires firms to have measurable and unfaltering procedures in place.

Good Netizen Conduct

The Internet has been referred to in such diverse terms as being a conservative and appropriate medium in which to conduct business, to being as uncontrollable as the proverbial Wild West. The Internet is as safe, or as uncontrollable, as each of its users allows it to be. Actively ensuring the dependable, proper, and respectful use of this highly exposed medium requires every individual who uses the Internet to become a good net citizen, or *netizen*.

The Centre for Safe and Responsible Internet Use (CSRIU) works with schools and educators to ensure that responsible Internet use is instilled at a young age. Respect for the medium can aid organizations in their next generation of workers.

In companies today, leaders must extend respect for the Internet throughout the organization. Practicing good *netizenry* can help ward off potential issues of negligence in the future. ISPs, possibly vulnerable to potential lawsuits, might begin to request minimum-security requirements from those companies to whom they provide service.

Service-level agreements (SLAs) between companies sharing just-in-time programs, as an example, could potentially require each party to be a good netizen. While SLAs are wholly negotiable, sections of an agreement could stipulate that each party involved in a transaction maintain a predetermined level of security, such as a formal plan for patching, firewall maintenance, and other pertinent requirements.

The continued pervasiveness of the Internet in everyday business requires all users, both corporate and individual, to ensure that the medium is used in a highly respectful fashion.

SWOT: Strengths, Weaknesses, Opportunities, and Threats

An organization can effectively use its IT infrastructure to aid its competitive posture by ensuring that internal IT systems are integral and integrated components of its business. A well-constructed security policy can ensure that an organization can concentrate on its core business while reducing system-related distractions to a manageable minimum.

Strengths, weaknesses, opportunities, and threats—commonly referred to as SWOT—is a form of self-analysis that can aid an organization in establishing and continually reexamining its security posture.

Table 11-1 can act as a guide to SWOT analysis.

Table 11-1 *Components of SWOT Analysis*

SWOT Analysis	Positive	Negative
Internal	Strengths	Weaknesses
External	Opportunities	Threats

This section considers the four components of SWOT:

- Strengths
- Weaknesses
- Opportunities
- Threats

Strengths

Deriving a positive business case for network security requires organizations to determine the most fundamental elements of their operation and quantify, to the greatest extent possible, those soft elements that typically represent the difference between success and failure.

Incorporating enhanced security measures can allow organizations to concentrate on their core business. Mitigation tactics used to reduce the likelihood of security breaches can result in fewer distractions for company users, because the system will potentially suffer less downtime. Customers and suppliers alike can rely on the system's consistency and, gaining ever more importance, the system's trustworthiness.

Remote users of every kind, whether they are working from home in the evenings or sitting in a hotel room 2000 miles from the office, can access the corporate server with the same level of functionality, ease, confidence, and security as if they were sitting mere yards from the server.

Bringing the need for security directly to every employee through stated job requirements and ongoing dialogues, as discussed in Chapter 7, "Engaging the Corporation: Management and Employees," allows every employee to fully comprehend what is at stake. The understanding, coupled with procedural guidance, allows users to proactively aid the organization in enhancing its security posture far beyond the scope of physical equipment. When users view themselves as integral to a process, human nature suggests that it is indicative of positive feelings they hold for both the functions and the overall goal. The end result is that they can feel a stronger connection to the organization, and positive morale could be an unexpected outcome.

An organization that enhances measures to protect its resources, both people and equipment, ensure that the attention of its users remains focused on the organization's central concern: its business.

Questions the steering committee can pose to itself to aid in determining strengths are as follows:

- Is our enhanced security an advantage because it ensures that employees are focused on the core business?

- Is our enhanced security an advantage because we have developed stronger bonds with our customers and suppliers?

- Is our enhanced security an advantage because we can process purchase orders taken by our branch offices faster than our competitors?

- Is our enhanced security an advantage as a marketing tool?

- Is our enhanced security an advantage that is used by our sales staff, as a value-added tool, that addresses the corporation's reliability and long-term commitment to promoting a safe environment in which to share information and conduct business?

Weaknesses

Every system has weaknesses, and instituting a program that continually attempts to identify and effectively address them can aid the organization in its quest for enhanced security.

While a business case attempts to identify the costs inherent in not implementing greater programs, it is important to recognize the total cost of ownership when developing system plans. From physical equipment to personnel training and product upgrades, the costs associated with enhancing security do not stop when equipment is installed on a network.

Equipment that analyzes network activity—whether appliances watch traffic as it flows across a wire or equipment acts as a filter, limiting destinations users can visit—inevitably introduces latency into a system. Time is measured in milliseconds, and while the latency is likely negligible for most users, all functions require certain time for execution; system latency is proportional to the functionality that is added.

Newly installed equipment might require training for the systems administrator and the requisite alternate administrator. Depending on the size of the organization, and the importance of the equipment, more than one alternate could be assigned. Certain equipment might even necessitate the hiring of specialized personnel, should they not already exist on staff. Also, the monitoring and maintenance of new equipment, in particular the work involved in analyzing log files, could result in greater work load for existing staff.

The security steering committee can pose the following questions to itself in an attempt to determine potential weaknesses:

- Are our users vigilant enough?

- Is our enhanced security so inflexible that we are removing potential efficiencies?

- Is the (present) lack of enhanced security known to customers, suppliers, staff, or even hackers?

- Is our lack of greater security negatively impacting our revenues?

- Is the company adequately insured against potential attacks? E-insurance can provide protection against viruses, unlawful system use, a DoS, and a variety of other potentially calamitous events. Network liability insurance is also available to contend with both external and internal threats. Insurance of this type could prove an opportunity for organizations, should they ever experience extensive damage as a result of an attack.

- Is the security implementation scalable, and can it grow with the business?

Opportunities

Building an enhanced network provides organizations with the ability to act. This is in stark contrast to the security position that many companies frequently find themselves in, which is one of reacting. Organizations have the opportunity to create an environment whereby employees become an integral part of the company's defense strategy. Users help fortify the company by adhering to guidelines that govern network segments and physical security.

Enhanced security can be used as a selling tool by the sales and marketing departments in promotions that stress reliability, consistency, and trust. Should it become clear that immediate competitors have not implemented similar security postures, the organization's adoption of an enhanced environment could be used as a differentiator when pursuing opportunities with customers.

Enhanced security measures could prove an ideal moment to renew SLAs with customers. If certain accounts are found to be lacking in their security postures, the discussion could be the impetus for those customers to follow a similar route in their own security development program. Regardless of the outcome, the resulting series of discussions would be perceived as adding value, which could serve to further solidify the relationship between the companies.

Questions the steering committee can pose to uncover opportunities include the following:

- Could greater opportunities be developed in the customer base, or would the ability to sign leading suppliers improve, with the establishment of enhanced security?

- Could greater sales be realized in the current customer base by enhancing security? Can sales personnel use the enhancement as a value-added tool that addresses potential reliability issues?

- Would certain costs decrease by implementing greater security? For example, physical property and receivables insurance could be reduced because of decreased vulnerability. If an organization uses SLAs to govern business relationships with its large customers, and security has been enhanced to ensure a safe and consistent flow of goods and funds, normal-level vulnerabilities that perpetually exist between partnered organizations would likely be reduced by tighter and more secure channels.

- Could the cost of doing business be reduced if enhanced security were put in place? Do identifiable areas exist where employees are manually overcompensating for lack of security?

- Can it be determined whether closest competitors have issues pertaining to their security postures? If it appears that one or more might have issues restarting operations after a widespread power outage, as an example, the organization's sales and marketing group could promote its own consistent high level of security.

Threats

Threats come in many forms, many of which are not visible until they are actual events. Recognizing issues as potential threats is a proactive step organizations can take to determine their tolerance, or aversion, to certain threats. The proactive process allows organizations to determine appropriate courses of action.

Questions a steering committee can ponder when considering threats include the following:

- Does a particular response to potential threats, or lack thereof, leave the organization unduly vulnerable? Could under-security lead to possible legal implications?

- Are an organization's electronic connections with its customers and suppliers well served and appropriately secured?

- Can the lack of enhancements negatively impact customer or supplier relationships?

- Can either customers or suppliers view immediate competitors as being better equipped?

- Could a serious breach (for example, system unavailability for 72 hours, loss of sales database, loss of backup, or infiltration of financials) severely threaten the organization?

- Is the organization suffering from higher levels of downtime compared to its competitors? Would less downtime result in greater concentration on the organization's core business?

Performing an analysis of this type can highlight issues that need to be addressed immediately and determine a prudent course for long-range security planning. It can also create a greater sense of confidence, knowing that the organization is doing all it can to proactively protect its business.

The marketing department could also perform similar analyses on the company's largest competitors.

Summary

Reviewing, renewing, and regenerating security fundamentals to ensure that they remain relevant are processes that serve all organizations. Given the litigious climate that exists today, assessing the potential for legal implications surrounding security can prove to be a prudent practice in which organizations can proactively engage.

Continual corporate self-examination of policies, practices, weaknesses, and threats can ensure that opportunities are recognized early in the business cycle, and effectively capitalized upon.

This chapter explored the following topics:

- The importance of a security wheel

- The relevance of scalability

- The implications of jurisprudence

- The necessity of a SWOT analysis

The Business Case for Network Security: Advocacy, Governance, and ROI presents technical terms and mitigation techniques in a format that is accessible to nontechnical corporate leaders. It provides executives with an extensive guide to securing the organization and a program to create effective security practices. It also explores the fundamental role employees can play in securing an organization. The book introduces IT executives to a program that can effectively garner support, build consensus, and rationalize ROI. It creates a financial model to address the subjective nature of security matters, effectively quantifying subjective organizational issues into concrete numbers that can assess individual risk.

Adherence to security policy fundamentals, coupled with a program that continually reviews and renews an organization's security posture, can foster an environment that can effectively address any challenge an organization might encounter.

End Note

[1]The Cisco Security Wheel, http://www.cisco.com/en/US/partner/products/sw/secursw/ps2113/products_maintenance_guide_chapter09186a008007d254.html#xtocid62413.

PART IV

APPENDIXES

APPENDIX A

REFERENCES

This appendix lists books, websites, and other resources that are referred to throughout this book, along with resources that were used during the research process.

NOTE   The website references in this book were accurate upon publication; however, they might have since changed. If the website is unavailable, you might want to conduct a search using a powerful search engine such as Google (http://www.google.com) and entering the document title as key words.

Berinato, S. with research by Cosgrove, L. "The State of Information Security 2003 Survey." *CSO Magazine*. Study conducted by PricewaterhouseCoopers and *CIO Magazine*. http://www.csoonline.com/read/100103/survey.html. October 2003.

Bosworth, S. and Kabay, M. *Computer Security Handbook*, 4th Edition. Wiley Publishing. 2002.

Briney, A. and Prince, F. "Security Survey: Disciplined Security." Information Security. http://infosecuritymag.techtarget.com/ss/0,295796,sid6_iss143_art294,00.html. October 2003.

Cisco Connection Online. http://www.cisco.com.

Cisco SAFE Blueprint white papers. http://www.cisco.com/en/US/netsol/ns340/ns394/ns171/ns128/networking_solutions_package.html.

"CSI/FBI Computer Crime and Security Survey 2003." Computer Security Institute and Federal Bureau of Investigation (CSI/FBI). http://www.gocsi.com/forms/fbi/pdf.jhtml.

"CSI/FBI Computer Crime and Security Survey 2004." Computer Security Institute and Federal Bureau of Investigation (CSI/FBI). http://i.cmpnet.com/gocsi/db_area/pdfs/fbi/FBI2004.pdf.

Department of Homeland Security. http://www.dhs.gov/dhspublic/.

Doraswamy, N. and Harkins, D. *IPSec: The New Security Standard for the Internet, Intranets, and Virtual Private Networks*. Prentice Hall PTR. 1999.

Fratto, M. "Don't Panic. Plan." *Network Computing* website. http://www.networkcomputing.com/1408/1408f1.html. May 1, 2003.

Hulme, G.V. "No Time to Relax." *Information Week.* http://www. informationweek.com/story/showArticle.jhtml?articleID=12803057. July 28, 2003.

"Information Security Breaches Survey 2002, Technical Report." Pricewaterhouse Coopers UK, Department of Trade and Industry UK. http://www.dti.gov.uk/industry_files/pdf/sbsreport_2002.pdf. April 2002.

"Information Security Breaches Survey 2004, Executive Summary." Pricewaterhouse Coopers UK, Department of Trade and Industry UK. http://www.pwc.com/images/gx/eng/about/svcs/grms/2004Exec_Summ.pdf. April 2004.

"Information Security Breaches Survey 2004, Technical Report." Pricewaterhouse Coopers UK, Department of Trade and Industry UK. http://www.pwc.com/images/gx/eng/about/svcs/grms/2004Technical_Report.pdf. April 2004.

Internet Requests for Comments (RFCs). http://www.cse.ohio-state.edu/cs/Services/rfc/.

Kirkpatrick, David. NEXT@CNN. CNN. January 11, 2004.

McClure, S., Scambray, J., and Kurtz, G. *Hacking Exposed: Network Security Secrets & Solutions*, 4th edition. McGraw-Hill Ryerson. 2003.

Newton, H. *Newton's Telecom Dictionary: The Official Dictionary of Telecommunications Networking and Internet*, 16th Edition. Pub Group West. March 2000.

Norton website. http://www.norton.com.

Paquet, C. and Teare, D. *CCNP Self-Study: Building Scalable Cisco Internetworks (BSCI)*, 2nd Edition. Cisco Press. 2004.

Snyder, J. "Taking Aim." *Information Security.* January 2004.

Symantec Corporation Norton website. http://www.norton.com.

Websense website. http://www.websense.com.

OSI MODEL, INTERNET PROTOCOL, AND PACKETS

This appendix provides a brief overview of the oft-mentioned OSI model terms found in this book, namely, Internet Protocol and IP packets. For more information on these topics, refer to the following Cisco website:

http://www.cisco.com/univercd/cc/td/doc/cisintwk/ito_doc/introint.pdf

OSI Model

- Open System Interconnection (OSI) reference model.
- Conceptual framework consisting of seven layers.
- Divides tasks involved with moving information between networked computers into seven smaller and more manageable task groups.

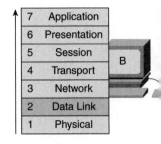

- Each layer is reasonably self-contained, so tasks that are assigned to each layer can be implemented independently.

Internet Protocol

- World's most popular nonproprietary protocol suite
- Used to communicate across any set of interconnected networks
- Equally well-suited for LAN and WAN communications

IP Packet

A *packet* is a unit of data sent across a network.

- Messages sent from one system to another are broken into smaller fragments.
- Protocol information, represented by a header, is prepended to those fragments before being passed down from upper to lower layers, in a process known as *encapsulation*.

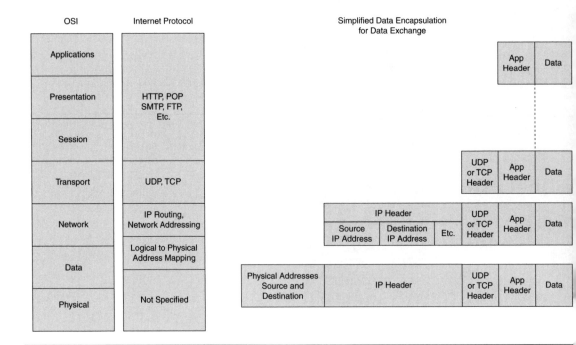

APPENDIX C

QUICK GUIDES TO SECURITY TECHNOLOGIES

The intent of the cheat sheets in this appendix is to provide the reader with quick supplemental information and quick reference of concepts that are covered in this book. Refer to Chapter 3, "Security Technology and Related Equipment," for more detailed technical explanations and the Cisco website (http://www.cisco.com) for more comprehensive information.

This appendix contains cheat sheets for the following topics:

- Cheat Sheet 1: Routers
- Cheat Sheet 2: Hubs and Switches
- Cheat Sheet 3: Perimeter Routers and Firewalls
- Cheat Sheet 4: Intrusion-Detection Systems
- Cheat Sheet 5: Virtual Private Networks and Authentication
- Cheat Sheet 6: Comprehensive Security Topology

Cheat Sheet 1: Routers

Routers perform the following tasks:

- Segment logical networks at the IP layer
- Route IP traffic (IP packets) according to routing information kept in their router tables
- Build routing tables manually or, usually, automatically by using routing protocols that exchange routing information between neighboring routers
- Usually keep only optimal paths in their routing tables

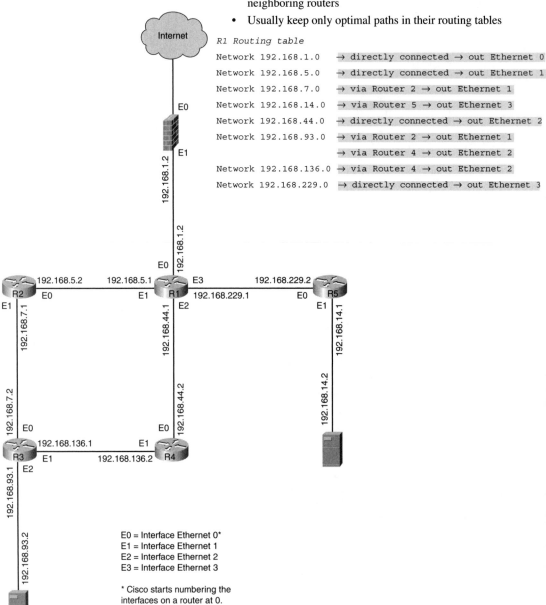

```
R1 Routing table
Network 192.168.1.0      → directly connected → out Ethernet 0
Network 192.168.5.0      → directly connected → out Ethernet 1
Network 192.168.7.0      → via Router 2 → out Ethernet 1
Network 192.168.14.0     → via Router 5 → out Ethernet 3
Network 192.168.44.0     → directly connected → out Ethernet 2
Network 192.168.93.0     → via Router 2 → out Ethernet 1
                         → via Router 4 → out Ethernet 2
Network 192.168.136.0    → via Router 4 → out Ethernet 2
Network 192.168.229.0    → directly connected → out Ethernet 3
```

E0 = Interface Ethernet 0*
E1 = Interface Ethernet 1
E2 = Interface Ethernet 2
E3 = Interface Ethernet 3

* Cisco starts numbering the interfaces on a router at 0.

Cheat Sheet 2: Hubs and Switches

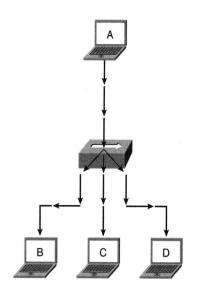

or more information regarding hubs and other LAN devices,
visit http://www.cisco.com.

What Is a Hub?

A hub is a physical layer device that connects multiple user stations,
servers, and network equipment.

Devices connect to the hub through dedicated cable, often referred to as
network cable or *patch cable* (which usually connects to a network drop
installed in a wall socket).

Electrical interconnections are established inside the hub.

Electrical signals emitted from one station are propagated to all stations
connected in the same hub.

Network bandwidth is shared among all devices connected to the hub.

What Is a Wireless Hub?

A wireless hub is also known as a wireless
access point.

A wireless hub operates under the same
principle as a wired hub by receiving a signal
and propagating it out.

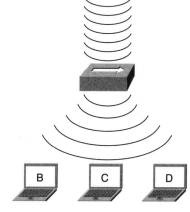

What Is a LAN Switch?

A LAN switch segments communication
between devices of the same physical
network, contrary to a hub, which
indiscriminately repeats signals to all
members of the same physical network.

For the most part, switches have replaced
hubs in wiring closets.

Network bandwidth is dedicated to each
station connected directly to the switch.

Modern switches are more versatile and
accomplish more tasks than the physical
segmentation work done by their
predecessors.

or more information on LAN switches, visit
tp://www.cisco.com/univercd/cc/td/doc/
sintwk/ito_doc/lanswtch.htm#xtocid2.

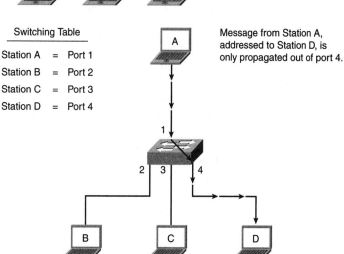

Switching Table

Station A = Port 1
Station B = Port 2
Station C = Port 3
Station D = Port 4

Message from Station A,
addressed to Station D, is
only propagated out of port 4.

Cheat Sheet 3: Perimeter Routers and Firewalls

For more information regarding perimeter routers and firewalls, refer to Chapter 3.

What Is a Perimeter Router?

- The first line of defense
- Performs the following basic security checks:
  - Validates source and destination IP addresses on incoming and outgoing network traffic
  - By default, performs stateless packet filtering and therefore is easier to hack than a stateful firewall

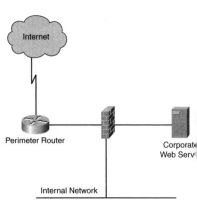

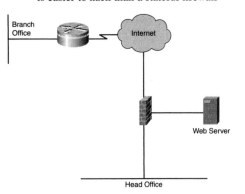

Can a Router be a Firewall?

Some perimeter routers can be upgraded to perform as stateful firewalls. Those upgraded routers/firewalls can also terminate VPN tunnels and perform some IDS tasks. Routers with these extra capabilities are often used by branch offices.

What Is a Firewall?

- A firewall is a network appliance dedicated to the meticulous filtering of all network traffic.
- Stateful firewalls meticulously record pertinent information of data streams transiting through it to permit or deny access.
- Default behavior dictates that traffic originating from the outside is denied access.
- Default behavior dictates that traffic originating from the inside is allowed out and that replies are permitted in.
- A firewall can be configured to modify its default behavior, for example, to let incoming outside traffic in, provided that the destination address is the corporate web server and only for the purpose of browsing the corporate web server. However, a hacker's traffic trying to access the internal network is blocked by the firewall.
- A firewall is commonly configured to perform Network Address Translation (NAT), where inside addresses are never revealed to the outside network.

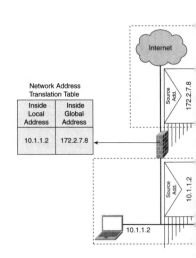

What Is Network Address Translation?

- NAT translates internal addresses (local addresses) to addresses used only when communicating on the Internet (global addresses).
- NAT is commonly configured on firewalls and perimeter routers.
- NAT provides additional security, because the true addresses of devices are not publicly known.

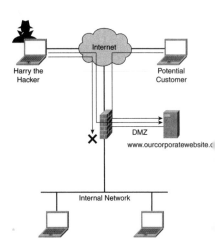

Network Address Translation Table

Inside Local Address	Inside Global Address
10.1.1.2	172.2.7.8

Cheat Sheet 4: Intrusion-Detection Systems

For more information regarding intrusion-detection systems (IDSs) and intrusion-prevention systems (IPSs), refer to Chapter 3.

IDSs

- IDSs analyze data streams in real time to detect attacks and viruses.
- A network-based IDS (NIDS) is located on the network and analyzes traffic for malicious activities.
- A host-based IDS (HIDS) is installed on a server or workstation and analyzes incoming data for malicious codes.

IDS Components

- **IDS Device Manager** —Configures sensors and is the central repository of alarms
- **IDS sensor** —Captures and analyzes traffic in real time

Actions Taken by an IDS

Upon discovering suspicious activities, an IDS can do the following:

- Logs an alarm
- Resets the IP (TCP) connection
- Blocks (shuns) further traffic from the suspect

Sensor Interface Operating Modes

- **Stealth** —Captures data without having a logical participation on the network
- **Command and control**—Announces suspicious activities that were detected as a result of data captured by the stealth interface

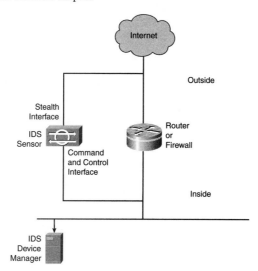

Alarm Severity Levels

- Informational
- Low
- Medium
- High

Traffic Analysis

An IDS analyzes traffic according to the following items:

- **Signature** —Looks for a match of a data string according to an attack definition database (similar to standard virus-detection software)
- **Pattern**—Learns what is normal traffic and then analyzes future traffic according to the previously created baseline

Alarms

Alarms, defined in the following table, are classified as follows:

- True-negative
- True-positive
- False-negative
- False-positive

	Negative	**Positive**
True	Legitimate traffic not caught by IDS sensor	Illegal traffic generating an alarm
False	Illegal traffic not caught by sensor	Legitimate traffic generating an alarm by sensor (commonly known as a false alarm)

Cheat Sheet 5: Virtual Private Networks and Authentication

For more information regarding Virtual Private Networks (VPNs) and authentication, refer to Chapter 3.

A VPN allows data to be sent securely over public networks, such as the Internet, through secure encrypted tunnels.

IPSec

IPSec is currently the most readily available VPN protocol. It provides the following features:

- Authenticity through authentication
- Confidentiality through encryption
- Integrity through hashing (integrity checking)

VPN tunnels from remote offices and telecommuters commonly terminate on VPN concentrators, which are dedicated appliances optimized for this task.

Preferred VPN Topology

Ideally, encrypting traffic originating from a remote office or a telecommuter would be permitted access through a firewall, terminating at the VPN concentrator.

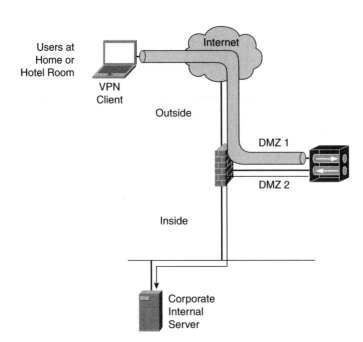

VPN and network security are better served when strong authentication is used.

Strong authentication refers to a minimum two-factor process, where the two methods must be used jointly.

Money withdrawn from a bank machine requires strong authentication, as follows:

- Something you have: bank card
- Something you know: PIN

Something You Know	Something You Have	Something You Are
Password PIN	Swipe card Proximity card Token	Biometrics • Retina • Thumb • Voice

Cheat Sheet 6: Comprehensive Security Topology

For more information regarding the equipment listed in this figure, refer to Chapter 3.

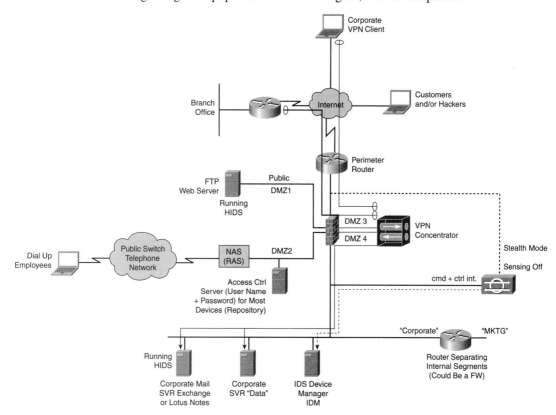

APPENDIX D

RETURN ON PREVENTION CALCULATIONS REFERENCE SHEETS

Refer to Chapter 9, "Return on Prevention: Investing in Capital Assets," for background and detailed information on the following calculations.

Security Costs Calculations

Asset Value (AV)

Cost of replacing information
\+ cost of replacing software and hardware and reconfiguration
\+ lost availability
\+ associated costs (loss of data confidentiality and integrity)

Total Asset Value

Annualized Rate of Occurrence (ARO)

The ARO is the probability that an attack might happen over a one-year period. It is represented as a percentage.

Annual-Loss Expectancy (ALE)

The ALE is the annual financial loss sustained should threats to a specific asset be realized.

Single Loss Expectancy (SLE)
X Annualized Rate of Occurrence (ARO)

Annual Loss Expectancy

Exposure Factor (EF)

The exposure factor is an asset's vulnerability to a given threat, represented in decimal value. The exposure factor of a web server expected to be 80% crippled by a DoS attack would be represented by a factor of 0.8.

Single-Loss Expectancy (SLE)

The SLE is the amount of financial loss sustained should a specific threat to a specific asset be realized.

SLE = Asset value X Exposure factor

Total Cost of Ownership (TCO)

TCO = Procurement Costs + Non-Recurring Associated Costs + (y * Recurring Associated costs)

$$TCO = P + N + (Y * R)$$

Where:
P = Procurement Cost
N = Non-Recurring Costs
R = Recurring Costs
Y = useful life of the equipment in years

TCO Present Value (PV)

TCO present value is cash flow (CF) in present-day dollars. Future expenses are applied a discount rate.

TCO Present Value = Procurement Costs + Non-Recurring Costs + (Time-Adjusted Recurring Costs)

TCO Present Value = P + N + (Time-Adjusted R)

An example of TCO present value with a three-year useful life is shown in the following table.

Year	Discount Factor When Discount Rate Is 10%	Cash Flow Out	Cash Flow Present Value
0 = (P + N)	1.000	$23,800	$23,800
1 = (Time-adjusted R)	0.909	$5,000	$4,545
2 = (Time-adjusted R)	0.826	$5,000	$4,130
3 = (Time-adjusted R)	0.751	$5,000	$3,755
Total	—	$38,800 (TCO)	$36,230 (TCO present value)

Financial Value Calculations

Net Present Value (NPV)

$$NPV = \text{Present Value Savings} - \text{Present Value TCO}$$

Present value of savings is calculated from the present value annual-loss expectancy (ALE). It is the savings realized by avoiding attacks following the installation of a specific security appliance.

Year	Discount Factor When Discount Rate Is 10%	Cash Flow (Without Present Value Considered)	Present Value of Cash Flow
Year 0–3 TCO	—	–$38,800	–$36,230
Year 1 savings	0.909	+$16,000	+$14,544
Year 2 savings	0.826	+$16,000	+$13,216
Year 3 savings	0.751	+$16,000	+$12,016
Total	—	$9,200	$3,546 (NPV)

Internal Rate of Return (IRR)

IRR equals the discount rate by which the net benefits must be discounted, over a time period, until the point that they equal the initial costs.

		10% Discount Rate		12% Discount Rate		15% Discount Rate	
Year	Cash Flow	Discount Factor	Present Value	Discount Factor	Present Value	Discount Factor	Present Value
Year 0–3 TCO	–$38,800	—	–$36,230	—	–$36,230	—	–$36,230
Year 1 savings	+$16,000	0.909	+$14,544	0.893	+$14,288	0.870	$13,920
Year 2 savings	+$16,000	0.826	+$13,216	0.797	+$12,752	0.756	$12,096
Year 3 savings	+$16,000	0.751	+$12,016	0.712	+$11,392	0.658	$10,528
Total	$9,200	—	$3,546 (at NPV)	—	$2,202 (at NPV)	—	$314 (at NPV)

Return on Investment (ROI)

$$ROI = \frac{\text{PV Savings} - \text{PV TCO}}{\text{PV TCO}}$$

Payback Period

$$\text{Payback Period} = \frac{\text{PV TCO}}{\text{Annual Net Savings}}$$

$$\text{Where Annual Net Savings} = \frac{\text{Total PV Savings}}{\text{useful years}}$$

GLOSSARY

This glossary assembles and defines common terms and acronyms used in this book and in the network security industry. Many of the definitions have yet to be standardized, and many terms have several meanings. Multiple definitions and acronym expressions are included where they apply. Many of these definitions can also be found on the Cisco website at http://www.cisco.com/univercd/cc/td/doc/cisintwk/ita/index.htm.

AAA   Authentication, authorization, and accounting. Pronounced "triple a."

access layer   Layer in a hierarchical network that provides workgroup/user access to the network.

access list   List kept by routers to control access to or from the router for a number of services (for example, to prevent packets with a certain IP address from leaving a particular interface on the router).

access server   Communications processor that connects asynchronous devices to a LAN or WAN through network and terminal emulation software. Performs both synchronous and asynchronous routing of supported protocols. Sometimes called a *network access server (NAS)*.

accounting   Process that enables the NAS or firewall to track both the services that users are accessing and the amount of network resources consumed by those users.

ACK   1. Acknowledgment bit in a TCP segment.
2. See *acknowledgment.*

acknowledgment   Notification sent from one network device to another to acknowledge that some event occurred (for example, the receipt of a message). Sometimes abbreviated *ACK.*

ACL   See *access list.*

address   Data structure or logical convention used to identify a unique entity, such as a particular process or a network device.

alarm   Message notifying an operator or administrator of a network problem.

analog   Electrical circuit that is represented by means of continuous, variable, physical quantities (such as voltages and frequencies), as opposed to discrete representations (such as the 0/1, off/on representation of digital circuits).

application layer   Layer 7 of the OSI reference model. This layer provides services to application processes (such as e-mail, file transfer, and terminal emulation) that are outside the OSI model. The application layer identifies and establishes the availability of intended communication partners (and the resources required to connect with them), synchronizes cooperating applications, and establishes agreement on the procedures for error recovery and control of data integrity. It corresponds roughly with the transaction services layer in the SNA model.

attack   Assault on system security that derives from an intelligent threat, for example, an intelligent act that is a deliberate attempt (especially in the sense of method or technique) to evade security services and violate the security policy of a system.

authentication   In security, the verification of the identity of a person or process.

authorization   Method for remote-access control, including one-time authorization or authorization for each service, per-user account list and profile, and user group support.

backbone   Part of a network that acts as the primary path for traffic that is most often sourced from and destined for other networks.

back door   Undocumented or unpublished access path to either a network or its components, such as routers, firewalls, and so on.

bandwidth   Difference between the highest and lowest frequencies available for network signals. The term is also used to describe the rated throughput capacity of a given network medium or protocol.

BIA   Burned-in address. Another name for a MAC address.

binary   Numbering system characterized by 1s and 0s (1 = on, 0 = off).

bit   Binary digit used in the binary numbering system. This can be 0 or 1.

blended threat   Combination of threats, or a single one, such as a worm, that attempts to wreak havoc in a number of possible ways. For example, a worm might initially cause damage to web pages on a particular server and then proceed to perform a DDoS or other similar type of attack.

broadcast   Data packets that are sent to all nodes on a network. Broadcasts are identified by a broadcast address. Compare with *multicast* and *unicast*.

buffer   Storage area used for handling data in transit. Buffers are used in internetworking to compensate for differences in processing speed between network devices. Bursts of data can be stored in buffers until they can be handled by slower processing devices. This is sometimes referred to as a packet buffer.

byte   A series of consecutive binary digits that are operated upon as a unit (for example, an 8-bit byte).

CA   Certification authorities. Servers responsible for managing digital certificate requests and issuing digital certificates to participating IPSec network peers. These services provide centralized key management for the participating peers.

cable   Transmission medium of copper wire or optical fiber wrapped in a protective cover.

CERT Coordination Center   Operated by Carnegie Mellon University (CMU), the CERT Coordination Center, or the CERT/CC, was the first computer security incident response team. Today, CERT/CC is a major reporting center for Internet security issues, offering both technical advice and information on security-related issues.

checksum   Method for checking the integrity of transmitted data. A checksum is an integer value computed from a sequence of octets taken through a series of arithmetic operations. The value is recomputed at the receiving end and is compared for verification.

CiscoSecure   Complete line of access-control software products that complement any dialup network solution, enabling the centralization of security policies.

client   Node or software program that requests services from a server. See also *server.*

client/server computing   Computing (processing) network systems in which transaction responsibilities are divided into two parts: client (front end) and server (back end). Both terms (*client* and *server*) can be applied to software programs or actual computing devices. This is also called distributed computing (processing).

collision   In Ethernet, the result of two nodes transmitting simultaneously. The frames from each device impact and are damaged when they meet on the physical media.

compactFlash card   Very small memory card that uses flash memory to store data. Developed by SanDisk in 1994, compactFlash cards are commonly found in digital cameras, music players, and other similar products.

cookie   Piece of information sent by a web server to a web browser that the browser is expected to save and send back to the web server whenever the browser makes additional requests of the web server.

CoOP   Continuity of operations. Special planning that provides the continuation of critical functions during emergency conditions such as natural disasters, accidents, technology glitches, and military or terrorist attacks.

countermeasure   Action, device, procedure, or technique that reduces a threat, a vulnerability, or an attack by eliminating or preventing it, by minimizing the harm it can cause, or by discovering and reporting it so that corrective action can be taken.

CPU   Central processing unit. The central processor (chip or brain) of the router, computer, switch, and so on.

cracker   Person who unlawfully accesses a network infrastructure to perform unethical activities. Cracking has long been associated with criminal, destructive, and malicious acts perpetrated on computers and the networks in which they reside.

CRM   Customer Relations Management. Software that is often used by sales organizations for the express purpose of managing sales activities.

CSI   Computer Security Institute. Founded in 1974, CSI is a membership organization that has information, computer, and network security professionals in the field of asset protection.

CSO   Chief security officer. Senior executive responsible for the security of an organization's network, communications, and business systems.

cyberpunk   Individual who might regard himself as *antiestablishment*. By maintaining their own technological ability, cyberpunks attempt to maintain their individuality so that they can effectively stand tall against the perceived power that corporations and major institutions hold over technology.

cypherpunk   Combines the efforts of cyberpunks and strong encryption algorithms to create a safe environment in which people can have private communications.

datagram   Logical grouping of information sent as a network layer unit over a transmission medium without prior establishment of a virtual circuit. IP datagrams are the primary information units on the Internet. The terms *cell, frame, message, packet,* and *segment* are also used to describe logical information groupings at various layers of the OSI reference model and in various technology circles.

DDoS attack   Distributed denial of service attack. Denial of service attack against a site or server launched from multiple sources. This is sometimes carried out by concealed exploiting servers that function as agents for transmitting the attacks. In many cases, the attacker will place client software on a number of unsuspecting remote computers and then use these computers to launch the attack. A DDoS attack is more effective than a simple DoS attack, because the volume of traffic is considerably higher, and it is more difficult to prevent.

decryption   Reverse application of an encryption algorithm to encrypted data, thereby restoring that data to its original, unencrypted state. See also *encryption*.

dedicated line   Communications line that is indefinitely reserved for transmissions rather than switched as transmission is required. See also *leased line*.

delay   Time between the initiation of a transaction by a sender and the first response received by the sender. Also, the time required to move a packet from source to destination over a given path.

DES   Data Encryption Standard. Standard cryptographic algorithm developed by the U.S. National Bureau of Standards.

destination address   Address of a network device that is receiving data. See also *source address*.

DHCP   Dynamic Host Configuration Protocol. Provides a mechanism for allocating IP addresses dynamically so that addresses can be reused when hosts no longer need them.

dialup line   Communications circuit that is established by a switched-circuit connection using the telephone company network.

digital   Use of a binary code to represent information, such as 0/1 or off/on.

DNS   Domain Name System. System used on the Internet for translating names of network nodes into addresses.

DoS   Denial of service. Forms of computer network communication sabotage through exploitation of computer communication protocols. The purpose of the attack is to overwhelm the target with spurious data to prevent legitimate connection attempts from succeeding. DoS attacks do not reveal sensitive data to the attacker, unlike attacks whose purpose is to penetrate the target system. In these kinds of attacks, the skillful attacker tries to choke down networks and servers in vital network junctions. A successful attack might cause considerable revenue and resources loss.

dotted decimal notation   Syntactic representation for a 32-bit integer that consists of four 8-bit numbers written in base 10 with periods (dots) separating them. It is used to represent IP addresses on the Internet, as in 192.168.67.20. This is also called dotted quad notation.

e-mail   Electronic mail. Widely used network application in which text messages are transmitted electronically between end users over various types of networks using various network protocols.

encapsulation   Wrapping of data in a particular protocol header. For example, Ethernet data is wrapped in a specific Ethernet header before network transit. Also, when bridging dissimilar networks, the entire frame from one network is simply placed in the header used by the data link layer protocol of the other network.

encryption   Application of a specific algorithm to data to alter the appearance of the data, making it incomprehensible to those who are not authorized to see the information. See also *decryption.*

false-negative   In intrusion detection, a situation in which a signature is not fired when offending traffic is detected.

false-positive   In intrusion detection, a situation in which a signature is fired incorrectly.

filter   Generally, a process or device that screens network traffic for certain characteristics, such as source address, destination address, or protocol, and determines whether to forward or discard that traffic based on the established criteria.

filtering router   Internetwork router that selectively prevents the passage of data packets according to a security policy.

firewall   Router or access server, or several routers or access servers, designated as a buffer between any connected public networks and a private network. A firewall router uses access lists and other methods to ensure the security of the private network.

frame   Logical grouping of information sent as a data link layer unit over a transmission medium. This often refers to the header and trailer, used for synchronization and error control, that surround the user data contained in the unit. The terms *cell, datagram, message, packet,* and *segment* are also used to describe logical information groupings in various technology circles.

FTP   File Transfer Protocol. Application protocol, part of the TCP/IP protocol stack, used for transferring files between network nodes. FTP is defined in RFC 959.

gateway   In the IP community, an older term referring to a routing device. Today, the term *router* is used to describe nodes that perform this function, and *gateway* refers to a special-purpose device that performs an application-layer conversion of information from one protocol stack to another.

hacker   1. Someone who works diligently on programmable systems until they perform optimally.

2. Person who unlawfully gains access to a network or system with a desire to perform a variety of possible acts, ranging from innocuous (and not harmful) to downright malicious.

hacking   Criminal or malicious actions directed at computer networks and hosts.

hacktivist   Politically motivated hacker who breaks into computer systems for premeditated socially-minded purposes.

hash   Commonly known as a *hash function*, it is used for hashing. See *hashing.*

hashing   Confirms the integrity of a message by converting its contents into a format that can only be understood by the receiver, by using an algorithm to convert data into a fixed-length result.

header   Control information placed before data when encapsulating that data for network transmission.

HIDS   Host-based IDS. host-based intrusion-detection system (HIDS). Operates by detecting attacks occurring on a host on which it is installed. It works by intercepting OS and application calls, securing the OS and application configurations, validating incoming service requests, and analyzing local log files for after-the-fact suspicious activity.

hijacking   Attack whereby a person, or persons, gains unlawful control of a communication, typically between two parties, and successfully assumes the identity of one of the parties.

HIPAA   Health Insurance Portability and Accountability Act. Enacted in 1996, this act presents standards for the maintenance and transmission of personal information regarding individuals. It is incumbent upon organizations in possession of, or potentially in possession of, information to be able to protect the security and confidentiality of electronic personal information. The act ensures that the interchange of said electronic data is standardized, and that privacy is ensured.

HIPS   Host-based IPS. host-based intrusion-prevention system (HIPS). Improves the security of hosts and servers by using rules that control operating system and network stack behavior. Processor control limits activity such as buffer overflows, registry updates, writes to the system directory, and the launching of installation programs.

honey pot   Decoys that are deliberately installed on networks to lure and trap hackers. A server or network segment is intentionally riddled with vulnerabilities consisting of interesting files and information, and then loaded with tracking software, enabling a hacker's movements to be effectively logged. Honey pots can also divert intruders' attention from mission-critical devices.

host   Computer system on a network. Similar to node, except that host usually implies a computer system, whereas node generally applies to any networked system, including access servers and routers.

HSA   high systems availability. HSA is a Feature on some Cisco routers which provides improve system availability.

hub   Hardware or software device that contains multiple independent but connected modules of network and internetwork equipment. Hubs can be active (when they repeat signals sent through them) or passive (when they do not repeat, but merely split, signals sent through them).

ICSA   International Computer Security Association.

IDS   Intrusion-detection system. Security service that monitors and analyzes system events for the purpose of finding attempts to access system resources in an unauthorized manner.

internet   Short for internetwork. Not to be confused with *Internet*. See also *internetwork*.

Internet   Largest global internetwork, connecting tens of thousands of networks worldwide and having a "culture" that focuses on research and standardization based on real-life use. Many leading-edge network technologies come from the Internet community. The Internet evolved in part from ARPANET. At one time, it was called the DARPA Internet. Not to be confused with the general term *internet*.

internetwork   Collection of networks interconnected by routers and other devices that functions (generally) as a single network. It is sometimes called an internet, which is not to be confused with *Internet*.

internetworking   General term used to refer to the industry devoted to connecting networks together. The term can refer to products, procedures, and technologies.

intranet   Network, internal to an organization, based on Internet and World Wide Web technology, that delivers immediate, up-to-date information and services to networked employees.

intrusion alarm   Alarm that indicates that an unauthorized activity has occurred, whether a policy violation (as logged by a Cisco router), a fragmented packet header, a denial of service attack, or another event.

intrusion detection   Security service that monitors and analyzes system events for the purpose of finding, and providing real-time or near-real-time warning of, attempts to access system resources in an unauthorized manner.

intrusion-detection sensor   Intrusion-detection appliance. It analyzes network traffic, searching for signs of unauthorized activity.

IOS   Internetwork Operating System. Cisco system software that provides common functionality, scalability, and security for all products under the CiscoFusion architecture.

IP   Internet Protocol. Network layer protocol in the TCP/IP stack offering a connectionless internetwork service. IP provides features for addressing, type-of-service specification, fragmentation and reassembly, and security. It is documented in RFC 791.

IP address   A 32-bit address assigned to hosts using TCP/IP. An IP address belongs to one of five classes (A, B, C, D, or E) and is written as 4 octets separated with periods (dotted decimal format). Each address consists of a network number, an optional subnetwork number, and a host number. The network and subnetwork numbers together are used for routing, and the host number is used to address an individual host within the network or subnetwork. A subnet mask is used to extract network and subnetwork information from the IP address. It is also called an Internet address.

IPS   Intrusion-prevention system. Security service that monitors and analyzes system events for the purpose of providing real-time or near-real-time protection from attempts to access system resources in an unauthorized manner.

IPSec   IP Security. Standards-based method of providing privacy, integrity, and authenticity to information transferred across IP networks. It provides IP network layer encryption.

ISO   International Organization for Standardization. International organization that is responsible for a wide range of standards, including those relevant to networking. ISO developed the OSI reference model, a popular networking reference model.

ISP   Internet service provider. Company that provides Internet access to other companies and individuals.

JPEG   Joint Photographics Expert Group. Standard for graphic image files.

Kb   kilobit. Approximately 1,000 bits.

KB   kilobyte. Approximately 1,000 bytes.

kbps   kilobits per second.

kBps   kilobytes per second.

LAN   Local-area network. High-speed, low-error data network covering a relatively small geographic area (up to a few thousand meters). LANs connect workstations, peripherals, terminals, and other devices in a single building or other geographically-limited area. LAN standards specify cabling and signaling at the physical and data link layers of the OSI model. Ethernet, FDDI, and Token Ring are widely used LAN technologies. See also *MAN* and *WAN*.

latency   1. Delay between the time a device receives a frame and the time that frame is forwarded the destination port.
     2. Delay between the time a device requests access to a network and the time it is granted permission to transmit.

leased line   Transmission line reserved by a communications carrier for the private use of a customer. A leased line is a type of dedicated line. See also *dedicated line.*

link   Network communications channel consisting of a circuit or transmission path and all related equipment between a sender and a receiver. It is most often used to refer to a WAN connection and is sometimes referred to as a line or a transmission link.

logging   Logging of security information is performed on two levels: logging of events (such as IDS commands, errors, and alarms) and logging of individual IP session information.

MAC   Media Access Control. Lower of the two sublayers of the data link layer defined by the IEEE. The MAC sublayer handles access to shared media, such as whether token passing or contention will be used.

MAC address   Standardized data link layer address that is required for every port or device that connects to a LAN. Other devices in the network use these addresses to locate specific ports in the network and to create and update routing tables and data structures. MAC addresses are 6 bytes long and are controlled by the IEEE. Also known as a hardware address, MAC layer address, and physical address.

MAN   Metropolitan-area network. Network that spans a metropolitan area. Generally, a MAN spans a larger geographic area than a LAN, but a smaller geographic area than a WAN. Compare with *LAN* and *WAN*.

MD5   Message Digest 5. Algorithm used for message authentication. MD5 verifies the integrity of the communication, authenticates the origin, and checks for timeliness.

message   Application layer (Layer 7) logical grouping of information, often composed of a number of lower-layer logical groupings, such as packets.

message digest   One-way hashing algorithm that produces a hash. Both MD5 and Secure Hash Algorithm (SHA) are hashing techniques that enhance security of data transmission.

modem   Modulator-demodulator. Device that converts digital and analog signals. At the source, a modem converts digital signals to a form suitable for transmission over analog communication facilities. At the destination, the analog signals are returned to their digital form. Modems allow data to be transmitted over voice-grade telephone lines.

multicast   Single packets copied by the network and sent to a specific subset of network addresses. These addresses are specified in the Destination Address Field. Compare with *broadcast* and *unicast*.

multivector worm   Worm that propagates in a variety of ways, making it difficult to mitigate.

NAS   Network access server. See *access server.*

NCSD   National Cyber Security Division of the Department of Homeland Security.

network   Collection of computers, printers, routers, switches, and other devices that can communicate with each other over some transmission medium.

NIC   1. Network interface card. Board that provides network communication capabilities to and from a computer system. Also called an adapter.
        2. Network Information Center. Organization that serves the Internet community by supplying user assistance, documentation, training, and other services.

NIDS   Network-based IDS. Network-based intrusion-detection system (NIDS). Operates by detecting an attack occurring at the network level and either takes a corrective action itself or notifies a management system, where an administrator can take action.

NIPS   Network-based IPS. Network-based intrusion-prevention system (NIPS). IPS that can act proactively, being able to detect intrusion attempts, thereby being able to potentially block an attack.

OSI   Open System Interconnection. International standardization program created by ISO and ITU-T to develop standards for data networking that facilitate multivendor equipment interoperability.

OSI reference model   Open System Interconnection reference model. Network architectural model developed by ISO and ITU-T. The model consists of seven layers, each of which specifies particular network functions, such as addressing, flow control, error control, encapsulation, and reliable message transfer. The lowest layer (the physical layer) is closest to the media technology. The lower two layers are implemented in hardware and software, while the upper five layers are implemented only in software. The highest layer (the application layer) is closest to the user. The OSI reference model is used universally as a method for teaching and understanding network functionality.

out-of-band Transmission channels outside the channels normally used for information transfer. Out-of-band transmission is often used for error reporting in situations in which in-band signaling can be affected by problems the network might be experiencing.

packet Logical grouping of information that includes a header containing control information and (usually) user data. Packets are most often used to refer to network layer units of data. The terms *datagram, frame, message*, and *segment* are also used to describe logical information groupings at various layers of the OSI reference model and in various technology circles. See also *PDU*.

password sanctity The process of acknowledging the relevance and importance of a password, and ensuring its inviolability.

patch Occasionally referred to as a *fix*, a patch is a programming solution for software issues, commonly known as *bugs*. The patch, usually developed by the original vendor, is distributed either as a full replacement of the original software or as an "add-on."

payload Portion of a cell, frame, or packet that contains upper-layer information (data).

PDU Protocol data unit. OSI term for packet. A packet of data consisting of control information and user information that is to be exchanged between communicating peers in a network. In general, a PDU is a segment of data generated by a specific layer of a protocol stack, usually containing information from the next higher layer, encapsulated together with header and trailer information generated by the layer in question.

phishing Internet identity fraud that typically uses spam e-mail messages and web pages that look legitimate, requesting users to fill in fake forms to steal their usernames, passwords, bank accounts, credit card numbers, and other personal information.

phreak Particular type of hacker who is known to break into a telephone network to tap into conversations or to engage in unauthorized long-distance calling.

ping Packet internet groper. ICMP echo message and its reply. This is often used in IP networks to test the reachability of a network device.

PIX Cisco Private Internet Exchange firewall. See also *firewall.*

port 1. Interface on an internetworking device (such as a router). Physical connection.
2. In IP terminology, an upper-layer process that receives information from lower layers. Ports are numbered, and each numbered port is associated with a specific process. For example, SMTP is associated with port 25. A port number is also called a well-known address.

PWC PricewaterhouseCoopers. Also known as PWC. A global consulting and auditing firm.

reconnaissance Gaining information about the network. Hackers conduct reconnaissance by listening to system messages, such as the status of packet delivery, which provide information (that is, IP addresses of devices).

remote-access server See *access server.*

ROP Return on prevention. A term coined for this book, return on prevention (ROP) is realized through a process that assesses and analyzes risk tolerance, explores organizational and governance needs, and examines network requirements. It applies appropriate financial methodology to aid an organization in effectively determining the true value of its proposed security posture.

ROSI Return on security investment. Value of network security with regard to the economic consequences of a security breach.

router   Network layer device that uses one or more metrics to determine the optimal path along which network traffic should be forwarded. Routers forward packets from one network to another based on network layer information. It is occasionally called a gateway (although this definition of gateway is becoming increasingly outdated).

routing   Process of finding a path to a destination host. Routing is complex in large networks because of the many potential intermediate destinations that a packet might traverse before reaching its destination host. Routing occurs at Layer 3, the network layer.

routing protocol   Supports a routed protocol by providing mechanisms for sharing routing information. Routing protocol messages move between the routers. A routing protocol allows the routers to communicate with other routers to update and maintain routing tables. Routing protocol messages do not carry end-user traffic from network to network. A routing protocol uses the routed protocol to pass information between routers. Examples of routing protocols are IGRP, OSPF, and RIP.

routing table   Table stored in a router or some other internetworking device that keeps track of routes to particular network destinations and metrics associated with those routes.

routing update   Message sent from a router to indicate network reachability and associated cost information. Routing updates are typically sent at regular intervals and after a change in network topology.

script kiddies   Derogative term to describe less crafty crackers who use readily available script to conduct an attack.

SD card   Stamp-sized flash memory card.

server   Node or software program that provides services to clients. See also *client.*

SMB   Small- to medium-sized business.

(358)

SMTP   Simple Mail Transfer Protocol. Internet protocol providing e-mail services.

sniffer   When written with a lowercase *s*, denotes a consecrated expression that refers to a program that is capable of capturing and analyzing network traffic.

Sniffer   When written with an uppercase *S*, refers to a protocol decoder and is a trademark of McAfee Security.

SNMP   Simple Network Management Protocol.

source address   Address of a network device that is sending data. See also *destination address.*

spammer   Sender of unsolicited advertisements through e-mail messages.

SPAN   Switched Port Analyzer. Feature of a Cisco Catalyst LAN switch. SPAN mirrors the traffic at one switched segment onto a predefined SPAN port. A network analyzer attached to the SPAN port can monitor traffic from any of the other Catalyst switched ports.

SSL   Secure Socket Layer. Encryption technology for the web used to provide secure transactions, such as the transmission of credit card numbers for e-commerce.

subnet   See *subnetwork.*

subnet mask   A 32-bit number that is associated with an IP address; each bit in the subnet mask indicates how to interpret the corresponding bit in the IP address. In binary format, a subnet mask bit of 1 indicates that the corresponding bit in the IP address is a network or subnet bit; a subnet mask bit of 0 indicates that the corresponding bit in the IP address is a host bit. The subnet mask then indicates how many bits have been borrowed from the host field for the subnet field. It is sometimes referred to simply as mask.

subnetwork   In IP networks, a network sharing a particular subnet address. Subnetworks are networks arbitrarily segmented by a network administrator to provide a multilevel, hierarchical routing structure while shielding the subnetwork from the addressing complexity of attached networks. It is sometimes called a subnet.

switch   1. Network device that filters, forwards, and floods frames based on the destination address of each frame. The switch operates at the data link layer of the OSI model.

2. Electronic or mechanical device that allows a connection to be established as necessary and terminated when there is no longer a session to support.

SYN   Synchronize (TCP segment).

synchronization   Establishment of common timing between sender and receiver.

T1   Digital WAN carrier facility. T1 transmits DS-1–formatted data at 1.544 Mbps through the telephone-switching network using AMI or B8ZS coding.

TAC   Technical Assistance Center (Cisco).

TACACS   Terminal Access Controller Access Control System.

TCP   Transmission Control Protocol. Connection-oriented transport layer protocol that provides reliable full-duplex data transmission. TCP is part of the TCP/IP protocol stack. See also *TCP/IP*.

TCP/IP   Transmission Control Protocol/Internet Protocol. Common name for the suite of protocols developed by the U.S. DoD in the 1970s to support the construction of worldwide internetworks. TCP and IP are the two best-known protocols in the suite. See also *IP*, *TCP*, and *UDP*.

threat   Expression of intention to cause harm or wreak havoc against a computer, network, or system.

topology   Physical arrangement of network equipment, nodes, and media within an enterprise networking structure.

UDP   User Datagram Protocol. Connectionless transport layer protocol in the TCP/IP protocol stack. UDP is a simple protocol that exchanges datagrams without acknowledgments or guaranteed delivery, requiring that error processing and retransmission be handled by other protocols.

unicast   Message sent to a single network destination. Compare with *broadcast* and *multicast*.

URL   Uniform resource locator. Type of formatted identifier that describes the access method and the location of an information resource object on the Internet.

USB key   Form of flash memory accessed through the USB port of a computer.

VPN   Virtual Private Network. Enables IP traffic to travel securely over a public TCP/IP network by encrypting all traffic from one network to another. A VPN uses "tunneling" to encrypt all information at the IP level.

VPN concentrator   Appliance optimized to terminate Virtual Private Network–encrypted tunnels. Enables IP traffic to travel securely over a public TCP/IP network by encrypting all traffic from one network to another.

vulnerability   One or more attributes of a computer or a network that permit a subject to initiate patterns of misuse on that computer or network.

WAN   Wide-area network. Data communications network that serves users across a broad geographic area and often uses transmission devices provided by common carriers. Frame Relay, SMDS, and X.25 are examples of WANs.

war dialer   Software that automatically dials preconfigured ranges of phone numbers and logs successful attempts at reaching another modem. Hackers commonly use war dialers to locate points of entry, for example, to dial in to a network.

war driving   Attempting to connect to a wireless network while strolling or driving in a neighborhood.

WWW   World Wide Web. Large network of Internet servers providing hypertext and other services to terminals running client applications, such as a WWW browser.

WWW browser   GUI-based hypertext client application, such as Mosaic, used to access hypertext documents and other services located on innumerable remote servers throughout the WWW and Internet. See also *Internet* and *WWW*.

INDEX

A

abuse, detecting, 77

access policies, 124
    clean-desk policies, 124–125
    closed-blind policies, 124
    departing employees, 123
    job categories, 123
    password sanctity, 124

access attacks, 15
    access strategems, 16
    data-driven attacks, 37
    impersonation attacks, 36
    man-in-the-middle attacks, 38
    password attacks, 36
    protocol exploitation, 37
    session hijackings, 37
    session replay, 38
    social engineering, 36
    software exploitation, 37
    Trojan horses, 37
    trust exploitation, 37
    viruses, 37
    worms, 37

access cards, 68-69

access control lists, routers, 107

access control servers (ACSs), 71, 106-107

access integrity, vunerabilities, 8

access points, wireless networks, 264

access warnings, routers, 259–260

access-control policies, 250–252
    three-strike access rules, 25

accounting, 66, 71–72

ACSs (access control servers), 71

ALE (annual-loss expectancy), 223-224

analog Internet access
    policies, 253
    authentication, 255
    dialup workstations, 254
    fax line use, 254
    inbound dialing, 255
    one-time passwords, 254
    outgoing traffic monitoring, 254
    password storing, 255
    war dialers, 253–254

annualized rate of occurrence (ARO), 223

annual-loss expectancy (ALE), 223-224

APM, 107–108

APM (automated patch management), 98–100, 107-108

application layer attacks, threat mitigation technologies, 108

applications
    as invasion targets, 45
    design issues, vulnerabilities, 5
    encryption, 60

ArcSight, 93–94

ARO (annualized rate of occurrence), 223

(363)

J-K

L

M

Q–R

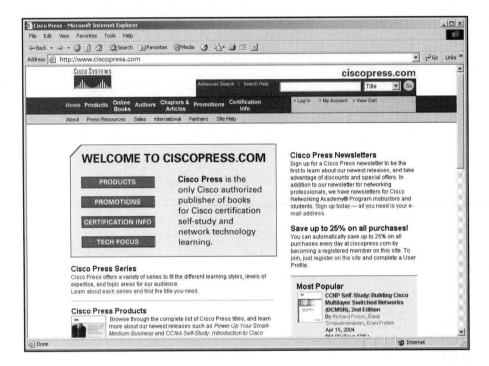